# Defined
# By
# God
# Not by
# Divorce

ANA REDDING

# ACKNOWLEDGMENTS

I would like to thank my parents for bringing me up with a high value for the ways of the Lord, and for encouraging my love for the Word of God. You have placed me in the path of truth and I am still walking in it. I would like to thank my wonderful mentor, Kewyn Appadoo, for the way he so generously invested in me, encouraged me, and granted all the time I needed to write this book. You have been instrumental in God's plans to make this happen. I would like to thank my loving, intelligent and empowering husband for cheering me on, for his support and collaboration in the writing and editing of this book, but especially for the way he has chosen, and continues to choose to believe and call out the best in me. You are my best friend and my most trusted life companion.

My heart is full of thanksgiving for friends and family who have made me who I am today, but the deepest gratitude in my heart is for my beautiful, kind, good, faithful, magnificent and brilliant God. He is the real Author, Perfecter and Finisher of my story.

# TABLE OF CONTENTS

Ana Redding

# INTRODUCTION

**Shawn Bolz prophecy** (18/05/18):

"It's like a refined wine. An aged message that came for people for resolution and restoration. Your message is ready to tell. There is nothing you can say that will defame others because you have an honorable and integrous heart. There is something in this story that needs to be told and heard. God is giving you permission tonight to be able to, in this new season with your wonderful husband, to take married couples on a creative healing journey. You need to know that God has planned this all along because of the healing that is going to be released through your story. It is a powerful story that needs to be told"[1].

Two weeks earlier I had my first meeting with the man who was going to be my 3rd year mentor at BSSM[2]. Questions were asked, answers were given, and it all seemed to be going well until he stopped and said: "I'm very happy with everything we've discussed, but there is one thing that concerns me."

---

1

https://www.youtube.com/watch?v=ZgDhBNfeVsA&feature=youtu.be&fbclid=IwAR3FsoaZ1n3lzEPmb8RAWOFXfY3IVxmNcgf96rxNdbqFOqMv--lmdjko_q0

[2] Bethel School of Supernatural Ministry

If we were in a cartoon, a giant question mark would have popped up above my head. A million thoughts flooded my mind. I was trying to anticipate what he was about to say - as if I could prepare myself, in a split second, to give the right answer, the one which would put his mind at rest and free him from any concern. My curiosity quickly gave way to perplexity, and then admiration when he asked: "In the end, what are you getting out of it?"

I gave all the right answers: the opportunity to work with him and be under his covering, to serve his vision and ministry, to be immersed in a culture that celebrates and propagates the testimony of Jesus Christ. Finally, when I mentioned that it would be very rewarding to see some of the testimonies I was going to write published and read all around the world, he interjected: "That's what I was waiting to hear you say, because of your heart to serve, but what will you get out of the year? Ana, I think that by the end of your 3rd Year I'd like you to have written and published your own book."

After a brief, silent pause, while I was trying to gather myself, I needed to make sure I'd heard him correctly: "Write my own book? Really?!" He was very assertive about it and proceeded to give me the gist of what the process would entail so I could prepare for it during the summer.

All the while I remember thinking, "I came here to find out how I can best serve him and he already had a plan to serve me!" I had just finished reading a book which had stretched and inspired me regarding the value and life-changing impact servant leaders bring into the lives of their teams and organizations[3], and here I was, face to face with a man who was a living example of that.

---

[3]*Developing the Leader Within You 2.0* by John Maxwell

2

In the following two weeks I experienced very mixed feelings. I was very grateful for the way God had guided my steps towards this mentor, and I was very grateful for being given the opportunity to do something which I hadn't planned, or even considered (at least in the near future). However, I was indecisive regarding what I was going to write about. I kept thinking of different book ideas (even considered 'stealing' a book idea from my husband, with his consent, of course) but I had no peace or enthusiasm about it. In the back of my mind there was always the possibility of telling my own story, but every time I thought about it, I wrestled with that thought. I always felt very uncomfortable with the idea of disclosing information about other people whose lives are, or were, connected with mine. So, I kept dismissing it. Until the Lord brought His seal of approval, the last night of the School of Creativity, with a prophetic word given by Shawn Bolz (quoted above).

This man of God called me, and my husband, by name, and proceeded to ask if a particular word made any sense to me. It just happened to be my former Portuguese surname, from my first marriage! I was now in another country, in another continent with my second husband and everybody knew me as Mrs. Redding. Apart from my husband, nobody else in the school environment knew my former surname, and I had never been introduced to Shawn Bolz, he did not know me. But God, who knows me, spoke through this Spirit-filled man to bring the clarity, confidence and affirmation I was lacking. He also did it in front of a crowd of witnesses, people with whom I had been running with, people who celebrated our journey and were cheering us on, people who knew the value of inspired storytelling and who would keep intentionally reminding me, and encouraging me, to complete the assignment I had been given.

That night, as God commissioned me to tell the story you are about to read, I felt validated, empowered and properly aligned for the task ahead. I was filled with a sense of purpose and destiny which drove me closer to God's heart, not just for my own sake, but for each one of you who are going to read this book and partake in our victories and breakthroughs.

I welcome you with open arms to come and sit at my table, hear me brag about God's goodness and then, with a hearty appetite, to reach out and taste, and see for yourself, that the Lord is good.

"I am God and there is no other; I am God, and there is no one like me. **I make known the end from the beginning**, from ancient times, what is still to come. I say 'My purpose will stand, and I will do all that I please'."

(Isaiah 46:10)

# 1 To know the End from the Beginning

*"It is not how you start that is important but how well you finish!"*

(Jim George)

My first thought when I read the above quote was: "It is arguable." Especially when storytelling is concerned. Everyone knows it is important to grip the attention of your audience from the very beginning. Why did I decide to use it, after all? Because, from the very beginning, I want to shift your focus from what it was to what is ahead: the potential and possibility, the promise actualized at the culmination of a perfecting process.

When we are aiming to go from A to B it is usually helpful to know where B is. If we continue to move aimlessly, unaware of our intended destination, we might end up in S, T or even Z! That's a lot of wasted time and wasted letters. Therefore, before I invite you to invest your time and energy to go on a journey through my process, I would like to tell you where we're heading and point out some of the reasons why I believe you will benefit from it.

Your circumstances do not define you. You are who God says you are and if you have gone through, or are going through, the painful and confusing experience of divorce, know that God continues to be fully invested in building a close, meaningful and life-changing relationship with you. He tells a better story, and your journey can be radically impacted if you choose to remain connected, instead of shutting Him out. I have experienced this first hand. You can experience it too.

This book is for anyone who is seeking to find their identity, their place and their purpose in life, as a child of God. It is also for those who feel trapped in what appear to be unending, repetitive cycles of hopeless relational brokenness but are determined to invest in their emotional health and pursue wholeness.

You will discover deeper and very practical expressions of God's empowering grace to forgive the unforgivable and to rebuild on desolate places. You will find language to help you understand and articulate your own process, and empower you to make informed choices, as you are invited and equipped to establish solid foundations for a successful relational future.

Divorce is a central topic but this book is not just meant for people who have gone through separation and divorce. It is also

*HOPE is the final destination.*

meant for those who are still married but know they are, or might be, on the brink of separation and possibly divorce, and for all of those who have in their hearts a calling to equip, disciple, inspire and empower people in the areas of inner healing and relational restoration. In whatever group you fit in, HOPE is the final destination.

## The beginning

I love my parents so much. They have made many sacrifices to provide me and my sister with a life filled with opportunities they didn't have. I know they love us deeply, but as we were growing up, I didn't always feel this way. My Father, a key person in my life, was not always very good at expressing his love. His childhood was ten times harder than mine and he did a much better job than his parents, but I still perceived him as being a very strict man because he was a perfectionist with zero tolerance for mistakes or messes.

The environment I was brought up in was very disempowering. I was consistently told, or made aware of how incapable, powerless and inadequate I was. Punishment, shaming and removal of love were used to 'discipline' us and, although I strived constantly for acceptance and love, I always felt I could never perform well enough to meet my father's, and later my husband's, standards and expectations. If you couple that with growing up in a legalistic church, devoid of grace, riddled with gossip and striving performance, you will understand why my relationship with God, especially the Father, was initially problematic. Misconceptions, misrepresentations and wrong projections from my personal warped relational experiences, where I didn't feel safe, secure, accepted, nor cherished, impacted deeply my formative years. When I eventually got married, I carried a ton of debilitating beliefs which, in turn, affected the way I related to my husband.

## The Promised Land

Today, this list of once sad and negative circumstances only serves to highlight the powerful, redemptive and beautiful restoration which has taken place in my own self and in my life. I've learned to trust God because

I have witnessed firsthand how perfect He is in all of His ways: especially in the way He deals with my heart and my soul.

I'm fascinated with His wisdom and I'm in awe of His goodness. I have learned the importance of loving myself well and extending grace to myself, as I have been given the beautiful and empowering capacity of seeing myself through God's eyes. This change in perspective also impacted my relational universe because I was able to apply this upgraded vision in the way I see and relate to others.

My intimate relationship with God continues to inspire me and increase my ability to lovingly and gracefully empower others to run the same restorative race. Thinking about this journey fills me with gratitude and erupting worship. I have truly *tasted and seen that the Lord is Good*!

## In between

Imagine you were given the opportunity to know the ending of a story right from the beginning? Would you want to skip all the chapters in between? I have told you already that the final destination is *hope* but this does not invalidate the importance and purpose of all the mundane (or not so mundane), nitty-gritty, catalytic, life changing, juicy episodes in between. That's why I want to invite you to take a sneak peek of my story. No spoiler alerts are necessary because there will be plenty of surprises, and interesting and meaningful details which will be added as the chapters unfold.

*In the midst of great turmoil, I continued to mend and grow.*

This is not a book about my love story with a man but about my love story with God. His presence and liberating truth infused me with life, hope and empowering transformation. In the midst of great turmoil and impending relational breakdown, I continued to mend and grow. It got to a point when

10

my first husband felt so safe around me that he openly admitted "he knew what he was supposed to do to cultivate a healthy marriage, but he felt it was too much work and he didn't think the investment was worthwhile." He left home, some time after he initiated another relationship and a few years later he filed for divorce which was granted on amicable terms.

I still believe our circumstances were not unredeemable, as all things are possible to our God. For a significant period of time I kept the door open and there was grace for my ex-husband to reconnect, but he chose to dissolve our covenant and so there came a time when I accepted his will and severed all heart and soul ties with the help of the Holy Spirit.

Today we have a cordial and respectful relationship. We share a son and I can say in all honesty that there is no sorrow or resentment in my heart. The closer I got to God's heart the more understanding I was given about my ex-husband's, and my own, struggles, unresolved issues and emotional wounds, and how unprepared we were to deal with those without a Kingdom[4] mindset.

The story I'm about to tell you focuses on resolution, restoration and creative healing. It carries a message of hope and a revelation of God's goodness and brilliant wisdom, even in the midst of great turmoil and confusion. You will see for yourself how His ways are undoubtedly better and higher than our ways. You will discover deeper but very practical expressions of God's empowering grace to forgive the unforgivable and to rebuild on desolate places.

You see, this book is not just about my story, but it is about your story too. It's not just about getting to know me better, it is about getting to know Him better. In the process, you will be empowered to know yourself better and equipped to deal with some of the hardest challenges that come with relational breakdown. You will also be empowered to empower others as you will be able to bring the inner healing and restoration you'll walk

---

[4] Kingdom of God.

through, to those around you who have been, or are being, directly affected by the overwhelming reality of actual or potential divorce.

The in-between episodes of my journey might even evoke some painful memories, suppressed back roads you don't really want to revisit, but they are not the end. They are there to set a context, to add clarity. They are there to give you the bigger picture, where you will be able to see the undeniable contrast between the beginning and the end, and increase your understanding of growth and personal development, throughout the different stages of the journey.

They are also an intentional part of the narrative to inspire you and raise your faith to believe that, if God has so beautifully guided someone else's steps from the murky waters of brokenness to the promised land of wholeness and abundant life, then He can do it again. He can do the same for and with you.

Your journey doesn't have to look like mine, I don't want to tell you what to do, but I want to share with you the 'equipment' and the 'dietary guidelines' I was given by God. If you eat nutritious food you will stay strong and healthy and if you use the right gear, like a reliable compass and a tested map, you will remain on track and reach your final destination. In the journey of life in the Kingdom your final destination is wholeness.

*It pleases God to bring us to Himself and to make us whole.*

The Master Storyteller makes known the end from the beginning and He declares *His purpose will be established, and He will do all that He pleases*[5]. What pleases Him? It pleases Him to bring us to Himself, and to make us whole:

---

[5] Isaiah 46:10

Long before He laid down Earth's foundations, he had us in mind, had settled on us as the focus of His love, to be made whole and holy by His love (...) Abundantly free! He thought of everything, provided for everything we could possibly need, letting us in on the plans He took such delight in making (Ephesians 1:7-10 MSG).

It pleases Him you haven't given up. It pleases Him that you are seeking, and it pleases Him you are choosing to believe He has the answers you are looking for.

## "It is finished!" (Jesus)

The end of the story has been rewritten by Jesus and it comes with a promise of victory. At this moment of your life, it might seem that the word 'end' doesn't evoke anything positive, but I would like to remind you that His ending is always surprising. He is an expert on breathing resurrection life into places which are steeped in confusion, hopelessness and death.

Let God be the Author, Perfecter and Finisher of your story and you will taste and see His plans to prosper you and to give you a hope and a future[6]. So, keep your hopes up and be of good cheer because your present experience is not your final chapter.

Let's go back to the beginning now.

---

[6] Jeremiah 29:11

"Then they cried to the Lord in their trouble and **He saved them** from their distress."

(Psalm 107:19)

# 2 UNRECOGNIZABLE

"Life is a mirror and it will reflect back to the thinker what he thinks into it."

(Ernest Holmes)

Who is this person? I couldn't believe my eyes...

Have you ever looked yourself in the mirror and struggled to recognize the person looking back at you? Or do you, like I used to, avoid mirrors altogether?

Although I had deliberately stopped looking at mirrors, there was a day I was compelled to look closer. Someone showed me a photo I could not ignore. This photo had been taken two weeks earlier, during my son's second birthday party. Next to me sat a beautiful friend, whose bubbliness and *joie de vivre* were so striking that the light she radiated caused the darkness in my soul to really stand out.

I was not ready to see what I saw, but there it was, unmissable, staring me in the face, a very broken reflection of myself. Vacant eyes, an aura of undeniable sadness and shoulders hunched under the weight of the world: "Who is this person?!"

I grabbed the photo, excused myself, ran to my room, locked the door behind me, threw myself on the bed and started sobbing uncontrollably. How did this happen to me?

After seven years in a difficult, emotionally draining marriage, stifled by judgement and accusation, and eroded by abysmal disconnection, I had lost myself and had lost my way.

As I stared at that photo, I remembered all the dreams I had since I was a little girl, about finding my life partner, my best friend, my companion. We were going to be very close and intimate, have great complicity, share everything and be very intentional about building a godly, happy family and a happily-ever-after life. Never for a moment did I contemplate the possibility of separation or divorce, because I hadn't even considered that disconnection could possibly be a part of our story.

## Different agendas

We both came into the marriage with very different agendas, though I was unaware of it at the time. He was in a season of transition in his life. He had ended a long-term relationship and was ready to embrace new challenges and experiences. I was attractive and popular and had several possible suitors at the time. I became a stimulating conquest and later a trophy that increased his visibility and status.

In turn, I had recently come out of a very destructive relationship, barely escaping with my sanity. It felt good to be pursued by a gentle and kind guy. This man was charming, hard-working and financially independent. Someone who gave me a sense of security. He became my 'high tower': the one where I could find protection, comfort and provision for all my needs. No pressure!

We were in our mid-20s. We dated for eight months and got married to the ideal, polite, almost perfect version of each other, charmingly portrayed at the beginning stages of a relationship.

I was convinced I had found my knight in shining armor. He didn't ride a horse, but he rode a cool motorbike and that was good enough for me. I didn't really see marriage as the beginning of something which requires investment, something that needs to be consistently built up. I saw it as a means to an end. I had arrived. I had found the one who was going to meet all my emotional and physical needs. How naive, and how selfish! I placed an overbearing burden on his shoulders to complete me and mend me, by performing as the perfect companion whose sole purpose in life was to make me happy.

Of course, he had needs of his own and they were very different from mine. We were both perfectionists, but our perfectionism carried different expectations and was manifested in different ways. I expected him to be fully devoted to me, in word and deed. He was brought up in an excessively meticulous household and he expected me to be fully devoted to the maintenance of the home, with all the practical chores it involved, in a timely and skillful manner.

> *We never managed to meet in the middle because we were too busy standing our ground.*

My main love languages[7] were, and are, touch and quality time; his main love languages were acts of service and words of affirmation. I felt devalued, even humiliated, when he chose to prioritize completing chores before spending time with me. I told him I shouldn't have to do things to earn his love and attention, those should be given for free. "Let's spend time being together and then we can focus on doing things", that was my motto. It even sounds good and spiritual: 'being' should come before 'doing'. It made sense to me, but to a person who needs to have a clean, tidy, organized environment in order to relax, it didn't make sense at all. We knew nothing about love languages and we never managed to meet in the middle because we were too busy standing our ground. In the end we always came out of this impasse feeling like "the other person doesn't really care about what is important to me." Basic needs weren't being met and the *cycle of trust*[8] was being repeatedly broken.

We weren't able to handle all these challenges in a healthy way because neither of us was healthy. When my brokenness clashed with his brokenness we reacted in different ways, but none of them involved kindness and grace. We were quick to point fingers and throw accusations, but we were not secure in our identity nor equipped to move past the problems into solutions. When our expectations weren't met, and in some cases were categorically denied, we did not know what to do, apart from criticizing, resenting each other and finding comfort in counterfeit

---

[7] Love languages: ways to express and experience love. You can learn more about this in the book "The Five Love Languages: how to express heartfelt commitment to your mate" by Gary Chapman.

[8] https://medium.com/@danaecouturewoodall/the-trust-cycle-6e4d1e2d4115 (simple informative article about the cycle of trust).

affections. It's not my place to discuss his 'coping mechanisms', but I can talk about mine: I developed addictive behaviors; compulsive comfort eating and mindless TV watching for long periods of time, till late hours into the night. Those were hours of my life I lost trying to get some relief for my troubled soul, a break for my afflicted mind and some pleasure and delight for my deprived body. The Comforter was there all along, waiting for us to turn aside and invite Him in. His grace would have been sufficient to meet all our needs. But, for a long time, we chose to hide our weaknesses from Him, and instead of strength we got shame, tons of it.

> *We chose to hide our weaknesses from God, and instead of strength we got loaded with shame.*

## Why God?

Seven hard years went by. At this point in life we had experienced cyclical patterns of turmoil and frustration. The man I had married had deep intimacy issues and an inability to communicate and connect on an emotional level. Our attempts to communicate were monologues which left me devastatingly alone after dealing with his impregnable silence. His heart had walls that were too high for me to climb and every time I tried, I would fall on my face and got terribly bruised and broken. I could never do anything good enough for his standards and that gave him the excuse to judge me and remove his love.

All the acceptance issues I faced growing up were back on the table and I felt rejected and looked down upon every single day. I felt physically exhausted, emotionally drained, lifeless and hopeless. I remember feeling alone, confused and overwhelmed, as if I was by myself in a dark, deep pit where there was no way up, no way out and I kept stumbling because most of the time I couldn't see where I was going. I was surviving. I had no bigger purpose in life other than to pick myself up every morning and plod through the day as best as I could so my boy wouldn't have to experience the destructive effects of living with a depressed mother. How did my life turn out so different from what I imagined?

We met at church, our inner circle of friends consisted mainly of Christian young adults and many of them were part of the youth ministry team, like me. We both started with good intentions. We did not set out to fail, but failure seemed to be our overbearing reality, and I could not understand how to fit it into my faith.

*Why God?*

*Why is this happening to us?*

*Why didn't you warn me?*

*Why didn't you stop us from ruining our lives?*

*Why did you let this happen?*

Do these questions sound familiar? Have they crossed your mind at any point? I used to ask God these questions all the time. Always in the midst of great despair: crying my eyes out, pounding my bed, banging doors and releasing my pain and frustration with loud shouts, when nobody else was around. God was so patient with me.

Little did I know that in doing so I was setting the course for victory. I stayed connected. Even in the midst of deep frustration and disappointment I didn't shut God out.  His presence was the only reality keeping me sane. We had a story together that I couldn't deny. I felt like I was dangling on a tightrope between life and death and I would certainly die if I carried on without Him, so I kept coming back to the secret place. I love my friend Yolondo Lupoe's definition of 'secret place': "where I experience His touch in the shaping of my history, His peace that settles my present, and His breath that commands my future."

Sometimes He spoke no words, but I knew in my heart that He was listening, and I could feel His tender love holding me close and soothing me. Other times He would give me specific Bible verses which brought encouragement and strength, or wisdom to deal with a particular situation, or address an issue of the heart. I couldn't see the bigger picture yet, but I didn't completely lose my way and die in the desert because I kept sitting at the table with Him, and He faithfully kept giving me my daily bread.

*I set the course for victory by staying connected to God, even in the midst of frustration and disappointment.*

Nevertheless, my marriage didn't seem to get any better. The same problems, the same issues, kept plaguing us over and over again, and although I was obsessively fixated in my conjugal plights, my ex-husband became gradually more indifferent. He got busier and devoted his time and energy to his professional career. He had his interests, I had mine. We lived separate lives. It got to a point when we were merely living under the same roof, discussing logistics and parenting a child together. "How can he go on living life as if nothing is wrong? Why is he not committed to make the success of this marriage, of this family, his priority in life?" I couldn't bring myself to forgive him for that. It was, in my eyes, an unforgivable betrayal. Meanwhile, in my time in the secret place (the time I spent in God's presence, connecting with His heart, listening to His voice, reading His Word), the Holy Spirit relentlessly reminded me that I needed to forgive my husband, but I chose to ignore His instruction and willingly disobeyed His commands, regarding this, for years.

Anyone who listens to the word but does not do what it says is like someone who looks at his face in a mirror and, after looking at himself, goes away and immediately forgets what he looks like (James 1:23-24).

That was me. I had forgotten who I was meant to be and was now staring at that photo and being bluntly confronted with a faded, shattered, almost unrecognizable reflection of myself. I was burdened by bitterness and offense, grieved by sorrow and loss, crushed by the pain of rejection and self-loathing. I had been poisoning myself

> *I had been poisoning myself for years as I counted my husband's trespasses against me.*

for years as I counted that man's trespasses against me. I was asking God for answers but all the time I was focused on highlighting the speck in my ex-husband's eye, unwilling to acknowledge the plank in mine[9]. I thought I was the spiritual one because I hadn't given up on us and kept pressing for an intimate, all in, holding-nothing-back connection. However, the ways I pressed in and pushed for, were so aggressive and lacking in grace that I got the opposite response. Don't get me wrong, I am not condoning or devaluing the negative impact that his inertia and neglect had on our lives, but there was a better way to deal with it: God's way.

My childhood dreams were God-given. I knew what I wanted in a marriage, but I wasn't equipped to pursue it. Out of His mercy and goodness, God kept instructing me in the way of forgiveness, love, freedom and life; equipping me so I knew the truth that would set me free. But what did I do with that knowledge? How did I steward the *revealed counsel of God*? I repeatedly chose not to act on it and, in the process, I paid a high price[10]. I truly believe things would have been very different for us if we had established forgiveness as a non-negotiable foundation from the very

---

[9] Matthew 7:3

[10] (On chapter 4 I am going to go a lot deeper regarding the destructive consequences of unforgiveness and the extraordinary healing and reward that follow the decision to forgive).

beginning of our marriage, but the truth was that we couldn't be reconciled with each other because we weren't yet reconciled with our Father.

## Orphan hearts in the making

We were both brought up in homes with a high value for hard work and achievement. Nothing wrong with that, unless it's taken to an unhealthy extreme. Both our families have a history of very determined ancestors who, having come from extreme poverty, had climbed their way up to comfortable middle class, through unwavering commitment and relentless hard work. A solid work ethic was passed to the next generations together with a no-nonsense, get-it-right, don't-make-messes code of conduct. So, from a very young age we were treated like mini adults and grew up believing that in order to be accepted and loved we had to work hard for it. Good performance with no mistakes equaled affirmation and reward. Mistakes and failures were not tolerated.

> *We couldn't be reconciled with each other because we weren't yet reconciled with our Father.*

To fail was to be weak and inefficient, and it would get you into trouble. It would bring punishment, anger, a lot of shame and removal of love. In other words, we grew up learning that *the expression of love* is to be guarded and conditional, based upon the other person's performance, as we seek to get our own needs met.

My parents are lovely people, they did the best they could and throughout the years I have seen so much transformation and growth in their lives as they've journeyed with the Lord. As I write these words, there is no resentment in my heart. This was the only model they knew, and they replicated it in their parenting. Through the renewal of my mind with the Gospel of grace, and the empowering of the Holy Spirit, I was able to forgive them. They have forgiven me many times when I have hurt and disappointed them, and I have forgiven them for inadvertently misrepresenting God's love.

Then, there was church - I had to forgive church too. We both grew up attending churches with a very legalistic culture, which reinforced the belief that good performance walked hand in hand with acceptance. We were not exposed to the Gospel of grace. We thought we were "saved by good works". It's not what people explicitly uttered, because that would be unbiblical, but it was what they modelled.

Unfortunately, in both environments, our homes and our churches, we were taught how to be critical and judgmental. Instructed in the 'fine art' of spotting flaws and shortcomings. Pointing them out, loud and clear, brought a kind of recognition of our capacity to intelligently assess the people around us. It was also a way to protect ourselves from being deceived or taken advantage of. Some people call this discernment without realizing that the root of it is self-preservation and self-promotion. Handling other people's faults with accusation and exposure became a way to make ourselves look good by making others look bad. It made sense at the time. We hadn't been shown a different way. We hadn't seen people love well and cover others as they sought to restore them. This was our default program and we interpreted ourselves and the world around us through those lenses. Of course, we ended up interpreting each other through those lenses too.

What happens when you believe that everybody else is looking at you with such relentless scrutiny? You become a master of disguise. To be known is very risky. To be known is not safe, so you become a master builder too: not of connections, but of very tall walls behind which you can hide your frailties and vulnerable spots.

My childhood memories are not the happiest ones, but my ex-husband didn't have it easy either. As he was growing up, he became an expert on how to remain entrenched behind walls so high no one could ever read his heart, myself included. The longer we did life together, the clearer it became how superficial our connection was, and I couldn't accept that without a fight. Communication got harder and harder and eventually that battlefield was abandoned. It became known as 'the land of monologue', as I literally did all the talking while he remained in complete, utter, frustrating, wanting-to-pull-my-hair-out silence. He just wanted to be left alone and carry on with life without having any drama interfering with his routine. He grew colder and more critical. No matter what I did and how hard I tried, it was never up to par. There was always something that was lacking or something that was below standard. And because my identity was intricately intertwined with my performance, I ended up reliving the familiar feeling that I was never enough, at least never good enough.

I was painfully unhappy. Every part of me was constantly consumed by this, and I felt like I was dying slowly, every day. I was so sad, depleted and depressed that I wanted out, but I couldn't see a way out. I was not financially independent and the idea of going back to live with my parents was off the table. They lived in a rural area and jobs were scarce or non-existent. I didn't want to become a financial burden to them and, besides, they were far away from my city and my friends. I would be even more isolated. I was also convinced I would lose my son's custody and that was something which was out of the question for me. From any angle I looked at it, it felt like I was going backwards. I was so desperate that many times I considered ending my life, but I couldn't do that to my boy. I felt trapped, just like the Israelites at the Red Sea, between certain death and no possible escape route. I was forced to remain and, although at the time it was tremendously hard, looking back, I am so glad I did. In that hopeless place, my wonderful God, with His mighty hand and His outstretched arm[11], empowered me to part the seas and to keep moving forward. Then, He pulled me out of that pit and led me on a journey through the *wide open spaces of grace*.

---

[11] Psalm 136:12

## Sonship!

What a journey that was. Back then, the 'land of grace' was not in our line of sight. We were not secure. We were not anchored. We had been building our lives on the sand of self-righteousness. We were striving to earn God's favor with the good works we managed to amass, but self-righteousness was hard to keep up and no fun at all. We had orphan hearts[12]. We were living from a place of lack, fending for ourselves and fighting ferociously for our rights because deep down we didn't believe anybody was in our corner; everybody was out to get us, even God.

I had grown up with so many mixed messages regarding fatherly love that I remember feeling constantly torn between running into God's arms and running away from Him. Although I experienced His loving presence and I longed to hear His voice (so I could devour His life-giving words!), at the back of my mind there was always the fear He was going to punish me as soon as I did or said something wrong. Back then I never felt completely safe in my relationship with God. I expected Him to, at any moment, throw me in the deep end and just sit there, watching from a distance, to see if I passed or failed the test. So, I approached Him with suspicion in my heart regarding His motives. Like Adam and Eve, yielding to the lies of the enemy, believing that He is holding something back and doubting His unconditional love and goodness.

I am writing these words and tears are running down my face. I had to stop and tell Him once again how sorry I am for having allowed my mind to

---

[12] You can find out more about the characteristics of an orphan heart in the book "The Father's Embrace" by Jack Frost; Also, the following link will lead you to an informative article listing the differences between the orphan spirit and the spirit of sonship: https://www.charismanews.com/opinion/39229-the-difference-between-the-orphan-spirit-and-a-spirit-of-sonship

entertain such wrong thoughts about Him. Back then, I did not fear[13] Him but I was afraid of Him. It's supposed to be the other way around.

What were we lacking the most? An experiential revelation of the unconditional love and acceptance of our Abba Father[14]. That is, and it will always be the cornerstone and the unshakeable source of our identity. First and foremost, we are sons and daughters of a good Father. That is the firmest foundation to build a life on. Yes, the Rock is Jesus [15] but Jesus came to reveal the Father heart of God. He is a good, loving, caring, wise, perfect Father who never leaves us or forsakes us. Clothed with that revelation we can remain secure, anchored, filled with an inner peace which surpasses rationality, even when there is a storm raging around us.

> *This is the cornerstone of our identity: first we are sons and daughters of a good Father.*

That wasn't us back then. We were blinded by wrong beliefs. "What you believe about God's goodness impacts every aspect of your life"[16], so our beliefs really needed to be challenged and changed by truthful ones.

For all who are led by the Spirit of God are sons of God. For you did not receive the spirit of slavery to fall back into fear, but you have received the spirit of sonship. When we cry, 'Abba! Father!' it is the Spirit himself bearing witness with our spirit that we are children of God, and if children, then heirs, heirs of God and fellow heirs with Christ, provided we suffer with

---

[13] The fear of the Lord: a reverential respect and awe which draws you near to His heart; the fear of doing or saying something which will bring separation or distance from God's presence.

[14] Ἀββᾶ (in the original Aramaic) - *Abbá*: "Father," also used as a term of *tender endearment* by a beloved child – i.e. in an *affectionate, dependent* relationship with their father; "*daddy*," "*papa*." (Strong's Concordance 5)

[15] Sorry Dwayne Johnson, but He holds the rights to that name :)

[16] Bill Johnson, *God is Good*, p.25.

him in order that we may also be glorified with him. I consider that the sufferings of this present time are not worth comparing with the glory that is to be revealed to us (Romans 8:14-18).

If we had the right beliefs about who God is and who we are in Him, we would have run into His arms and invited Him to invade our situation. With God, suffering is never in vain or senseless. With Him in the equation, healing, restoration, reward, expansion and a glorious destination are always available. That's what Jesus conquered for His children. His Kingdom is not a decreasing Kingdom but an ever increasing one[17].

*The right beliefs will be the building blocks for what you want to see edified in the next season of your life.*

Whether you are divorced or not, the right beliefs will be the building blocks for what you want to see edified in the next season of your life. They can change the end of your story. What do you want to rebuild? The same kind of building you had before or a new upgraded version, with foundations which will weather the storms and sustain ongoing increase?

## From glory to glory

This chapter is not meant to depress you. Instead, it is meant to give you a clearer picture of where I'm coming from. I called myself a Christian, but I was not living in the freedom Jesus conquered for me. I was trapped, dying inside, consumed by bitter unforgiveness, drifting through life, with no higher purpose, just trying to survive. There was so much darkness, deception and confusion I wanted you to know about because, against this dark backdrop you will be able to see the light shine so much brighter.

---

[17] Isaiah 9:7

The truth revealed in my story, as a daughter of God who chose to trust Him and follow His wise ways through the hardship and suffering of separation and divorce, will open your eyes and your heart to a higher reality, the Kingdom reality. God is for you, not against you. He didn't cause your affliction, but He is the answer to it.

I also hope the truth you have encountered so far has caused you to reflect, released you to look beyond your own struggle, and empowered you to become more empathetic. Empathy is more significant than you think (we will be looking into it in greater depth in the next chapters). Your spouse or ex-spouse is a child of God too. He loves his son or his daughter and He wants them to grow into the full stature of Christ as well.

I am now seeking to live a life where I am increasingly led by the Spirit and I know in my heart that I am a daughter and an heir of God, and a fellow heir with Christ. Our story depicts a trajectory that goes from glory to glory, so I invite you to come along because, from here on, it only gets better!

# Q & A

I want to keep in your line of sight, from the very beginning, that reading this book is not just about knowing me and my story. It is very much about you and the story of transformation that you will get to tell as you open your heart and let the revelation in it impact you and lead you closer to God. He is the source of all the healing and restoration you need. The following questions, suggestions and exercises are to be used as a reflective tool to facilitate an encounter with the Truth. Remember, I needed first to take the plank out of my own eye so I could *see clearly* to remove the speck from my brother's eye (Luke 6:42). Do you want to see clearly? Do you want to have a clearer understanding of who and where you are and what to do next? This is the time to bring yourself fully. He is a safe place. You can be honest and vulnerable. He is also secure in His love. He can handle your doubts, frustrations and disappointment. Whenever you find yourself stuck, just ask the Holy Spirit to give you the answers and to "guide you into all the truth" (John 16:13).

There are two boxes to provide the opportunity for individual and joint reflection (for those who want to work on or improve their marriage). I advise you to always start alone with the Lord and let Him minister to your heart, before you engage in joint reflection with your spouse.

As you go through this process, I would like to remind you that some things will probably require time and perseverance, so make the decision to give yourself grace. Sometimes the Holy Spirit will bring conviction and correction, but He is loving and kind. He will never do it through accusation or condemnation as His desire is to empower you and to build you up.

# M y s e l f  &  G o d

- Are you connected with God or do you need to reconnect with Him? Ask the Holy Spirit to guide you back home: to the heart of the Father. Have an honest and open-hearted conversation with the Lord; Don't forget to stop and listen to what He is saying. (If you feel you are stuck, ask someone you trust, who is connected with God, to help you reconnect).

- Do you believe God is real, good, and a rewarder of those who seek Him? (Hebrews 11:6); If not, ask for the gift of faith.

- Did you feel the need to repent of something while you were reading this chapter? If you did, ask the Holy Spirit to guide you into full repentance[18]. Repentance is a gift[19].

- Do you need to forgive someone? Who do you need to forgive? Are you ready to do it? (Ask the Holy Spirit to bring clarity, guidance and empowerment in this process. If you don't feel ready yet, keep moving forward with the expectation that change is in the air).

- Are you secure in your identity as a son/daughter of a good God? If not, what is the root of your insecurity?
  (Ask the Holy Spirit to reveal this to you and take notes; Ask Him to help you identify any lies you have been believing, and ask Him to reveal the truth).

- Do you believe He is for you, not against you?
  (If you believe He has something against you be completely honest with God about it;

*Don't leave the secret place without giving Him a chance to encounter you with His healing love; Don't leave without having your relationship with Him fully and authentically restored).

---

[18] *Repentance* = change the way you think

[19] 2 Timothy 2:25

# T o g e t h e r

*(For those who want to work towards the restoration or improvement of their marriage)*

- Did you step into marriage with a specific agenda? Does it match God's agenda? Come with an open heart, make the decision that you are not going to be offended and discuss this with each other, with honesty and kindness; Ask the Holy Spirit to lead you in finding out God's agenda, in revealing motives of the heart, and together surrender your agendas to the Lord.

- Do you know your love languages? Pick two or three main ones. (I you haven't yet, go online and check out the "5 Love Languages"[20]).

- Do you know your spouse's love languages? Talk it through with your spouse.

- Discuss practical ways you can receive and express love more effectively in your daily lives.

- What lenses do you use when you look at your spouse? (Write it down on a piece of paper but don't share it with your spouse yet; If you're stuck, ask the Holy Spirit to show you what "lenses" you are using).

- Ask God to give you a different 'pair of glasses'. Close your eyes. What is He showing you about your spouse you couldn't see before?
  Take notes and then share with your spouse the contrast between the old and new lenses.

- ✦ Get 2 photos of each other (one you can carry with you, and one you can put on display); write on them or attach a speech bubble post-it where you can write the words which express God's perspective of your spouse.

---

[20]https://www.sheknows.com/love-and-sex/articles/1059295/what-are-the-5-love-languages/ (simple informative article outlining the five love languages).

The following section will be at the end of every chapter. Use it to record any reflections, experiences, encounters, prophetic words and dreams which have brought increased revelation, mind renewal and even transformation. In the end you will be able to trace back the way your journey unfolded, with God guiding your steps. You will have a clearer overview and this bigger picture will be an unforgettable piece of your eternal story with the Lord.

# LifeLine

Revelation & Transformation log _____/_____/_____

"Carry each other's burdens and in this way you will **fulfil the law of Christ.**"

(Galatians 6:12)

# 3 Catalytic, Empowering People

"Give someone permission to speak into your life. Make sure it's someone you trust. And when the person says something you don't want to hear, listen very carefully."

(Mark Batterson)

What you are about to witness is really the beginning of change. This shift began to take place in my soul and my heart when I invited and allowed godly, empowering people to walk alongside me and speak truth into my life.

Throughout my turbulent marriage and also during my separation, I not only kept attending church, but I also remained working in ministry as a volunteer. I was part of the Teen & Youth leadership team. Unfortunately, in some churches, marital problems, impending separation and, especially divorce, are sometimes addressed as either gossip or *taboo*: we'd rather pretend it's not there, and we don't like to talk about it because we find it uncomfortable or even embarrassing. So, during this time many people moved awkwardly around me. It doesn't mean that no one cared, they just didn't know what to do or what to say, so they pretended that nothing was wrong and completely avoided the subject. But God!

This is a book where you are going to witness many moments of deep gratitude for what God has done and the way He has done it. I might even sound somewhat repetitive at times, but I will do it unapologetically. I am so grateful for the way God was in my corner in this very difficult season and how He put amazing people around me.

My direct leaders at church truly came alongside me and embraced my vulnerability with respect, empathy and tender, loving care. They saw in me what I couldn't yet see; they didn't label me as troubled, messed up or full of issues, and restrict me because I was struggling in my marriage, but poured into me. They invested in me and empowered me in a way that made them instrumental in my journey towards restoration. They modeled godly leadership, and in doing so, influenced the development of my leadership skills, which allowed me to become a more effective leader in my own life. They were used by God to be catalysts of empowering change. Let me tell you all about it.

## Brought up in a Disempowering Culture

As I shared before, both at home and at church, it was difficult to assert my identity and find my voice. I never felt fully accepted, so I never felt safe to be fully known. I grew up feeling as though there was always some reproach or remark coming my way, no matter how hard I tried. I remember, on many occasions, being punished or simply having something abruptly taken off my hands because I wasn't getting it right, I wasn't doing it properly, or because I was making a mess. The unsettling exasperation, the harsh words or the look of disappointment and reproach in my father's eyes, instead of the acceptance and approval I so desperately craved, caused so much shame and self-reproach. Those crushing feelings had a devastating and lasting effect on the way I viewed and tackled future challenges. In those memories, which were gradually suppressed, failure became the prevalent reality because I was never given the chance to clean up my messes, guilt free, and get back on track towards a satisfying and fulfilling sense of achievement and completion. I always felt as though there was something wrong with me, as though I was never enough. I thought God viewed me that way too.

Church is supposed to be a place where we can find family, a welcoming community that lends strength to us, a *living organism* of cooperation and purposeful growth where we are surrounded with loving and empowering people who see us through God's eyes and are committed to equip us for the good works we are purposed for[21]. However, sometimes churches don't reflect the heart of God, especially when unrealistic expectations are put on people and very little grace is given for real life issues and processes to be dealt with in a healthy way. I have experienced both.

The church I attended until I was eighteen fostered a culture where religious, legalistic mindsets were prevalent and rarely questioned. To be fully known, in other words, to let others into your vulnerable places and processes, meant there was a high probability that you were going to become a target of comparison, condemnation, accusation and even rejection as a form of punishment. You could very well end up isolated, labelled as 'damaged goods' and left to deal with painful shame on your

---

[21] Ephesians 2:10

own. I hope you have never experienced and will never have to experience this the way I did, particularly during my teenage years.

There is always a process of restoration and ongoing trimming involved, if we want to grow into the full stature of a son and daughter of God[22], and there is a godly way of partnering with people who are growing. It is true that when we invite Jesus to be the Savior and Lord of our lives, we immediately become a new creation in our spirits. However, there are systems of beliefs, assimilated during a lifetime and manifested in behaviors, which require a relational journey with the Lord, a daily renewal of the mind through the Word of God and the increasing infilling of the Holy Spirit.

What would happen to babies in the natural if, while they are learning to walk, we punished them with shameful criticism and accusation, and removed our love and presence every time they fell down?[23] Would that benefit their development or become a stumbling block to it? Why do some of us still think it's okay to do this to our spiritually developing brothers and sisters? Maybe a better question would be: Why do well intentioned people, who love Jesus and want to become more like Him, actually end up acting towards others in ways which are so opposite to what He taught and demonstrated?

> *When we are driven by fear instead of love, we can easily lose sight of God's grace.*

In my own experience in a disempowering church environment, this reaction was mostly rooted in the fear of men: "If I don't punish you with visible disapproval, expressed through the removal of my affection and consequent disconnection, then people will think I agree with you, or that what's happening to you is happening to me too. Therefore, I will not

---

[22] John 15:1-15

[23] I have heard the 'baby first steps' analogy in two messages, one by Bill Johnson and another by Steve Backlund.

associate with you until you've got it all figured out and have proven you are beyond reproach!"

Environments where the focus is put on self-preservation, instead of collaborative restoration, can easily become competitive and hostile. When we are driven by fear instead of love, we can easily lose sight of God's amazing grace and become unable to extend it to ourselves and others. Highlighting other people's mistakes means deflecting everyone else's attention from my own. As mistakes are not tolerated, and are usually punished, it's not safe to be authentic about our struggles and failures. We start to hide or 'embellish' information which can lead to punishment, and we work hard to make sure people around us only get the edited version. Today, as I look back into some of the barren landscapes of my past with greater and deeper understanding, I can see the core of the problem.

At the heart of the disempowering culture I experienced, both at home and at church, were people in authority who didn't know how to deal with mistakes or messes in a constructive way. Whenever they were confronted with a challenge or disruption of the *status quo*, control through punishment, drama and disconnection was a way to get others to comply, to do what they wanted and get what they needed. It stemmed from fear and insecurity, and the need to have everything under control to be able to feel secure and safe again.

> *At the heart of a disempowering culture there is fear and insecurity.*

## Roots of Insecurity

I'm not just pointing fingers here. If I was, I would have to point at myself too. Without realizing it at first, as the years went by I too became an expert in ways to deal with fear and insecurity (which were not always sound or healthy), especially after I became a parent. When I started growing in the awareness and knowledge of what it means to be a powerful person, committed to raise powerful people, I eventually went through some very painful reality checks. I realized that, even though in some areas I intentionally parented my child in a very different way than I had been parented, I still mimicked many controlling, manipulative and punitive behaviors in the way I related to my son. My intentions were good, but my debilitating belief systems had not been challenged and transformed. Therefore, I kept replicating what I had experienced, at the expense of connection.

When my son Daniel moved to England to live with me, he was seven years old and he was not an English speaker. God blessed me with the finances and the logistic capacity to be very present and support him well during the initial integration process. His transition was smooth, he was doing several extra-curricular activities he loved and after 6 months he had become a fluent communicator. He loved primary school, he was happy and thrived in it. Unfortunately, his transition into secondary school was very difficult and painful. He suffered with bullying and didn't always know how to pick his 'friends'.

I was able and knowledgeable to approach the school and work with them towards remedial solutions but, as a single parent, I was struggling to keep it together in our home environment because I was fearful and insecure. I was afraid that Daniel was going to get physically or emotionally hurt (or both) and I was always second-guessing my parenting abilities. I was also very self-conscious and still very afraid to mess up and suffer the wrath of the 'parenting community' around me. I told myself that all my decisions, judgements and restrictions were because I loved my son and I wanted to protect him, but this wasn't always the case. True love casts away all fear[24],

*People can't give grace to others if they don't have it for themselves.*

---

[24] 1 John 4:18

and fear was still very prevalent in my home. I was more focused on saving face than I was on the saving grace of Jesus.

In the following years, in the moments of deeper awareness and greater understanding of myself and my process, the Lord led me to repent from not always addressing my ex-husband, my son and myself, with grace and kindness, and empowered me to move forward with the certainty that there was nothing I had done or failed to do which was beyond redemption. Coming face to face with my own shortcomings, in an honest and authentic way, produced humility and empathy. It changed the way I regarded others and their processes and cleared the way for forgiveness to become a prevalent reality in my life.

I know I have been forgiven, just as I have forgiven the people who abused their authority in ways which so negatively impacted me. I am thankful to God for granting me the gifts of insight and empathy and the capacity to forgive what once caused deep indignation and anger whenever I thought about it. I have realized these people were perpetuating a model they had assimilated without asking questions. Moreover, they too were terrified of failing and had no grace for themselves. They couldn't give what they didn't have, so they had no grace for us either. I am also convinced they weren't aware of how they were passing on a poisoned legacy to the ones who were closest to them.

## The Fear of Failure: a Poisoned Legacy

The fear of failure stops you in your tracks before you even get started. It paralyses you. You'd rather not even try than face the possibility of dealing with the unwanted, crushing feelings which come with blame and shame[25]. It also hinders creativity and innovative thought because you are no longer willing to try new things. New things are risky, and you don't want to take unnecessary risks, no matter how small they are. You can't see what you

---

[25] https://www.habitsforwellbeing.com/shame-resilience-theory/

can win or achieve because you are painfully focused on what will be taken away from you if you don't achieve. Fear has front stage, and you can never build something solid on a foundation of fear. Eventually you stop dreaming because you are not willing to go through awkward learning processes, while you are not an expert. Every initial, unfamiliar step becomes a painful experience riddled with over-the-top anxiety: "What if I fall?"

But then, how can we become experts on anything if we are not willing to make mistakes and learn from them? If we are growing, stepping into new, upgraded levels, from glory to glory, we will make some mistakes on the way up. Instead, "what if in the end I fly?"[26] becomes the question.

When His disciples were arguing about who was the greatest among them, Jesus didn't rebuke their desire for greatness, but redirected their attention to what real greatness looks like: to become like a child. How do children learn? Through trial and error and through what is modelled to them. Now, I am fully convinced 'good practice makes perfect' and that there is reward on the other side of perseverance, but it has taken me years to change my fearful perspective of growth. Today I know that growing through 'trial, error and improvement' doesn't always have to be a painful experience if I learn how to enjoy the ride and continue to extend grace to myself and others. The secret is to learn from other people's mistakes too (harvesting their wisdom), and to keep making new mistakes - because if we are making the same mistakes over and over again, that means we are not really learning our lessons.

*The fear of failure stops you in your tracks before you even get started.*

Back then I didn't have a clue on how to do this well, neither did my ex-husband. We were both terrified and disgusted with the idea of failure. I

---

[26] Erin Hanson

was so deeply steeped in this fear that, although I have experienced ongoing breakthrough, to this day, I find myself being triggered[27] when I face new challenges or learning curves. I still have to be intentional in pursuing increasing levels of freedom in this area of my emotional intelligence.

Seven years in a marriage where we felt stuck: two people who didn't believe they were powerful but acted like they were each other's victim, who were so afraid to fail they were paralyzed within the problems, unable to move constructively towards any solutions. But God!

Fear was my initial tune, but Jesus' song over me was very different and it kept getting louder and louder. I am so grateful to God for the way He helped me navigate such scary waters, so I didn't have to remain alone, unknown and stuck in a crippling, sterile state of mind. Through the truth revealed in His word, the power encountered in His presence and the community He put around me, He showed Himself faithful.

> *A victim mindset keeps you stuck in the problems, unable to move constructively towards any solutions.*

## Servant Leaders

As a young adult I moved to another church where I became an attending member and a volunteer worker for the next fifteen years. At the time this narrative starts, seven years into my marriage, the Youth pastors, Paulo and Vanda Caio, were the leaders who line managed me. In the process they

---

[27] A lot of the time, susceptibility to triggering occurs as a result of a traumatic event; the person is triggered by anything that reminds them of that event or experience. A trigger is something that sets off a memory tape or flashback transporting the person back to the event of her/his original trauma. When something or someone triggers you, it means that they're actually setting off one of your subconscious beliefs.

became close, dear friends. Their input in my life was so far above and beyond what I expected and could have hoped for, that I am still today, and for the rest of my days will be, reaping the abundant life they sowed in me, and building upon the firm foundations they helped me lay.

These leaders demonstrated a very different way of doing things (at least very different from what I had experienced until then), and their leadership style impacted me profoundly. Their love for the Word and the Presence set a template I sought to emulate. The way they empowered and released their team members, rooted in love and in the security of their relationship with the Holy Spirit, got my full attention. I loved the way they honored people and the way they valued and fostered connection - which really stood out in an environment where people in ministry had very entrenched religious, utilitarian mindsets and practices.

Paulo and Vanda were intentional in making time in their busy schedule to connect with people, especially with those who worked with and under them (their inner circle) [28]. They planned regular meetings and social gatherings but also one-on-one sessions. They weren't there just to be served, instead they approached us with a servant heart. That model gave us a template to follow and equipped us to do team/family in a more connected and collaborative way.

Paulo and Vanda weren't just interested in talking at us (yes, they still brought their vision, guidelines, instructions and correction), but they were genuinely interested in hearing what we had to say. I'm not just talking about opinions and ideas regarding the ministry. They were interested in building a real, deep connection of the heart with those who were running the race with them. I found that irresistible.

---

[28] Danny Silk, *Keep Your Love On*, p. 124-127

Sometimes we just need to be heard. When someone is willing to listen, with no ulterior motives, no hidden agenda, merely because they want to know you, the real you, it is a powerful invitation for the heart to open and the soul to fully show up. So I did. I opened up my heart to them and shared the good, the bad and the ugly. They didn't avoid the difficult subjects but listened attentively

> *As I recognized my leaders' authority, I positioned myself legitimately under their covering.*

and gave valuable feedback. They were trustworthy and reliable. Nothing of what was discussed between us was ever mentioned anywhere else. Because they listened and they cared, were careful with my heart and showed integrity, I invited them to speak into my life.

## Discipleship: a Mutual Choice

As I recognized my leaders' authority to bring vision, guidance and correction, I positioned myself legitimately under their covering. No longer just a servant, but now a friend, in the truest meaning of the word. That is what discipleship is really about. I choose you, you choose me, we do life together, we speak into each other's lives and we lend our strength by carrying each other's burdens. In the process, I discovered the role we play in each other's restorative stories is second to God's role. No, I'm not inflating our significance, I am merely repeating what Jesus demonstrated in his relationship with his immediate family (his disciples), and what God clearly reveals in His word: we fulfil the law of Christ when we carry each other's burdens (Galatians 6:2). What is 'the law of Christ'? It's a 'law' where every commandment, precept, decision and choice, in language and deed, hangs on the principle of love[29].

---

[29] Matthew 22:36-40

Use your freedom to serve one another humbly in love. For the entire law is fulfilled in keeping this one command: "Love your neighbor as yourself" (Galatians 5:14).

Love does no harm to a neighbor. Therefore, love is the fulfillment of the law (Romans 13:10).

It is not always easy but it is simple. And it was the simple Gospel these leaders put into practice as they kept me, a person next to them (*their neighbor*), under their wings. They covered me, kept believing in me and loved me well as they sought to equip, empower and restore me in a *spirit of gentleness*[30]. Instead of being judgmental and controlling, they were compassionate, empathetic and refreshingly authentic about their process. Yes, I'll say it again: their authenticity was like a breath of fresh air. I felt safe and covered, like I had room to breathe and permission to be fully myself, to finally be authentic. And I did. I tentatively brought my vulnerability to the table, and I wasn't punished for it!

*The role we play in each other's restorative stories is second to God's role.*

In return, I was also challenged and given the opportunity to make a choice to continue to love them well and extend grace and covering whenever they gave me access to their vulnerability. And I did. How could I not extend to them what they had so generously given to me?

When Paulo and Vanda chose to disciple me, they embraced the whole package, and now you have a considerably clearer picture of how much luggage I was carrying. There were days when I had stories of victory to tell and glimpses of hope to share, but those were an exception at first. Most of the time I experienced great emotional turmoil. I struggled with low self-

---

[30] Galatians 6:1

esteem, ongoing self-doubt, unrelenting, vicious self-talk and I lacked self-confidence. I was desperate to make up for the acceptance, affirmation and validation I still wasn't getting at home. The condition of my heart, my compelling emotional needs and existential aches, became clearer and clearer to the naked eye, the more we did life and ministry work together. They knew my first motivation was not an altruistic one. On the contrary, I was hanging on to the accomplishments in that quadrant of my life, as if they were pieces with which I could continue to build a life-saving raft in the middle of the no-land-in-sight, inescapable, inhospitable, overwhelming ocean my life had become.

They were aware of all of this, but because they were insightful and full of faith, they could see the desire in my heart to change and grow. They could see beyond what I could see, and they kept championing me. They were in it for the long haul. And it was a long one. It took about five years to fully step out of victim mode and see myself through the eyes of an empowering Father.

## No Longer a Victim

Do you remember the questions I frequently asked God, listed on the previous chapter? They all started with "why":

*Why God?*

*Why is this happening to me?*

*Why didn't you warn me?*

*Why didn't you stop us from ruining our lives?*

*Why did you let this happen?*

If you read between the lines, you can unravel at their core a victim mentality or mindset. I found myself in the midst of heartbreaking circumstances and instead of tracing back my willful steps, I blamed God for not stopping me. I assumed He was in control. He is in charge, but He's chosen not to be in control. That's why we have free will.

What did I do with that freedom? What choices and decisions did I make? They weren't always good, and they weren't always grounded in

> *Life didn't just happen to me, I happened to life too.*

God's will. I didn't always ask for His input when it was time to choose or make life changing decisions. And there I was, further down the road, asking questions as if life happened *to me*, not taking responsibility for my own actions or realizing I had happened to life too. Did you know "our beliefs drive our destiny, because what we believe to be true actually ends up creating the world we live in"?[31]. The more I thought about my thoughts in the light of the Gospel, the more I was convinced that my mindset needed to shift.

I began to confront the familiar lies which conveniently put the blame for my unhappiness on my parents, the church, God and my husband. Yes, I had gone through some rough patches in my life. Yes, I had experienced the deep emotional pain that comes with rejection, but now I was not alone anymore. In His Word, God makes it clear that "He has not given us a Spirit of fear, but of power and of love and of a sound mind"[32]. We are no longer victims, because of the way He fiercely loved and loves us. We are now

---

[31] Danny Silk in People Helping People (online course LOP Academy), lesson 3.

[32] 2 Timothy 1:7 (NKJV)

called "more than conquerors"[33]. I knew I needed to explore the mind of Christ and "be transformed by the renewal of my mind"[34] ; to possess the truth that was going to

> *Transformation comes by the renewal of the mind.*

set me free and empower me to face fears and insecurities; to take ownership for my decisions (whether good or bad); to learn to clean up messes quickly and shamelessly, and move forward with hope. For that to happen I needed help, support and accountability. I did not know where to begin but my loving leaders did. They were a gift from God, and I cherished their friendship and held on to them for dear life. Paulo and Vanda were catalytic in the way they set about this change of trajectory in my life, and in the way they were committed to make it sustainable and increasing.

They offered to help in practical ways, and they followed through with it. Our communication lines were always open. I felt secure and supported and I was not afraid to ask for help whenever I felt I was drowning in the ocean of hopelessness I mentioned before. They were truly, faithfully there for me, but always making sure I was the one taking ownership of my problems and addressing my heart issues. They made sure I was being equipped, empowered and strengthened to grab the burdens they were helping me carry, and take them to the only One who can carry all the heavy burdens without being crushed by them. As a matter of fact He invites us to let go of our burdens, throw them at His feet and embrace the beautiful peace and freedom birthed in the supernatural exchange which takes place when burdens become light, yokes are made easy and we find rest for our souls[35]. This realignment was foundational because it started to break off familiar cycles of powerlessness and propelled me into a proactive, constructive movement which gradually gained momentum.

---

[33] Romans 8:37

[34] Romans 12:2

[35] Matthew 11:28-30; Psalm 55:22

Paulo and Vanda always modeled faithfulness and commitment in the way they served and did family, and they let me be part of that in more ways than one. They were also brilliant mentors in the areas of planning, managing time, resources and teams. I learned invaluable skills with them, not only by observing them but also by being released and given the opportunity to do all of the above. They invited me to teach, prepare training sessions and workshops, lead small groups and also lead worship. In time, they asked me to organize larger events and coordinate multipurpose teams. It's important to highlight that they were neither opportunistic nor irresponsible. They kept me close and they gradually increased the level of responsibility required of me, while being available to provide counsel, guidance, support and correction. Their goal was not to exploit me, which is what happens when there is delegation without development, but to place me in multiple learning contexts, intentionally chosen to grow, empower and even promote me.

Every task and every challenge set before me became an opportunity, not only to prove myself, grow in self-confidence and develop a skill set, but also an opportunity to get outside the confines of my imploding universe. An invitation to explore faith beyond the boundaries of my past experiences, to fly higher and see the bigger picture of what God was doing in other people's lives and in some way become a part of it. To serve others well I had to step up and believe God was real and powerful to meet them where they were at. The decision to press in for other people's sake also freed me, many times, from my own worries and anxieties, and allowed me to focus on the solutions that our God, who's bigger than any problem, can provide.

> *When our faith rises our capacity to receive is enlarged.*

When faith levels rise, our capacity to receive more of God's empowering presence and anointing is always enlarged[36]. That's what started to happen to me and it will happen to you

---

[36] Ephesians 3:14-19

too. As you consistently partner with Him, you will experience breakthrough and growth. Make the decision to celebrate – with a thankful heart – every step forward, yours and the people's around you.

## Celebrating Growth

This beautiful couple really brought a new meaning to the expression "running the good race." As we ran together, they did not add to my burdens, on the contrary, they chose to remain connected, to value me and look at me as a daughter of God. They never labelled me as the troubled one, the emotional or needy one, the one with marriage issues, or the one on the brink of divorce. They were patient and kind but also tenacious. They did not give up on me but kept believing in me because they saw me through our heavenly Father's eyes.

> *It's in the middle of our messy processes that we most need to draw near to God.*

As they championed me and called me up, they tangibly represented Jesus in a way I hadn't seen represented in church before, and by doing so they helped rebuild and solidify a bridge of trust between me and God.

"Religion only celebrates perfection but family celebrates progress."[37]

Do you remember the example of the baby learning to walk? What do loving parents usually do? They celebrate every single step! They cheer the baby on effusively with encouraging words and promptings. They take photos and make films. Everything in their facial expression and body language tells the baby how proud and delighted they are with the progress achieved, no matter the number of steps taken. That is the perfect picture

---

[37] Wendy & Steve Backlund, sermon at Mount Chapel, Weaverville, December 2018.

of our good God. He never said He would keep away while we got everything just perfect enough for Him to associate with us again. On the contrary, He said that He will never leave us nor forsake us[38], not even during messy processes. In fact, I propose to you that, it is when we are intentional and draw near to Him during messy processes that we see the fullness of His glory revealed[39].

Can you look at your present circumstances and retrace your steps back to bad decisions or poor choices? Can you identify negative or self-sabotaging patterns or behaviors? Can you identify areas where you need spiritual and emotional healing? Is there room for you to grow? Do you want to grow?[40]

He always wants to grow us. He is an empowering Father. He is absolutely invested in completing the good work He has started in us[41], but that doesn't mean He is going to do all the work on His own. It's a partnership. Empowerment doesn't happen when we are not engaged. He does not force us to embrace maturity, but He is ready and willing to partner with us towards it, every step of the way.

---

[38] Deuteronomy 31:6, Joshua 1:5 and Hebrews 13:5-6 (If you look up the contexts, you'll see that this word is connected with taking ground, conquering new geographical and spiritual territories and believing that when God is our helper we don't need to fear men or circumstances).

[39] I will share with you, in future chapters, more about how I've seen *His strength being made perfect in my weakness.*

[40] If any of these questions stand out to you and you feel you need to take time with the Lord to go over them, I suggest you include them at the Q&A personal reflective time with God.

[41] Philippians 1:6

## Together we are Stronger

Whatever relational issues or relational breakdown you have been going through, whatever you are experiencing now, the desire of my heart is that you finish this chapter believing that you too can undergo a change of trajectory and you don't have to carry such heavy burdens on your own. Bring them to the Lord and He will gladly relieve you[42]. Ask Him to point you in the direction of godly people and they will represent Him well by locking arms and carrying some of those burdens with you, until you are ready to fully let them go.

I hope you have been able to see the bigger picture, beyond the underlying limitations and shortcomings of some of the people I mentioned, who were trapped in the wrong mindsets, and unable to rise up to the fullness of their identity as God's sons and daughters. We have all been there at some point. I pray that, if difficult memories were re-lived, evoking similar episodes and characters from your own story, you were able to understand them better and forgive them for the way they have hurt you, failed you or even breached your trust.

I hope you have understood the intention of my heart when I described my journey through religion and out of religion. I never stopped believing in the Church. The Church, Jesus' Bride, is getting perfected every day. It's an ongoing process, which means it is not complete yet. When we start pointing fingers, we forget we too are being perfected and haven't arrived yet. The Church is God's idea, and because it's

*We need to connect with the Jesus inside of each other.*

His idea He is the one who knows how to build it. He has made the necessary blueprints, tools and gifts, available to those who are willing to connect with Him, not through religion, but through Spirit and Truth. We need each other, and above all we need to connect with the Jesus inside of

---

[42]Psalm 55:22

each other. Only then the full picture of His glory can be clearly displayed to the world: "We are being built together to become a dwelling in which God lives by His Spirit"[43].

If you are a leader or part of a church staff, my prayer is that you didn't feel devalued and you didn't approach my narrative in a defensive mode. Remember, this chapter is about catalytic people who partnered with God to change my life. They were church leaders like you. There is so much value in what they taught me, in the way they invested in me, and in how they tangibly represented Jesus and facilitated a deeper connection with Him. My desire is that you can learn from them too. I included this part of my story with no intention to gratuitously criticize the Church, on the contrary. I wanted to paint a picture so real and so vivid that key matters could not be dismissed or ignored. I wanted it to awaken some of you and especially to inspire all of you. You can really make a difference in people's lives. If you know the Holy Spirit is calling you to commit yourself afresh to build those around you in a different way, then draw closer to Him, don't lean on your own understanding. Depend on Him and know that He will guide you, refresh you and empower you to do it with excellence. Continue to get equipped, keep moving forward with integrity and only look backwards to learn lessons and give thanks for how far you've come and how much He has done in your life.

Whether you are in leadership or not, my prayer is that you were encouraged to reflect on your own journey, and to decide to reach out to the men and women God has put around you. My ex-husband had several opportunities to connect with these leaders and benefit from their counsel and support, but he chose not to open up and he decided to plod through things on his own. His journey was considerably different from mine, and who knows if we might still be together if he had not chosen to run solo?

---

[43]Ephesians 2:22

"Vulnerability is the most accurate measurement of courage" [44] : be courageous, reach out and ask for help. It might not be a leader or someone on church staff that is going to run the race with you. They are limited on the number of people they can meaningfully connect with. They are there to equip the saints for the works of ministry[45], so pick a saint. Approach a brother or sister in whom you see fruit, and who is willing and committed to do life with you and help you carry your burdens, not add to them. Learn from them so you can become a source of strength and support to others in the future. We were never meant to run this race alone.

> We were never meant to run this race alone.

## Authority Redefined

If you went through an experience somewhat similar to mine while growing up, you might have trouble trusting people, especially those in authority, and you might even have trouble surrendering to the rulership of Jesus and acknowledging Him as your Lord and King. What I can share with you regarding this is, even in that place of mistrust or resistance to surrender, the Lord has met me there, time and time again. He is not afraid of your doubts and He is bigger and stronger than any fear or trauma. Every time He brings correction, He also brings the grace to embrace it and act on it. He does it lovingly and never through shame or condemnation. He has patiently held my hand and led me on a journey of inner healing and restoration. He has nurtured me back into the ability to trust people again, and He has continued to reveal how good and kind of a King He is.

---

[44]Brene Brown - https://www.youtube.com/watch?time_continue=14&v=psN1DORYYV0

[45] Ephesians 4:12

I pray you approach God confidently, with trembling reverence but not afraid of Him. As Bill Johnson often says: "He is better than you think, so change the way you think." The One who, after proclaiming "all authority in Heaven and on Earth has been given to Me"[46], grabbed a towel and washed His disciples' feet, has completely redefined authority for me. Remember He paid a price for our freedom, even knowing that we could use that freedom to reject Him. He doesn't want to control you against your will, but if you trust Him with your life, surrender to His will and invite Him to be not just your Savior but your King, you will begin to experience and understand what it means to be "seated in the heavenly realms with Him"[47].

Under His rulership we step into the authority He has conquered for us, to empower us to establish His Kingdom on Earth: in our hearts and minds, our families, and in our relationships as it is in Heaven. Peace beyond understanding, perfect love, wisdom, beauty and abundant life are the realities of Heaven that He wants to bring into your life and the lives of those connected to you.

God is with us always[48], individually but also corporately. He delights in community. He has designed you for family. I would have never made it this far without the extraordinary intervention of catalytic people God sent my way when I was so broken and lost: Paulo and Vanda Caio, and Lidia Ferreira (you will find out more about her incredible role in the next chapter), from the bottom of my heart, thank you for the way you have loved me and invested in me.

---

[46] Matthew 28:18

[47] Ephesians 2:6

[48] Matthew 28:20

# Q & A

## M y s e l f  &  G o d

- When you pray, or talk to God, do you take time to really listen to Him?[49]

- What is He saying now?

- Are you happy with the idea of being fully known by God? If not, why not? (Ask the Holy Spirit to show you if you are believing any lies, and to lead you back into all truth).

- While reading my story did you feel like there is someone you haven't yet forgiven? If that's the case, ask the Holy Spirit to bring clarity and empower you to forgive.

- Were there moments when you felt triggered? [50] What triggered you? (If your answer is yes, ask the Holy Spirit to show you the root of that fear, pain or trauma; ask Him to disclose all truth and lead you into inner healing):

  - If you feel stuck, like you can't do this on your own, ask the Holy Spirit who can help you (informal or formal therapeutic help).

- Do you see yourself as a powerful person who takes ownership of your choices or do you tend to blame others and see yourself as their victim? What is God saying about this?

---

[49] https://hellochristian.com/7248-kris-vallotton-8-ways-god-wants-to-speak-to-you

[50] A lot of the time, susceptibility to triggering occurs as a result of a traumatic event; the person is triggered by anything that reminds them of that event or experience. A trigger is something that sets off a memory tape or flashback transporting the person back to the event of her/his original trauma. When something or someone triggers you, it means that they're actually setting off one of your subconscious beliefs.

- Are you afraid of trying new things? Do you worry constantly about what others will think and say about you? Are you afraid of change? Do you feel the need to be in control of everything? Ask the Holy Spirit to deliver you from the fear of men and the fear of failure, to show you that you are safe in His hands and to give you the gift of faith to believe that He really knows what He is doing.

- What value do you place on the truth? Are you willing to be vulnerable and authentic and ask for help? When?

# T o g e t h e r

*(For those who want to work towards the restoration or improvement of their marriage)*

- Do you feel fully known by your spouse?

- Do you want to be fully known? If not, why not?
  (If you feel ready to do it, discuss this with your spouse and make a parallel with your dialogue with God about this).

- When you engage in a conversation with your spouse do you feel really heard?
  Are you a good listener? (Check out some tools to become a good listener)[51].

- Can you identify familiar patterns of blame and shame in your relationship?

---

[51] Tools to become a good listener – follow the links
https://www.mindtools.com/CommSkll/ActiveListening.htm

https://www.forbes.com/sites/womensmedia/2012/11/09/10-steps-to-effective-listening/#7ef7851f3891

- Do you need to forgive each other? What is the Holy Spirit saying?

- Has God pointed out people (names/faces) that can 'run the race' with you?

- When are you going to approach them and ask for help?

✳ In your spare time, draw a timeline with important events/dates in your life. You can draw it as a graph chart signaling the highs and the lows. If you're artistic you can include drawings, pictures, poems and even songs. Then, take the time to share your life journey with your spouse. The goal is to be fully known and understood so you can build a deeper connection.

As you go through this process, remember some things will require time and perseverance, so make the decision to give yourself grace. Sometimes the Holy Spirit will bring conviction and correction, but He is loving and kind. He will never do it through accusation or condemnation as His desire is to empower you and to build you up.

If you have someone you trust "running the good race" with you, my suggestion is that you share this process with them and, if you and your spouse are comfortable with the idea, invite them to mediate the reflective conversations (especially if you feel like you are stuck and are having difficulty communicating).

# LifeLine

Revelation & Transformation log          ___/___/___

"Beloved, I pray that in all respects you may prosper and be in good health, **just as your soul prospers.**"

(3 John 1:2 - NASB)

# 4 The Master-Key of Forgiveness

"To forgive is to set a prisoner free and discover that the prisoner was you."

(Louis B. Smedes)

**Pay what you owe me!**

Once upon a time, in a far, far away land, there was a woman who had accrued such a massive debt that a lifetime of uninterrupted hard labor would not be enough to pay it off. Her situation was so serious that she was summoned by the King. He wished to settle the account with her. As she anxiously climbed the steps leading to the throne room, she remembered the law of the land and her heart skipped a beat: "He is going to take my freedom away" she thought, picturing herself no longer as a free woman but as a slave. A wave of fear came crashing down on any hope she might have left for her future and heavy tears started rolling down her cheeks. Standing by the door, she took a deep breath and composed herself: "This King is a good King. I will ask for mercy". This thought brought her some comfort. Desperation brought her the strength and boldness to throw herself at the feet of her King and plead her case with every fiber of her terrified being. She appealed to the King's patient heart, she proposed a phased payment plan and she even promised to do something she knew was impossible: "I will pay you everything". The King knew she would not be able to fulfill her promise, but he was so moved by her desperate condition that he decided to rule against his own interests and forgave, not part of the debt, but her entire debt!

She was beside herself when she left the palace. Her life had changed in one hearing with the King. In one moment where the words "I FORGIVE YOU" propelled her from death to life. She now had hope and a future. She felt light as a feather and excited about the days ahead, not as a slave but as a free woman. With a million plans swirling and twirling in her head, she realized that she needed money to put some of those plans in motion. Lost in her thoughts, she was not yet far from the palace when she saw a neighbor that owed her a substantial amount of money (but nothing compared to the enormous amount she owed the King). She approached her neighbor with a menacing look on her face. He was taller and stronger than her, but he felt so embarrassed with the situation that when she held him by the neck, trying to choke him, he immediately fell on his knees.

"Pay what you owe me!", she demanded. He started pleading with her, asking her to be patient with him: "Just wait a few more months and I'll pay you everything". It seemed like history was about to repeat itself, except it didn't. This woman who had just been on the other end of a similar exchange and had experienced such unmerited, extravagant, generous, merciful forgiveness, decided to not forgive her neighbor's smaller debt and threw him in jail until he could pay her every cent back. Unbelievable! The King had just modeled something extraordinary and she hadn't learned anything from it.

Her other neighbors who saw what she had done were very upset, and they went and reported to the King all that had taken place. The King was shocked with her harsh judgement and right there and then he decided to change his previous verdict. He summoned her again and this time his tone was very different. He said to her: "You wicked woman! I forgave you all your debt because you pleaded with me. Shouldn't you have been merciful to your neighbor, as I was merciful to you?" So, in anger the King threw her in jail, into the hands of the tormentors, until she could pay all her debt.

Does this story remind you of another story you have heard before? That is because this story is inspired in one of Jesus' parables. It is called the "Parable of the Unforgiving Servant" and it is recorded in Matthew 18:21-35. The reason why I replaced the male servant with a female one is because the woman in this story could very well be me.

> *I loved Jesus but had stepped outside our covenant and was not representing Him well.*

It took me many years to forgive my husband for giving up on me, and on us. I considered his passivity as an unforgivable and disloyal breach of our wedding vows. I could not think about it without experiencing heart-wrenching, gut-piercing pain. The wounds of rejection were drilled through to the very core of my childhood dreams, and so I believed he deserved to be punished. I chose to ignore that punishment is not our business anymore because Jesus took upon Himself "the punishment that brought us peace"[52]. Taking justice or punishment into my own hands meant I took justice out of God's hands, and by doing so, stepped away from the King's rule and the King's grace. I wish I had yielded to the Holy Spirit sooner. In my obstinacy I was the one being punished, as I came to experience firsthand what it means to be in the hands of the tormentors.

---

[52] Isaiah 53:5

## The Torment of Unforgiveness

"And in anger his lord turned him over to the prison guards to torture him until he repaid all he owed." (Matthew 18:34 - NET)

The original Greek word used in this parable to name the *prison guards* is *basanistēs*[53]. In the main English versions, it has been translated as 'jailors', 'tormentors' or 'torturers'. The history of its usage sheds significant light regarding its range of meaning in the Greek[54]. It was initially used in the practice of the inspection of coins and it meant "touchstone". As the testing of gold with a touchstone became a common practice among traders, the word for "touchstone" came to mean a method of testing. Because jailers were the ones who tormented prisoners, the word derived from "touchstone" was also applied to jailers who caused torment on men by testing them. The 'testing' could range from interrogation, through to the more harrowing kind of testing which involved outright torture. Therefore, it eventually gained the meaning of "one who elicits the truth by the use of the rack"[55], which could be an "inquisitor", a "torturer" and also a "jailer" (because the business of torturing was sometimes assigned to them). This meaning co-existed alongside with "being tormented by disease" too.

When I researched this information, my experience in the purgatory of unforgiveness made a lot more sense. I was already a new creation, I loved Jesus, I loved the Word of God, I believed He was my Savior and Redeemer, and I longed for His presence. However, I had stepped outside our covenant. I was not living in the fulness of the freedom He conquered for me. I was not representing Him well in the way I was relating begrudgingly towards my husband. The gold in me was tarnished and not recognizable. For it to shine it had to be touched by the Rock, sanded by the sharpness of

---

[53] τοῖς βασανισταῖς or, in its lexical form, βασανιστής: G930 - Strong's Hebrew and Greek dictionary.

[54] Article by Johannes Schneider, "βάσανος, etc.", in *Theological Dictionary of the New Testament*, ed. by G. Kittel & G. Friedrich (Eerdmans, 1964), vol. 1, pp. 561-563.

[55] https://www.biblestudytools.com/lexicons/greek/nas/basanistes.html

the truth, polished by the glory of His presence. The longer it took to initiate this process the thicker the build-up of obscuring layers became, and I ended up in a very dark place.

"How can he go on living life as if nothing is wrong? Why is he not committed to make the success of this marriage and family his priority in life? I have wasted all these years of my life and He is the one to blame! Why doesn't he want to connect intimately with me? My self-esteem is on the floor, I feel adrift and I can't see a promising future for us and it's all because of what He has done to me. Why doesn't he demonstrate or receive affection? Why doesn't he want me? Why? Why? Why? Me, me, me..."

A multitude of painful questions and lamentations tortured me continuously. They were the last thing I thought about before trying to go to sleep, the first thing that popped into my mind when I woke up, and they hit me relentlessly throughout the day. There was no rest from this. You can argue that those were inflamed arrows thrown at me by the enemy of our souls, and there is some truth in it, but I also think that in some of those moments my metal was being tested as I had a choice between forgiving, extending grace and believing the best or believing the worst and carry on counting my husband's trespasses against me. Every moment I chose to bury myself in the pit of offense, bitterness and anger, the more those muddy waters contaminated my heart, intoxicated my soul and poisoned my body. It only takes a quick search on the internet to find a large number of scientific studies which confirm with solid evidence what the Bible has revealed long ago: bitterness, anger and hostility can affect a person's mental and physical health.

A cheerful heart is good medicine, but a crushed spirit dries up the bones (Proverbs 17:2).

I ended up engulfed in deep sadness and hopelessness which drained my strength and made me lethargic. I started having panic attacks, severe migraines and heart palpitations. On many occasions we rushed to the hospital because I was convinced I was about to have a stroke or a heart attack. After many years of this, I had cried floods of tears and had no strength left. I was dying slowly. Shackled to the rack of unforgiveness, I was being stretched to the very end of myself. It can be a very scary and dangerous place if you are there on your own, but I wasn't alone. As I drew closer to God, He drew closer to me[56] and through *the valley of the shadow of death* He shepherded me, continued to whisper the truth, and showed me the way back to love and life as *He guided me to still waters and green pastures.*

---

56 James 4:8

## The Wide Open Spaces of Grace

# Lidia

I met Lidia when I was 14 years old. She and her husband were hired by my church to be, amongst other things, Youth Pastors. My youth leader and later my friend, counselor, ministry leader and mentor, Lidia saw something in me that not even my parents could see. She demonstrated grace in an environment riddled with legalism and condemnation and her intimate relationship with Jesus permeated everything she said and did. Because of that, Lidia stood out in the crowd like a well-lit city on a hill. I felt attracted to what she carried and, in my heart, picked her as a role model. She was instrumental to my emotional health, not only during my teenage years but especially during the years my first marriage was precarious. She was a precious gift from God, a tangible representation of Jesus walking alongside me in a tipping point season.

Four years after I met Lidia and Manuel Ferreira, they moved to another church (the same one I moved to when I turned nineteen) and, although I didn't do it to follow them, it was nice to see their familiar faces there, and to continue to be connected with someone who had been with me in some very important and also very difficult moments of my journey as a teenager and a young adult.

Fast forward ten years into my marriage, when I was part of the Youth team and doing life with Paulo and Vanda, and Lidia was still working as one of the senior leaders in this church. It was a very large church and she coordinated all the ministry teams within the areas of Family and Education. She was Paulo and Vanda's line manager and she knew what was going on in my personal life. She was aware of the deterioration of my marriage in the previous years and she was always one to offer an encouraging word or just a listening ear, with no judgement attached.

Lidia also was, and is, an accredited psychotherapist. She was an extremely busy lady and yet she still gave me the precious gifts of her time and attention. In a year, my life dramatically changed because Lidia generously offered free counselling sessions, once a week. By doing so, she played a very significant role in my spiritual and emotional growth and well-being.

## Therapy: a Precious Gift

A lot took place in these sessions. At the time, and for many years to come, I did not have the language to articulate what happened in therapy but today, looking back, I know that Lidia taught me mindfulness and the ability to become more reflective in my process, instead of being mindlessly reactive. I was equipped with reflective tools which allowed me to become more self-aware regarding the underlying beliefs that motivated my behaviors and reactions. She also consistently modelled how to hear God's voice. We always prayed together, and the Holy Spirit was always invited to lead the conversation.

*The ability to become more reflective in my process.*

In this safe environment, my heart gradually became more open to discuss very intimate and vulnerable issues I had to deal with in my broken marriage. Every question she asked me became an opportunity to hand over pieces of a puzzle which she handled carefully and wisely in order to make sense of the very confused and fragmented picture my stories painted. Patterns I couldn't see, because I was in the eye of the storm, became very clear to Lidia. When she was convinced that I had laid everything on the table, that I 'had no cards up my sleeve', she knew important pieces were missing, which needed to be revealed in order to reach truth, freedom and wholeness. "Something doesn't add up Ana. There are secrets, hidden things that need to be called to the surface", she said to me. And from thereon, every single session we prayed for the truth to be manifested and for hidden things to be brought to the surface, "like olive oil droplets emerging in water" (which was the vision the Holy Spirit had given her).

As the weeks and months went by, something else happened in my heart. I was no longer in defensive/offensive mode all the time. As I approached the challenges which arose in the difficult interactions with my husband, with a reflective mind frame, little by little I started to break relational patterns which had brought a lot of pain and frustration.

I began to focus my mind on God's words and thoughts about me in the moments I needed to be rescued from the hurt of rejection, and rescue me He did: on so many occasions it felt like God's strong arm came down from Heaven, and in one go swooped me by my waist and pulled me up to higher places, above rejection and misunderstanding, close to His heart. I still wasn't getting what I needed from my husband, but I was getting what I needed from my Heavenly Father.

> *I began to focus my mind on God's words and thoughts about me.*

In that place of greater safety and rest I had time to breathe deeply again and I gained an increased capacity to move my gaze away from my navel. I was no longer in survival mode. As I renewed my mind and moved closer and closer to God's heart, I knew I could not continue to live in unforgiveness for much longer.

I started to look at my husband's behaviors and reactions with a desire to reflect about and understand his motives too. Out of that intentional process, empathy was birthed. Very tenuous at first, but just enough to create a window of opportunity that the Holy Spirit didn't miss. He kept talking. I am so grateful that He didn't give up on me and was so patient and committed to my restoration.

More than ever my heart was ripe for forgiveness. I knew that I couldn't move forward without stepping through that door. I wanted to follow Jesus and He lived in the wide open spaces of grace and forgiveness, while I was stuck, restricted and held back in a prison, in the land of offense and past hurts. I wanted out.

To be completely honest, the decision to forgive my husband was, at first, a very selfish one. I didn't want to go back to the painful, oppressive emotional turmoil I had been immersed in for so many years. I had tasted peace and some amount of freedom and I liked it. I wanted more.

*Following Jesus into the wide, open spaces of grace and forgiveness.*

I didn't pretend I was very excited about the thought of finally forgiving my husband, because I wasn't. Instead I was very honest with God. I have learned He always honors authenticity: "Lord, I know I can't do this on my own. No part of me wants to forgive this man for the many years he has willingly chosen disconnection. If this forgiveness thing is going to happen, you have to be the one to make it happen. I want to obey you. I can't wrestle with you about this anymore. I love you, I need you and I want to be closer to your heart so, yes, I decide to forgive my husband". As I surrendered this very old, stale and entrenched stronghold into the hands of the good King, a warm blanket of peace covered me. I could feel the pleasure of the Lord so tangibly in that moment. He had been waiting for that to happen for a long time. I cried and cried as a string of once painful memories unfolded in my mind and I felt empowered to forgive every single hurt, offense, disappointment and disloyalty with unreasonable, extravagant joy. I knew God was answering my prayer there and then.

The capacity to genuinely forgive, not only the behaviors but all the wounds and consequent suffering endured for more than ten years, was not of this world. I knew at that moment that a supernatural power to forgive had been released from God's heart into my heart. In the process I became a little more like Him. The result is always measurable in added love and abundance of life. It felt like scales fell from my eyes and I was filled with a love for him, for myself and for life in a way I hadn't experienced before.

No longer focused on my pain and emotional survival, I was released to look beyond myself and see the other person more clearly, with compassion and empathy. I continued to seek to understand my husband's own struggles and shortcomings in the light of his upbringing and former relational experiences.

I felt big chunks of my heart turning from stone into flesh again as I experienced kindness and love bubbling up inside of me towards this man whom I had begun to see through the Father's eyes as a beloved son of God. I was filled with the Fear of the Lord, a reverence for His truth and nature deposited in

> *A supernatural power to forgive was released from God's heart into my heart.*

that man. I began to respect my husband in word and deed because the way I started to think about him changed and that change became visible.

Everything else changed radically when this happened. God's glory began to shine brighter and brighter in me, through me, around me. Having been given supernatural ability to forgive what I once considered unforgivable, tremendous freedom, openness to life and the world around me, and joyful restoration ensued. This was a defining moment in my life. The type of event that defines life in terms of "before" and "after this". Prior to this I was a very sad, depleted and depressed woman. The overwhelming sense of rejection, together with bitterness, sorrow and resentment, felt like waves of brokenness crashing over me, draining me from anything that was good and beautiful. After this, as I chose to climb up on the steps of forgiveness and waved goodbye to the pit of hopelessness where I had been imprisoned for more than ten years, I finally came out, breathed in the fresh air of freedom, and grabbed an extra portion of hope for the future. My life would never be the same again.

Meanwhile, serious things, which were hidden, were finally made known in another supernatural move of God who could now entrust me with delicate information about my husband, because He knew I would not use it against his son. This is when light triumphed gloriously over darkness.

## Godly Setup

I still remember that day so clearly. It was a Saturday, we went to a friend's wedding. For quite a while I had stopped enjoying wedding ceremonies. They always evoked memories of my own special day, filled with so many expectations that came crumbling down. It caused so much sadness and pain that I used to cry from beginning to end. Fortunately, people around me thought that I was just very moved by the couple's happiness so there was no fuss about it and they just let me be. This wedding was different. I was genuinely happy for the bride and groom. I was fully present to celebrate them and cheer them on, even though my marriage was in dire straits. We left the church and headed to the reception venue without knowing our lives were about to be rocked again.

In my country, Portugal, a land of luscious vineyards and exquisite, ancestral winemaking heritage, fine wine is expected to be a part of a wedding banquet. Drinking with moderation is accepted and encouraged within the Christian communities, especially in a wedding reception. A few hours into the reception, I saw my husband chatting with a friend. They were on their own, away from all the other guests. It seemed like they were having a serious conversation. It didn't take too long to find out what was really happening. After a few glasses of wine, my husband was not drunk, but he was relaxed and loose enough for his friend to feel comfortable to approach him with a difficult subject: our marriage. You see, that friend had known my husband since they were very young. They had gone through a lot together and shared many memories from their teenage years through to their adulthood, where their paths separated geographically and vocationally.

This friend was now a pastor and he could tell that something was off between us. When he started asking all sorts of probing questions, my husband, instead of shutting down and hiding behind silence or vague replies, this time was completely honest, opened up his heart and revealed the good the bad and the ugly. His friend proceeded to tell him that he needed to be honest with me and he offered to accompany my husband

and support him on that initial conversation. Surprisingly, against all the odds, my husband agreed. Furthermore, by the grace of God, that pastor had the wisdom to seize the moment and to propose that such conversation should happen right there and then. The stage was set for truth to be revealed. They pulled me aside and brought me into a conversation that marked the beginning of the end of the world as I knew it.

The pastor, my husband's friend, started the conversation explaining why he approached him in the first place. He was very honoring in the way he did it. He told me that he knew I was a godly woman and he wanted his friend to realize that, and to move towards reconnection. For that to happen we needed to build upon the truth. After that introduction he encouraged my husband to make a commitment, which they had previously discussed, and he did. With his friend standing there as a witness to his resolution, my husband explained that there were important things I didn't know about which he wanted to share with me, and that he was going to do it once we got home. I could tell his friend's presence gave him the courage he needed to step into something that was very difficult for him and that he wouldn't have stepped into on his own. To this day I marvel at the way God lovingly set all of this up, answering my prayers and all the while providing my ex-husband with a safer, friendlier setting to do the right thing.

We stayed in the reception for a few more hours but I couldn't wait to get home. My husband's words and especially his tone were enough to convince me that he had something very significant to reveal. The ride home was in absolute silence. I knew he didn't want to risk starting any conversation yet. He was still mustering up the courage to honor his commitment. I respected that and did not initiate anything but waited patiently until he was ready to talk. That alone was evidence of the striking transformation God had already done in me.

We never sat down to talk. After arriving home, we went through the normal night time routines, still in absolute, eye contact avoidant, awkward silence. When we finally went to bed, there was nothing left to do, nowhere else to escape to, and with his eyes staring at the ceiling, he started to share a series of events and circumstances that had taken place from before our wedding till our present day. I let him talk without ever interrupting him. He made very serious, potentially devastating confessions, but in the end I wasn't devastated at all.

Tears rolled down my cheeks and disappeared into my pillow as I lay there in absolute silence, mourning, for a moment, the demise of a love story that I thought was real but instead was full of dead ends and hidden back-alleys. But that was all it was, a moment. Unreasonable peace permeated the moment and still permeates the memory. He asked for forgiveness and I realized that I had already forgiven him, for everything, without even trying. When I reluctantly decided to forgive him a few months earlier, completely unaware of all he had just disclosed, I was given such a deep revelation of God's grace that it really became sufficient for the challenges ahead (namely this sobering reality check moment). Furthermore, I started feeling increasingly joyful. It made no sense.

*Unreasonable peace and increasing joy? It made no sense!*

As he laid next to me, waiting for a reaction, an outburst, an ultimatum asking him to get his stuff and leave (he told me later he was convinced I was going to do that), he didn't really know what to think and what to do with my calm, composed, accepting, forgiving self.

Later he shared how he had experienced mixed feelings. There was a sense of relief, of getting rid of heavy burdens that had been oppressing him for so many years, and a liberating honesty which allowed him to be authentic and not have to perform all the time to make sure he wasn't caught off guard. However, he also experienced great fear, which made him regret some of his confessions as soon as they exited his lips. I now possessed information which could hurt him and cause unpredictable ripple effects within our families and our church community.

While he was there wondering how on earth he had put himself in such a vulnerable position, sharing, of his own accord, things I would not have been able to find out at all if he hadn't revealed them to me, I was going on an internal joy ride. This unusual joy, after what should have been a heartbreaking disclosure, rose from the awareness that it was all in the light now, which meant it could be addressed, dealt with, healed, made whole. The truth had been manifested, hidden things were brought to the surface and I finally had all the pieces of the puzzle. Everything – behaviors, reactions, words, patterns – which didn't make sense before, made complete sense now and brought insight. It was like I had been given a very clear road map in the middle of a once very obscure and scary maze.

*In the light, it can be dealt with, healed and made whole.*

His fears were unfounded. I firmly believe one of the main reasons God orchestrated all of this was because He knew He could entrust me with sensitive information about His son as I wouldn't use it against him. And I never did. I only shared it with my close leaders Paulo, Vanda and Lidia, because they were journeying with me. I was accountable to them and they would never disclose this information themselves; and later I shared it with my husband (my godly life partner in whom I trust and know would never disclose it either).

There were many moments throughout the process of separation and divorce when I was tempted to use that information to get the upper hand, to get people's sympathy or simply to win an argument with a family member on his side of the family, to prove that things are not always what they seem. I thank God that he has kept me from doing such a terrible thing. As I told you before, the Holy Spirit filled me with the Fear of the Lord. This man was, and is, a son of God and the father of my son, and I made a decision right there and then, as I was lying in that bed, that if he wanted to share any of it with our son or closer relatives, it would be his decision to make, because I would never, under any circumstances, release that information.

As you can tell, it's not going to happen in this book, or any other book either. I am sorry if I somehow disappointed your expectations as you were reading this narrative waiting for the moment where all would be revealed, but you see, covering my ex-husband's frailties was one of the wisest, most honorable, most righteous and graceful things that God has empowered me to do. We all have harbored frailties which only the blood of Jesus can wipe away. Should we use our new-created selves to cast the first stone at anybody when He who is perfect chooses to not condemn but to lovingly forgive? God's perspective is the right one and he gives us eyes to see the gold in others, even when it's tarnished. My ex-husband is a good man and a good father who stumbled but got up again and has been on his own journey with the Lord. He found a good church where he reconnected with God and made friends for life. He is involved in the ministry and plays an important role in reaching, serving and empowering new believers to consistently come to church and be involved in all the family building activities it promotes. He chose to walk on a different path than mine, but I wish him well. If it goes well for him and he prospers[57], then it goes well for my son, and consequently it goes well for me.

## Jesus' Teachings on Forgiveness

Remember the story with which I started this chapter? I chose it because it illustrates so well the Father's perspective about forgiveness.

Jesus' parables were brilliantly crafted to transport people into the alien, unseen realities of the Kingdom of God. The multilayered storylines reveal secrets about God's heart and thoughts, His nature and His ways, and make them available and understandable for the ones who are invested in finding the truth. The ones who are willing to turn aside, leave behind the boxes

---

[57] 3 John 1:2

they have been given by religion, ideology and culture, and are willing to look closer and dig deeper into the challenging but mind-renewing, heart-transforming, life-changing pictures Jesus paints with His words.

> *The same measure of mercy you give to others will be given to you.*

To set the context for this parable, Jesus had just told them the "Parable of the Lost Sheep" which led to a conversation about forgiveness. Peter in his upfront style asks: "Lord, if my brother sins against me, how often should I forgive? As many as seven times?" Peter proposes what he thinks is a large number, but Jesus proposes a significantly larger number[58] to communicate the truth that we should forgive as many times as necessary. In Heaven's economy of reconciliation, God doesn't count people's sins or trespasses against them[59].

To further illustrate his point, that we should forgive as many times as necessary, Jesus tells the "Parable of the Unforgiving Servant". The servant represents everyone. A lifetime of toil, striving, good intentions and even good works is not enough to produce a pure, selfless heart. Perfect, righteous love is the mark, and we all fall short of that. Every one of us had a debt which God has already forgiven. On the cross, Jesus settled the massive debt that held us captive to a destiny of bondage and death. He paid the price to bring us all together in Him[60]. When we enter this new covenant, we enter through mercy and forgiveness and we are expected to model it. We represent Him and make His love visible to the world when, out of thankfulness and appreciation for the grace and mercy He extends to us, we choose to forgive others of their much smaller debts towards us.

---

[58] Matthew 18:21-22

[59] 2 Corinthians 5:18-19

[60] Galatians 3:26-28

What if we choose not to forgive? Aren't we free to make that choice? We are, but forgiveness is an unmerited gift to begin with, it comes from mercy and it seems that the measure of mercy we extend to or withdraw from others is the same that will be extended to or withdrawn from us.

Jesus concludes this parable by saying: "So my heavenly Father will also do to every one of you, if you do not forgive your brother or sister from your heart" (Matthew 18:35). I learned the hard way, if I really want to walk on the path of freedom and abundant life, "to forgive or not to forgive?" is no longer the question. As I have pointed out before, in the Kingdom of God King Jesus has made sure our trespasses are not counted against us, therefore, if we want to experience and be included in this reality, forgiveness is no longer an option, it's a mandate[61]. "To obey or disobey?", that is the question.

At first it might seem unfair to *let people off the hook* so easily but you will soon realize that what you are actually doing is managing yourself, severing ties with pain, hurt and torment and using the master-key of forgiveness to open the door for Jesus to be welcomed back into that broken part of your heart, to bring freedom, healing, redemption and full restoration. It requires trust in God, expressed in the belief that He is wise, just, capable and willing to right all the wrongs, even when we can't see it happen straight away or we don't fully understand His sovereign and perfect ways.

At the end of the day, when I have to deal with hurt and disappointment caused by offense, betrayal or disloyalty, and I find myself struggling to forgive, this is what works for me and I hope it works for you too: I remember that decision is going to affect my relationship with God, my access to His presence. I remind myself that, what I really have before me is a choice between intimacy or distance, which ultimately means a

*A choice between life and death.*

---

[61] Matthew 6:12-15

choice between connection or separation, or in other words, a choice between life and death. Simple.

My son, pay attention to what I say; turn your ear to my words. Do not let them out of your sight, keep them within your heart; for they are life to those who find them and health to one's whole body (Proverbs 4:20-22).

Do you remember the moment I was staring at a distorted reflection of myself, in shock? I was now about to find out how much that reflection had changed. I had chosen life and I had been spending a lot of time "intently looking into the perfect law [of love] that gives freedom"[62], so when I sat with my friends at church, the day after my ex-husband's disclosures, to share the great breakthrough we'd had, they were astonished and perplexed. It was extraordinary to watch them stare at me and be significantly more startled and dumbfounded with my new reflection, filled with outrageous joy and hope, than they were with the unsettling nature of the information I shared. You see, I once was dead, and now I felt fully alive with hope and a future, that's what living in God's perfect will does to you, even when the outcomes are different than the ones initially expected:

But whoever looks intently into the perfect law that gives freedom, and continues in it - not forgetting what they have heard but doing it - they will be blessed in what they do (James 1:25).

---

[62] James 1:25

# Q & A

## M y s e l f  &  G o d

- Remember the story of the "Unforgiving Servant", at the beginning of this chapter? I would like to invite you to read it again and to consider your immediate response in some of its key moments, with absolute honesty.

  What do you feel and think when...

- ...the King forgives the entire debt?
- ...the woman is making plans for her future?
- ...the woman is aggressive and merciless towards her neighbor?
- ...the woman throws her neighbor in jail?
- ...the King changes his judgement?
- ...the King rebukes the woman?
- ...the woman is thrown in jail?

- What is the Holy Spirit highlighting in this story for you?

- Have you forgiven those who have hurt you, including your spouse or former spouse?

- If the answer is no, remember that the decision to forgive is yours but once you make that decision you can firmly believe that the Holy Spirit will empower you to do it wholeheartedly.

- If you can't make this decision on your own, reach out to a trusted, Spirit filled friend, leader or therapist, so you can move towards freedom and life.

# T o g e t h e r

*(For those who want to work towards the restoration or improvement of their marriage)*

- Please share with your spouse what the Holy Spirit highlighted for you in the story of the "Unforgiving Servant".

- Is there anything that you want to confess to your spouse so you can ask for his/her forgiveness and start building on the truth? (If your answer is yes, please ask the Holy Spirit to guide you in asking forgiveness not only for a behavior, action or attitude but also for all the consequences which followed).

- If you have forgiven your spouse, share your process with him/her.

- If you are unable to forgive your spouse, please share that process too, and let him/her know what you are going to do to get help with this. (If you are the spouse on the other end, be patient, respect his/her process and ask the Holy Spirit to guide you both in the next steps towards reconciliation).

- ✦ Cut two paper hearts for each of you. One is "the heart before forgiveness", the other is "the heart after forgiveness". Write down words or simple sentences which express the content of your heart in those two very different contexts. In the end, put the forgiving hearts on display to remind you this is the heart of God for you and in you.

# LifeLine

Revelation & Transformation log          ____/____/____

"Therefore, if anyone is in Christ, that person is a **new creation**: The old has gone, the new is here! All this is from God, who reconciled us to himself through Christ and gave us **the ministry of reconciliation**."

(Corinthians 5:17-18).

# 5 RECONCILIATION IN SPITE OF SEPARATION

*"You can't go back and change the beginning, but you can start where you are and change the ending."*

(C.S. Lewis)

What happened after my ex-husband's disclosures turned out very different from what he had imagined initially, and very different from what I had imagined it would be in the end. He was convinced that I was going to "invite" him to grab his possessions and leave. That would have made things somewhat easier and simpler for him because it would release him from any decision-making leading to separation. When I demonstrated genuine forgiveness and the desire to move towards reconciliation and the restoration of our marriage, he didn't know what to do with that. It meant he had to finally take a stand about his level of involvement and commitment in our relationship. Too much had happened, too much had been said for life to go on 'as usual'. Still, after that initial disconcerting realization, that was exactly what he tried to do: go on with life as usual.

Twice, dinner was booked with Paulo so they could have a one-on-one guy chat, (I knew Paulo could bring so much wisdom, guidance and support), twice, my ex-husband found last-minute lame excuses to cancel. Paulo was still willing to meet with him, but he left the ball in his court: "Whenever you feel you are ready to talk just give me a call". But that call was never made. Lidia also offered marriage counseling sessions, but he never felt comfortable with the idea and never wanted to go, so I went by myself.

Weeks and months went by and my heart started to doubt if any tangible change was ever going to take place. We were still walking on the old, familiar treadmill of disconnection that had characterized most of our story as a married couple. I really believed that after that moment we were positioned to start over again, to build something solid and authentic on a foundation of truth. I was not totally mistaken though. Truth and authenticity had definitely moved into our home and taken up permanent residence.

## A Bespoke Heart

Although things were not happening the way I expected, I continued grounded in God's words and promises. His presence filled me with peace, recalibrated my hope and showered me with a healing love that drenched my frustration and overflowed into my everyday challenges with my dismissive spouse.

Communication improved significantly in the sense that he started to feel safe to express what he was thinking and feeling, even if it meant being honest about not wanting to talk to me or spend any time in my presence, or openly disregarding something I valued and considered to be a priority. My respectful and drama-free responses freed this man to finally open up and be completely honest about his thoughts and feelings. He wasn't intentional about sharing them with me, but he had the space and opportunity to not have to hide or disguise them anymore for fear of punishment or reproach.

Some days were harder than others: rejection, even in its most polite form, is never easy or fun to deal with. Nevertheless, it was a character-building experience for me and a liberating experience for him. It was only possible because God's comforting power strengthened me every step of the way. Looking back, I know there was a special grace given for that season of honest, difficult and painfully blunt communication. I was so secure in God's love that I did not only survive but was even able to thrive while my husband continued to withdraw his love and to demonstrate his lack of desire to connect on a deeper level with me.

*God provided my ex-husband a window of opportunity for a heart change.*

The whole time, this most unusual, unreasonable, almost difficult to explain phenomena was happening within me. The only way I can describe it is, as if there was a change in the architecture of my heart. In this new design, a bespoken "love pouch" was built in. A new airtight compartment designed to hold something precious, to preserve it and not let it go to waste while I was waiting for the moment when it would be appropriate and safe for my love for this man to be fully released. The few times I had tried to do it, I had been bluntly and painfully rejected, but instead of shutting down my love for him God empowered me to keep it alive. It became a win-win situation because, although it was not a withdrawal or self-preserving mechanism, it equipped my soul to deal with the imminent rejection, while it protected my tender heart by keeping it temporarily on hold, but still available, open and expectant for connection. At the same time, I knew deep within that this was not only for my sake, it was also for my husband's sake: to grant him time, to increase the window of opportunity for a heart change.

## Resolution

A heart change did happen in my husband, but not entirely the one I was looking for. He became increasingly more respectful and considerate in the way he addressed me, but we continued to have a very superficial connection. Taking advantage of the higher ground God had brought us to, where we felt secure to assert ourselves truthfully and respectfully, I continued to press in for my childhood dreams, knowing that companionship and complicity were not a fantasy but indispensable pillars for a meaningful and connected married life.

In this period of time, which lasted a few months, I felt like I was living in the tension between the rest and peace which came from the assurance that God was faithful to make a way for a different future, and the restlessness which sprang from the unwillingness to conform to any standard below what God had showed me in His Word and in the lives of happily married couples I knew. This tension started to spur me towards positive action, and as we kept moving in circles I got more and more convinced that a line needed to be drawn in the sand, if we wanted to escape beyond familiar dead ends and genuinely move forward.

That day came when I explained calmly, but wholeheartedly, that I couldn't go on living under the same roof with a man who was willing to share chores and parenting logistics, but was unwilling to share his heart and his bed with me. I was calm but assertive in the way I elicited his assertiveness. I told him how painful it was for me to keep that up: we were not officially separated but we lived as though we were. I presented him with two mutually exclusive options: "We work on fixing our marriage, we get help and move in tangible ways towards full

*An empowering choice.*

restoration, or we go our separate ways." Some may call it an ultimatum, I call it an empowering choice. He listened calmly and then told me that he was going to think about it. I was hoping he was going to choose to stay and build a new life together, but to stay meant to choose me and once again that was not his choice.

The freedom that permeated this whole process was such that, after years of being unclear, vague, indecisive, and even at times obscure about his motives, he finally felt liberated to openly express his decision. He was completely and refreshingly honest as he admitted that "although he knew what it took for a marriage to succeed, he felt overwhelmed by it because it required too much hard work. He was already stretched enough professionally, he had no time or energy left to invest in our marriage." He proceeded to inform me that he had made arrangements with a friend and that he was going to move out the following week.

At that moment, I experienced very mixed feelings. He was actually telling me that "there was a way, but there wasn't a will." This man did not love me enough to choose me and to pursue a covenant relationship with me, period! However, if on one hand I had to draw on God's empowering grace in order to deal with painful rejection again, on the other hand, I really appreciated his assertive honesty. The ease experienced in that moment of added clarity contrasted deeply with the emotional confusion and strain we had experienced for so long. There was almost a sense of relief and respite as I looked into this new, open door. On the other side I could see change and definition of something which had been stuck in "no man's land" for more than ten years. Finally, I knew where he stood, and consequently where I stood, in this marriage.

*I chose to guard my heart from offense and unforgiveness.*

This was not the end I expected but truth continued to abide and guide my steps and, as I chose to guard my heart from offense and refused to partner with any thoughts rooted in unforgiveness, punishment, vengeance or retribution, my path kept getting clearer and clearer, brighter and brighter, as the fullness of God's glory began to be manifested in many ways in my life and the lives of our families[63].

## Alabaster

I don't want it to sound like I had suddenly attained some sort of magical power which allowed me to sugarcoat all offense and simply forgive and forget. I didn't just whizz through all the difficult conversations which were bound to happen with all the people closely involved in our lives, on both sides of a family that was about to be split up.

It was a difficult, one day at a time process, which I wouldn't have been able to plod through without the help of the Holy Spirit. The first weeks and even months following my spouse's move, were filled with opportunities for growth. Patience, gentleness, kindness, longsuffering and self-control were in high demand as I faced difficult questions, criticism, judgements and even accusations from people who had biased views, because they had limited knowledge of our story, but still thought they knew best. "If only they knew the whole story they would

*I knew whatever I said and did would have an impact in people's lives in the present and in the future.*

sympathize and agree with me": Time and time again this thought tempted me to reveal details which would have changed people's minds and would persuade them that I was in the right and my ex-husband was in the wrong. But I knew that was a very dangerous road to follow. I had witnessed other divorce stories unfold where so much destruction had come from hateful, prideful, polarized dissension. Family members broken, children wounded

---

[63] Proverbs 4:18

and traumatized, bridges burnt almost beyond repair, compromising any possibility of future reconciliation. I was filled with an acute awareness that whatever I said and did was going to affect and impact significantly not just my life but the lives of those who were closest to me in the present and in the future.

> *God's wisdom enacted will have a tangible impact in the quality of our emotional health and relationships.*

I had just come out of a long period of emotional oppression and spiritual bondage as a result of leaning on my own understanding and reacting to things the way I saw the world around me react. I knew better now. I had learned my lesson. That experience had filled me with the *Fear of the Lord* regarding the way we are meant to consider and deal with other people's hearts. It taught me to trust God's brilliant wisdom, as my eyes were opened to how His ways are indeed better and higher, leading to a fruitful and abundant life that we can tangibly measure in the quality of our emotional health and our relationships.

Trust God from the bottom of your heart; don't try to figure out everything on your own. Listen for God's voice in everything you do, everywhere you go; he's the one who will keep you on track. Don't assume that you know it all. (Proverbs 3:5-6 MSG)

That's how I did it. One conversation at a time, one challenge at a time. Each moment of frustration, exasperation and aggravation. Every time I felt overwhelmed with sadness or anger, every time I felt treated unjustly and everything in me wanted to take justice into my own hands. Every one of those times, I remembered His ways and held it together until I got into my room and closed the door on the world behind me. There, where no one else could see or hear me, I gave it all to God amidst floods of tears and effusive outbursts. He was strong enough to handle all of those destructive feelings, and powerful enough to send them far away from my heart. He was good enough to fill me with a peace and a love that surpassed understanding and He empowered me to do what was unreasonably good and righteous. Beautiful exchanges happen when you trust God with the vulnerable, weak and tired places in your heart and soul.

When I was reminiscing about these moments and asking God if I had forgotten any important details of learning value for my readers, the Holy Spirit whispered the word "alabaster". I asked Him what was the meaning of that word and He reminded me of the episode of the woman who shed heartfelt tears while she poured out an alabaster jar, containing a very expensive perfume, on Jesus' head and feet (Matthew 26:7-13). I looked it up and read that story again.

The Holy Spirit highlighted how she was following God's instructions and purposefully acting according to His will. That was a history-making moment. Because she was following God's higher ways, unfamiliar and unpopular to the others around her, she was misunderstood and became a target for reproach and harsh judgement. Know that when you decide to do the right thing and refuse to participate in gossip, slander or other vindictive acts, there will be many people around you who will criticize you and consider you weak. But when you start going even beyond that, choosing to follow the better, higher ways of righteousness the Holy Spirit shows you (which usually involve unreasonable kindness and treating others with loving honor and respect[64]), then people around you will be completely baffled and will actually feel convicted. That's when you might experience reproach and

*If you ask Him, the Holy Spirit will equip you to live out the higher ways of righteousness.*

---

[64] Romans 12:10

judgement, even from well-intentioned ones who cannot make sense of the way you are handling or letting go of things they believe are worth keeping or fighting for.

My heart melted when I heard the Lord tell me in my spirit: "Every time you came to me and gave me that offering of sacrifice, when you didn't do what you wanted, didn't take matters into your own hands but trusted me with all things, it was like you were pouring an alabaster jar with very costly perfume over me all over again. You honored me and let me rule, invited my will to be done and my Kingdom to come on Earth, to your circumstances, to reveal Heaven's ways."

2000 years later and we are still reading this woman's story and celebrating her act of obedience because it had eternal ramifications! If you read it to the end you will see that she didn't have to plead her case because Jesus Himself pleaded her case. He spoke on her behalf and promoted her in front of all that were looking down upon her. What a beautiful, restorative God. As I continued to partner with His will and His ways, as I continued to represent Him well, I too experienced God's grace and favor following me and promoting me during the difficult and convoluted seasons of separation and divorce.

I felt so secure in His love and soothing presence, I did not need to protect myself against "the other side." As a matter of fact, God's empowering grace positioned me on neutral ground: there was no 'me' against 'them', there was always us. My ex-husband is always going to be the father of my son and his family are always going to be connected to me through my son, and that is something the Lord has always highlighted and equipped me to steward well. He unlocked my heart to receive greater understanding and increased empathy regarding people's motives and struggles, even those who didn't always see eye-to-eye with me and were really trying to do their best but not always being successful at it.

If you are facing imminent separation or divorce, what you do and say on this leg of your journey may have repercussions to your relational universe for many years to come. The way the Lord guided me to handle sensitive information, and the way He empowered me to treat parents and in-laws with wisdom, care and honor even in the midst of painful offense, disappointment, and unfair treatment was, once again, supernatural. There were harsh words that could have been rightfully uttered which never exited my lips, and truthful information I omitted to cover some people's reputation and protect other people's hearts. Unknowingly, step by step, word by word (whether uttered or silenced), under the wise guidance of the Holy Spirit and the Word of God, I was led to protect connection and equipped to put foundations down for bridges of reconciliation to be rebuilt in the future.

## God's Higher Ways When Dealing With our Children

My son Daniel, who had just turned five, handled the initial stages of our separation very well. The reports we had from school were that he remained his happy self. Two things contributed to that: his routines with mum and dad were only slightly changed and he never once saw us argue or fight. He was so used to doing different things, at different times, with either mum or dad, but never with the two of us, that when his father moved out and he spent every other day with him he didn't find it odd. However, I believe that the most important factor in this process was the way we established healthy boundaries regarding the involvement of

*We both decided that we would never use our son as a bargaining chip.*

our son in these matters. We had always been very careful about not exposing our son to any arguments or heated discussions between us. We had agreed very early that we wanted to protect him from that, and it didn't change with the separation. We both decided that neither of us would ever use our son as a bargaining chip and put pressure on him to be involved in issues that were really beyond his age and emotional capacity.

Fast forward two years and my life had changed tremendously. In the meantime, I had emigrated to England and was finalizing my son's move, so we could start a new life together where I was able to support us and still be a present mother. This was not an easy process. I had to travel back and forth many times but, whenever I did, I always stayed at my in-laws' house so I could be near my son. They always welcomed me with open arms and treated me with great respect and appreciation. They valued me more then than they did before, and I know the increased favor was the fruit of the way things had been handled throughout the separation process.

As time went by and my son grew older, his parents' separation became more tangible to him. He became more aware of, and had to deal with, some of the unsavory realities that come with having disconnected parents. (We eventually got divorced, but I will be talking more about this in chapter seven).

When my ex-husband introduced his new partner to Daniel, he didn't respond to her presence in a positive way. The time leading to the move to England was particularly challenging for the family and when my son finally joined me, his relationship with his father was very broken. Daniel felt that his father had preferred his girlfriend to him, and he felt rejected and very resentful. I was never happy with that. I knew for my son to be emotionally healthy and whole his relationship with his father had to be restored. For this to happen I was very intentional about speaking positive words about his father. Again, my faith played a major role in this process. I believed God's counsel to be the higher truth and I decided to put it into practice.

Do not let any unwholesome talk come out of your mouths, but only what is helpful for building others up according to their needs, that it may benefit those who listen (Ephesians 4:29).

The fact that he hadn't been a committed husband didn't overshadow his consistent commitment as a father, in love with his son from the moment he laid eyes on him. Daniel didn't need my opinions about my ex-husband, he needed information that could help him understand and reconnect with his father, so I made the decision not to hinder their communication in any way and encouraged, facilitated and created regular opportunities for positive connection.

In the following five years we took it in turns. When we travelled to our home country we stayed with my parents and my sister, but I also made sure we stayed with my ex-in laws so my son could be near his father. When my ex-husband was available to travel and visit Daniel in England, I opened my home for him to stay with us so they could spend as much time together as possible. My ex-in-laws also visited regularly, and they always stayed with us.

*My son didn't need my opinion about my ex-husband, he needed information that could help him understand and reconnect with his father.*

There were many opportunities for Daniel and his father to mend bridges and work on their connection until it was lovingly restored. I was very happy when that happened because I knew how important it was for my son. However, there was a consequence of that relational restoration which I hadn't foreseen: when Daniel became a young man, he decided he wanted to live with his father again. It was a very difficult, even heartbreaking decision for me (in the next chapter I dive deeper into this life-changing event). I spent some heart-wrenching moments in God's presence seeking for guidance, direction and comfort. In the end, I didn't regret releasing him. I knew it was the right thing to do because this was not just about me, but it was about celebrating the beautiful restoration we hoped and believed for: a father who turned his heart to his son and a son who turned his heart to his father.

## Ties Severed with Respect and Honor

We had been legally divorced for more than five years when I finally decided to sever all heart and soul ties with my ex-husband. I resisted doing it for so long because I did not want to be responsible for closing that door completely. I still believed that God could and can restore anything, but in all honesty that door had already been closed, a long time before, by my ex-husband. It "takes two to tango". A covenant always involves partnership and the other part had already made the decision to dissolve our alliance. After having a heart-to-heart conversation with my dear friend Vanda, I realized those ties conflicted with my prayers and desires. I was asking God for a new start and a new husband who loved Him and myself, and at the same time I was letting my heart be divided by the possibility of reconciliation. Don't get me wrong, please. If there is a strong possibility for reconciliation to happen, because both parts are considering it, then do not turn away from it. God is in the business of reconciliation. That is His main activity. *Where there's a will there's a way*, especially when God is invited to be at the center of it all. Nevertheless, when two free people have gone separate ways because one of them freely decided to throw away the zipper head which bonded them together, then there is no point in holding on to that split-apart, headless zipper trail. God also branches out in restoration and redemption and He is an expert at it.

*Those heart and soul ties conflicted with my prayers and desires.*

When I finally decided to do it, I knew I was meant to make it 'official' by writing a letter to my ex-husband. What I didn't know was, even after all that time, how hard it would be to write it:

Dear C.

I hope this letter finds you well and that, in spite of the struggles and challenges, your days with Daniel are positive.

Where shall I begin?...This is a very difficult letter to write. I still have some doubts about how to best express what's in my heart, but I know I must do it. I have decided it is time to start a new chapter of my life and to fully open the door to the possibility of starting a new family with someone who really wants to share his life with me.

It seems like a logical and natural decision that requires no justification or explanation, however, I felt moved to acknowledge, accept and articulate in words, before God and before you, the end of a story that you have concluded long ago, but to which I hadn't added the final full stop yet.

Just by briefly looking back, I can see with added clarity (increased with time, distance and inner growth), that we actually had everything to become a successful partnership. We were so different, and because of that, so able to impact each other's lives with everything that each one of us could uniquely bring.

Your tenacity and entrepreneurial spirit could have given legs and motion to my idealistic and contemplative spirit. My emotional depth and creativity could have established you while adding solidity and novelty in your daily, hit-and-run relational busyness. You could have brought organization, order and structure to my world, I could have brought challenges, disorganization, flexibility and surprises to yours. In the mixture of it all, in the middle, there we would have found virtue. Together we could have been complete, stronger, more efficient, more humane, more! If only we had given each other the freedom to be who God created and purposed us to be…

We needed perfect love instead of constant criticism and judgement, but we chose to hold on firmly to our valid reasons why we were, felt and thought a certain way. It was more important to be right than to be connected and so we remained distinct, divided, incomplete. Our worlds never really touched, never collided, never mingled. Because of that, we both lost, big time.

I've lost count of how many times I asked God's forgiveness for not really giving Him the opportunity to manifest His glory in our marriage. I hope you have done that too.

Even now, I still struggle to write these lines without feeling a profound sadness and sense of loss which crush my heart.

Even now, the Holy Spirit is whispering that I must close this door if I want to fully open the doors for complete inner healing, so I can continue to move forward. This is the main reason why I'm writing this letter: it's a vital, tangible part of what has been a continuous process of inner healing. It is tiring and consuming to go through this daily, having to choose to forgive you and myself all over again.

You did your best, I did my best, but we never gave God a chance to do His best. Still, His grace continues to be enough if we decide to dwell in it. Life goes on and the Good News continue to bring truth, light and hope for the future.

In this new season of our lives, I wish you happiness and I pray that, above all, you can experience the fullness of the abundant grace of God like a child, free, secure and full of peace, because you know that there is absolutely nothing you can say, give or do that can surpass who He's made you to be in Him and through Him. It is really finished. He has done everything and given everything. He is everything! Compared to this truth, everything else, even our well intentioned efforts, is nothing more than mere poo :)

I hope you have caught and understood my heart

May God bless you

I had a deep sense of God's presence while I was writing. The Holy Spirit inspired me to communicate in an honest, authentic way but with a respectful and honorable tone, using inclusive language and steering away from everything that might sound or feel accusatory. I remember crying non-stop while I wrote this letter. At some points I had to stop writing because I was sobbing so deeply. I was finally mourning for

*A clear sense of closure was completely established.*

everything that had been stolen and destroyed, for what could have been and never will. In the end, I was filled with great peace and a weight was lifted. A clear sense of closure was completely established when I received brief, but very positive feedback.

The lyrics of a well-known song came to mind when I decided to wholeheartedly shift my gaze towards the horizon ahead: "It's a new day, it's a new dawn, it's a new life".

## Family Reconciliation *a la Kingdom*

Separation didn't bring devastation into the family because I didn't seek retribution or judgement but was forgiving, extended grace to relatives, covered my ex-husband, guarded the hearts of all family members involved, and intentionally facilitated connection. It was not a one woman show, because I was not alone or isolated in a bubble but was dealing with people who actually wanted to do the right thing in the end.

I understand your story can be very different from mine in that respect. You may be dealing with a spouse or former spouse who continues to be abusive or disrespectful whenever you interact. You may also be dealing with other broken individuals who are a product of dysfunctional family dynamics. In situations like these, putting healthy boundaries in place is essential but that doesn't mean you stop believing that change can one day come. Your emotional and social landscape may differ from mine but your spiritual landscape doesn't. You are still a son or daughter of God and you have Christ, the hope of glory, living within you. As you choose to renew your mind with His thoughts and invite His presence into this process, He will give you grace and equip you to thrive as you are transformed more into His likeness. This transformation will impact every choice you make, independently of what other people throw at you. I know the way I positioned my heart in God's truth, and grounded myself in it, significantly impacted my decisions, my choices and the lives of those around me. My story would be very different if I had done it my way instead of His way.

Today, I can sincerely say that all has been redeemed by God's loving grace, which infused every stage of the process with a solid foundation for family reconciliation. Our parents, especially my father, did come out emotionally bruised and hurt initially, but God brought so much healing and poured out so much grace that all has been forgiven and full reconciliation has taken place between the families. We remain friends and wish each other well. We go out for meals together, celebrate birthdays and other special occasions together and

*My story would be very different if I had done it my way instead of His way.*

even plan days out together. My son has a good relationship with my husband Mat, who has always welcomed my ex-husband into our family gatherings (and vice-versa), and they are both very respectful and friendly in the way they relate to each other.

One of the funniest moments in my life happened during the Christmas season, in the first year of my second marriage. Daniel travelled to England to spend Christmas with us. With him came his paternal grandmother. She had a great time with us and in the end she couldn't compliment my husband enough. It was beautiful to watch this woman, who in the past struggled to see any flaws in her own son (and believed that all our major issues originated in my person), become so warm and maternal towards me and very vocal about "what a lovely man Mat is and how much she loves him." She kept congratulating me for "having found such a great husband" and she was genuinely happy with my happiness, even if it didn't include her son anymore.

But I saved the best for last. The funniest highlight of her stay was when I went to church with both mothers-in-law. I wish I had a camera on me to capture some people's reactions when I introduced these two very friendly ladies who accompanied me as "my ex-mother in law and my current mother in law." Their locked arms and big smiles left many articulate people amusingly speechless. What an unusual sight...

For my thoughts are not your thoughts, neither are your ways my ways," declares the LORD. "As the heavens are higher than the earth, so are my ways higher than your ways and my thoughts than your thoughts (Isaiah 55:8-9).

Can you hear His voice inviting you now, right where you're at? He's saying, "Come up higher; If you do, I will help you change your story."

# Q & A

## M y s e l f  &  G o d

- As you read my own story, did any faces, names, or difficult conversations from your own story come to mind?

- Have you considered asking God what are his thoughts about the people who have misunderstood, antagonized or treated you unjustly?

- Ask the Holy Spirit to reveal how your heart is positioned towards those people.

- Have you forgiven them? What have you forgiven them for? (If you haven't, ask the Holy Spirit to lead you and empower you to do it).

- God's heart is for reconciliation. Ask Him if there is anything you need to change in the way you are considering others, the way you communicate with them and what you are saying to and about them.

- Are there any heart and soul ties that you need to actively sever so you can move on towards complete inner healing? (Ask Holy Spirit if there are, and what to do).

- Ask the Holy Spirit to show you God's ways and wisdom to lead you in the path of genuine and sustainable reconciliation. Be prepared to take notes.

# T o g e t h e r

*(For those who want to work towards the restoration or improvement of their marriage)*

- Please, share with your spouse what the Holy Spirit revealed to you in your personal time with God as well as any relevant breakthrough.

- Ask the Holy Spirit to help you imagine an ideal scenario of reconciliation which extends to your spouse, your children and other close relatives. (Don't dismiss it if it looks too good to be true. There is nothing that His perfect love can't redeem).

- Share that scenario with your spouse and build each other's faith up. Remind each other that God's heart is for reconciliation and He is backing you up on this.

- Ask God what are the next steps that He wants you to take towards reconciliation with your spouse and other members in your family. (Be sensitive to specific timing and opportunity: you don't want to hinder God's healing process or even put yourself in a situation where your safety or integrity may be at risk).

    - Trust God's timing and follow through with the steps he has given you.
    - Be accountable to your spouse, or a trusted friend, and 'report' on progress.

- Draw a "Map of Reconciliation". X marks the 'spots' or people you are aiming to reconcile with. Following God's instructions write down the next steps to move towards reconciliation for each one of those Xs. Keep updating your map with God ordained steps until all Xs are reached. (Maybe log dates and other details you consider interesting, curious or important).

# LifeLine

Revelation & Transformation log          ____/____/____

"Now without faith it is impossible to please Him, for the one who approaches God must **believe** that He exists and **He rewards those who seek Him.**"

(Hebrews 11:6 - NET)

# 6 The Desert: a Place of Encounter

"What makes the desert beautiful is that somewhere it hides a well."

(Antoine de Saint-Exupéry)

Ten years on my own. For someone who had always dreamt of finding a life partner and building a happy family, some stretches of this long-winded journey were very hard. Whatever season of your personal and relational journey you are in, one of the hardest places to be is in the "hallway". You are longing for doors to open which will transport you into another landscape, another sought-after dimension of your destiny. You knock, and you keep knocking, and the doors which open lead you to another corridor, another "hallway" where you are required to wait. In the waiting you can despair and lose sight of the dreams and promises of God, or you can hold hands with faith and hope and continue to ask, seek and knock[65].

Why didn't I give up and abandon my quest? Because every step of the way, God made Himself known to me. How He revealed His secrets, His mysteries, His heart, enticing me into intimacy with Him, bringing me into a place of value and identity as His daughter and His beloved, was precious and made me who I am today. In the deepest valleys I experienced the greatest floods of His presence, grace, favor and provision. This was a journey where God transformed me into a giver, where I used to be a taker, and instructed me in the higher ways of covenant.

I pray that your vision of Him as a good God and a perfect Father is so clear by the end of this chapter that you remain firm in the decision to believe He is faithful and trustworthy, and His timing is also a revelation of His goodness.

This vision is for a future time. It describes the end, and it will be fulfilled. If it seems slow in coming, wait patiently, for it will surely take place. It will not be delayed (Habakkuk 2:3).

## Starting Anew

I had come such a long way from 'shaking like leaves' while filling up my car with gas (my ex-husband always did it because I was afraid I was going to do something wrong and blow up the car!), but emigrating to another country and starting anew, that took it to a whole other level. Finding a teaching job (with all that entailed), communicating in a language which

---

[65] Matthew 7:7

was not my own, adapting to a new culture, setting up a home from scratch with very little money, finding the right church and getting involved, and last but not least, being a single parent away from most of my closer family and friends.

There was so much happening, and I had already gone through so many life-changing epiphanies and experiences, that I didn't realize this was just the beginning of an extensive and profound inner healing and inner growth process. I was definitely on the mend but still broken on so many levels. My fragmented heart and soul needed to be pieced together by the Master Potter. The wheel was spinning and although I felt a bit lost and dizzy at times I was certain of one thing: I was not spinning aimlessly, and I was not alone. God had His strong, firm, but caring and tender hands on me and He was committed to reshape me into wholeness.

> *God was committed to reshape me into wholeness.*

Before I made the decision to move to England, I prayed and asked God for His direction, and the Holy Spirit gave me this verse of the Bible: "Whether you turn to the right or to the left, your ears will hear a voice behind you, saying, 'this is the way; walk in it'" (Isaiah 3:21). So, I knew God was giving me the freedom to choose and that in the process I could count on His ongoing counsel and wisdom. He was not going to be silent and He was not going to lead me astray. Nonetheless, with this promise came the requirement to elicit, expect for, pay attention to, and follow His instructions. Was I successful at that? Was I willing and quick to relinquish control and elicit His counsel in every area of my life? I wish I could reply "absolutely!", but I can't.

With the realization that this was a time of rebuilding came a heightened awareness that, if I was aiming for a different outcome, I was required to build in a different way. In the previous years I had been gradually equipped to dismantle a wrong belief system regarding my expectations of others. I could identify lies which had deceived me and negatively shaped my past relational experiences, and the greatest lesson I learned was that to make others responsible for my happiness and success was not a good idea. I had learnt that I am the only one who manages myself and, in the depths of my heart, I knew that I was never again going to seek my primary source of love and affirmation in a man, because I could only find that in Jesus, my loving King and perfect Bridegroom.

The decision to no longer lean on my own understanding, like I had done before, deeply impacted the way I regarded possible romantic involvements or relationships. There were so many moments when I felt lonely and craved emotional and physical comfort, but the awareness that I was not going to find complete fulfillment in a man and the certainty that a wrong association could be irreversibly damaging, kept me on the straight and narrow. I was not prepared to 'gamble away' my relational future and with it my dreams of a happy family. I was determined to get it right this time and I was totally dependent on God's counsel to open my heart to the one He would unequivocally point to.

However, if this resolution to solely depend on God's counsel seemed to make sense within the confines of my past experience, I wasn't always willing to trust God in the unknown and the unpredictable. In other areas of my life I wanted to control the outcome. I wanted to do it my way, not just because I was stubborn and proud, but because I still had doubts about God's intentions, and I was still steeped in self-righteousness. I still needed to do good in order to look good.

Mine was not a linear journey. Here and there I got sidetracked on a few distracting 'rabbit trails' because it took a while for the truth, that had already been fully embraced by my spirit, to be fully established in my soul. I had spent a lifetime desperately seeking for value and affirmation from others, especially the ones closest to me, and I was still very hungry for it. On top of that, I knew my parents were worried about my future and the perception I had of the people back home, without any of this ever being openly discussed, was that they were waiting to see whether I was going to succeed or fail. Subconsciously, I began to approach the challenges at hand as an ongoing proficiency test: this was going to be the time to prove my value and ability to achieve and make a life for myself. The pressure was on and performance was very much at the head of the table again.

> *It was vital to discover my identity as a daughter of a good God and perfect Father.*

What I didn't know was that the process of self-discovery I had just embarked on, was going to lead me into a long "expedition into the desert", a journey where I wouldn't have been able to survive without "a pillar of cloud by day and a pillar of fire by night" [66]. Perfectionism, self-sufficiency and self-righteousness were about to be confronted and challenged in a fight to the death. The real testing was not one of performance but of motive. It was essential to continue to discover my giftings, my purpose and destiny as a free, powerful person and a leader in my own life, but most importantly, it was vital to discover my identity as a daughter of a good God and perfect Father.

"Jesus passed the test of sonship in the desert where Satan tried to get Jesus to abandon his sonship — then his ministry began. We too must have a desert to test whether or not the Father's love is really all we need." (Jack Frost)[67]

## "What do you need?"

Do you know? Can you answer this question clearly? Don't feel bad if you can't. I couldn't, back then. Now I can, but just because time and process have given me perspective. At the time I thought I needed a good job, more

---

[66] Exodus 14:24

[67]https://richardconlin.wordpress.com/2015/01/28/spiritual-slavery-to-spiritual-sonship-by-jack-frost/

money, a good school for my son and a good, loving husband. Nothing wrong with that but, from a distance, looking at the whole picture, I can see now that those were secondary needs, like the leaves on a tree. A closer look at the roots and different, deeper needs become visible, and those were the ones which came first in Heaven's economy.

I was still a very inflexible person, too quick to judge and very hard on myself and others. I was still riddled with shame and the fear of failure. I experienced high levels of anxiety and worry regarding financial provision. I felt overwhelmed, like there was always too much at stake, caught between not feeling able or enough and feeling I had to overperform and overachieve to compensate for my latent inadequacy. Striving and duty permeated most of my attempts to succeed as I worked hard to increase my capacity and become self-sufficient. I trusted myself, and to some extent God, but I couldn't fully trust other people.

*I needed a deeper revelation of the unmerited, liberating, empowering, sufficient grace of God.*

What did I really need? I needed a deeper revelation of the unmerited, liberating, empowering, sufficient grace of God. I needed to trust God completely, relinquish control of every area of my life, and enter into His rest, even when I didn't fully understand His ways. I needed to stop second guessing God's motives and to wholeheartedly believe "He is a rewarder of those who seek Him"[68]. I needed to invite Him into all the guarded 'rooms' in my heart so He could heal me and strengthen me, and I could fully love and fully trust others again. I needed to know Him more intimately and "figure out what pleases Him and do it"[69], so I could fulfill my identity and purpose as His daughter, His betrothed, and His ambassador on this Earth.

---

[68] Hebrews 11:6

[69] Ephesians 5:10 MSG - Romans 8:8

Once again, His mind-blowing faithfulness was about to transform my existential landscape. In the following years I saw God's hand blessing, equipping and empowering me with resources, divine connections, professional and training opportunities which grew me and opened up my horizons immensely. Nevertheless, what impacted me the most, because it brought greater inner healing and transformation, was the way God revealed Himself over and over again as a good Father and a true Friend in every one of those circumstances. He continuously sent me the message that He is for me, not against me, and that He is faithfully committed, reliable and fully present.

> *God continually sent me the message that He is faithfully committed, reliable and fully present.*

I have many stories I could tell from this period of my life, but I also have a limited number of pages, so I have carefully considered which ones were more relevant and emblematic of this revelatory and transformational season.

## Unexpected Provision

Just before my son Daniel moved to England, I had a car crash. It doesn't seem like a very good start for a section about provision, but with God in the equation *all things* did *work together* in a surprising way. It happened when I was driving home after a normal day at school. I worked at a school in Birmingham and it took me about one hour to return home. That day I had done most of the travelling. I remember feeling tired but happy that my long drive home was about to come to an end. I was looking forward to relaxing and I was considering what I was going to do in the evening when, at a very busy junction, the driver of a big van didn't respect the 'give way' sign and stormed into the main road, where I just happened to be passing through.

The driver tried to brake but it was too late, and the van hit my car on the passenger door. The collision was strong enough to ram the door in. I was completely taken by surprise and as I hit the brakes myself, trying to make sense of what had just happened to me, I only had enough time to notice that the big, white van with racing cars painted on it, was getting away. That description was all I had. I had no other information that I could give to the police. I wasn't able to see the face of the driver, and I didn't know the car make, let alone its license plate number.

I remember thinking how unbelievably wrong it was for that driver to run away without checking whether I needed any assistance. Many other thoughts and feelings followed: indignation, frustration, powerlessness to mend an injustice, disorientation and fear, and more. The busy traffic continued to hustle and bustle all around me but I felt like I was still frozen, alone, caught up in that moment of unexpected, irreversible, destructive assault: "There is nothing I can do about this...what am I going to say to the police and the car insurance people?"

That very moment, a lady approached me and asked me if I was okay. She then proceeded to tell me that she was driving in the opposite direction at the time of the collision and she had seen everything. She ended up giving me her details so I could nominate her as an official witness in case the police wanted to record her testimony. What an amazing blessing. We were on an extremely busy road where it was particularly difficult to find parking, but even under those circumstances, after a long day at work, when everyone just wants to get back home, this lady decided to go out of her way and tackle all of those inconveniences to offer her help and testimony as a precious eyewitness. But it doesn't end here.

I drove home, still pretty discombobulated, and when I got out of the car and started to carefully assess all the damage, asking God for His help and guidance, my attention was drawn towards the hinge of the ruined door and I realized that something, a plastic strip of some kind, was halfway stuck into it. When I pulled it out to take a closer look, I couldn't believe my eyes: I was holding in my hands a very important piece of the other vehicle:

its license plate! What a glorious moment that was! I remember being in pain but still walking repeatedly in circles around my car, laughing out loud and praising God: "Father, you are so good, you look after me in such an incredible way; you are in my corner, you have got my back!".

I still needed to go to the hospital because I had severe whiplash in my neck, but my heart was bursting with joy and confidence. I felt like a child who gets a boost of courage and boldness to face anything just because a loving parent is right there, holding hands and lending strength. The next day, when I went to the police station to report the hit & run incident of which I had been a victim of, I didn't just have a license plate number to give them, but I carried the actual plate with me!

The whiplash injury was no fun and I had to take time off work because of it, but the positive repercussions of this incident far outnumbered the negative ones. The insurance company proposed to write off my car and offered more money for it than its actual value (it was an old car), but then they gave me the opportunity to buy it back from them for a nominal fee. My uncle who is a talented mechanic fixed it and in the end I still had a car plus the exact amount I needed to pay my future landlord: two months of rent and the equivalent security deposit. Unforeseen, complete provision was a tangible and victorious outcome of this ordeal.

I had been looking for a rental property and had picked an old house because of its lovely location, its home-making potential and of course, rent within my means. A big group of friends from church together with my uncle, aunt and cousins (the only precious family members who lived nearby), came to help me clear out the overgrown jungle which had once been a garden, and for the next few months I cleaned, painted and decorated our new home. When my son joined me, our house was comfy, cozy and fully furnished. God was so faithful in the way He orchestrated all things so they could work together for our good[70]. I don't believe anything

---

[70] Romans 8:28

evil comes from Him. That accident was an attack of the enemy, something that was meant to kill, steal and destroy[71], but once again God came to my rescue and repurposed for good what the enemy intended for evil[72]. I didn't just get the provision I needed but I got a relational experience which opened up a tangible revelation of God not only as a provider but as a caring, loving, powerful, attentive Father who rescues me, looks after me and works all things for good in the lives of His children.

## Divine Connections

There were so many people who were God's arms and feet, in so many different ways, during this pioneering season of my life. I am grateful to, and for, every single one of them. I cannot mention them all, so I have used the previous criteria and picked two of the most relevant and emblematic examples of the way God used people to look after me, to make Himself known and to grow me.

> *I was given hope for a better and purposeful relational future.*

I want to start with Jim and Marie Morris, the dynamic duo! I met this beautiful couple at church. I lived for one year with them before my son came to live in England with me. They provided the home environment I desperately needed while starting a new job and trying to 'find my feet' in a new country. Their beautiful relationship rekindled the belief that happy marriages are possible and real, and their narrative exposed me to an extremely important ingredient: hope for a better and purposeful relational future.

---

[71] John 10:10

[72] Genesis 50:20

They inspired me to continue to pray for a godly husband and a God-ordained marriage, and helped set the course for positive and faith-filled expectations. They were in their second marriage, had met and got married in their forties and had been happily married for more than thirty years. God was at the center of their lives and of their covenant. They had intentionally 'built their house on the Rock'[73]. It was beautiful and uplifting to be a part of this and to see up close how God's presence and truth can powerfully redefine and reshape people's lives and relationships, 'enlarge their tent', and increase their influence and legacy.

Eight years later they helped us organize our wedding reception and invited us into their home for the last three months before we travelled to America, as we no longer had a home of our own. Jim and Marie are in their early seventies but still super active, coordinating teams, preparing and providing training, and travelling several times a year on mission trips to Eastern Europe where they equip the church and impact the surrounding communities with the Gospel of the Kingdom in word and deed. We have learnt a lot from them, and we feel privileged they are part of our lives and our story.

Then, there is my dear friend Rose[74]. She was one of the most significant divine connections I was blessed with in this period of my life. I am still in touch with her and when in England we always spend time together. I will never forget the way she enriched and touched my life in a time when I was a single parent, in a foreign country, starting from scratch.

I met Rose at church. She took me under her wing and had an extraordinary impact on the quality of life my son and I enjoyed. She took us to see places and attend events we could have never accessed or afforded on our own. We travelled together to Ireland, Wales and other parts of England and spent most school holidays together. She was, and is, a very good friend, loyal, reliable and extremely generous with her time and her resources. My

---

[73] Matthew 7:24-29

[74]This is not her real name as she requested her identity not be disclosed.

perspective of what it means to be a generous person changed tremendously by doing life with Rose.

---

*The stage was set for a different outlook on life and a greater openness for new challenges and opportunities.*

Rose is adventurous and determined and she is always open to try new things and face new challenges. I was the complete opposite, which didn't change overnight, but as she provided opportunities for adventure and new experiences it was very impactful to observe the way our children were growing in confidence, resilience and the willingness to face their fears and keep an open mind to try new things themselves. Eventually I understood the value of facing life with the same willingness and openness: the stage was set for a different outlook on life and a greater openness for the new challenges and opportunities God wanted to guide me through.

Rose also was, and still is, an Early Years teacher and an experienced foster carer. I learnt a lot just by watching her interact with her little girl and having long conversations about real-life parenting struggles and challenges, and what constituted good practice in those particular situations. I eventually became a foster carer myself. In my mind and my heart, Rose will always be deeply connected with the crazy adventure of parenting. I witnessed some of her struggles, she witnessed many of mine. To be very honest, one of the hardest things I had to do was being a single parent.

## Amazing Grace

Let me go back in time again, when God gave me a beautiful baby boy. I longed to be a Mum, so I welcomed my pregnancy with a joyful heart. I didn't know the next eight months would bring some of the hardest moments of my life. My pregnancy developed into a high risk one and we started going to appointments and routine checks at the biggest, best-equipped maternity in Lisbon. If I had been booked to give birth at my local hospital, as was the normal procedure, my son wouldn't be here today. Daniel was a miracle baby.

Because we had access to equipment which signaled early on that the baby was in distress and had an irregular heart-beat, I was prepped for an emergency c-section which literally saved his life. Daniel was born prematurely, and he had to stay in an incubator for a week, followed by another week in the neonatal ward; which meant that a few days after the birth, when I was finally discharged, I came home without my baby. The next two weeks, time stopped. My days consisted of going to the maternity early each morning and coming back home late each night, without my baby.

Throughout the whole process, God's 'cloud' of *peace beyond understanding*, encircled me and I could feel His tangible presence every step of the way. My baby got stronger and stronger and the day we finally brought him home was a day of great joy and celebration.

At this point, Daniel was still tiny, but when he started eating and sleeping well he grew and developed into a beauty of a baby. People would stop me everywhere I went just to look at him and engage with him. He was a gift from the Father in a very difficult season of my life. I loved my son dearly and devoted myself to him. We were very close but not exclusive. His father fell in love with him and became a good dad, very present in his son's life, even when geographical distance got in the middle.

In England, parenting on my own, I was a loving mother, but I was also on a painful growing journey. I didn't know how to empower my child well because I was still learning what it meant to be a powerful person myself. I knew the power of words, so I tried my best to use words which built my son up, however my words didn't always match my heart posture. I took choices away from him because of my need for control, rooted in an insecure and fearful parenting style. I communicated without words that I didn't trust his choices, that he had no ability to choose well and he couldn't do things to the standard I liked, so I'd better do them for him. His problems were my problems to solve but I didn't do well with mistakes and messes.

The truth was I still didn't love myself well, I didn't fully accept myself and I didn't know how to extend grace to myself. This lack of grace and acceptance was projected onto my relationship with my son, especially when dealing with his errors or blunders. I mostly resorted to punishment (usually referred to as 'consequences') and removal of love, and very seldom walked him through formative and restorative discipline. A milder version, yes, but still a version of the disempowering parenting I had experienced which I swore I would never emulate.

Today I have the ability to put words to the process, but at the time I couldn't articulate it like this. I knew in my heart that something was amiss with my parenting, but I lived in the tension of wanting to address those things, to become a better mum, and the desire to run away from them because I couldn't really pinpoint what was at the root of our malaise.

There were so many moments when the painful thought that "I was never going to be enough as a parent" rose up. I was plagued with ongoing self-doubt about whether I was doing a good job or not and, subconsciously, every day I battled the fear of failure which whispered in the back of my mind that, if I didn't get it right all the time, I was going to irreparably compromise my son's future. It was, in some way, a kind of torment. I always wanted to be a mum, but I had never planned to do this parenting thing on my own.

One glorious Sunday, John Partington, who was at the time the National Leader of the AOG[75] in Great Britain, came to our church. When the worship time was over and he grabbed the microphone, before he started preaching he asked where I was. I was on the worship team that day and when he saw me singing the Lord gave him a word for me. Before he gave

---

[75] Assemblies of God

me the word he asked if the little boy who had just walked across the room was my son. I confirmed he was correct. This was an auditorium big enough for 500 people, but Daniel had just walked from one end of the room to the other to go to kids' church. As he walked, John's attention was drawn to him and the Holy Spirit revealed a calling on his life.

This man of God started to prophesy over Daniel, declaring words of life and affirmation over his identity and speaking words of empowerment and hope over his future and destiny. He then proceeded to tell me that the Lord wanted me to know "He was proud of me because I am a good mother and I was doing a good job raising my son." My friend Rose was right next to me, sharing that beautiful moment when my heart was deeply touched by God's grace. He kept repeating it as if to make sure I really got it. I had tears running down my face because I knew I wasn't always doing a great job as a mum, but I was blown away by the fact that God was choosing to focus on what I was doing well and cheer me on, rather than focusing on what I wasn't getting right yet.

*If God believes in me, why shouldn't I?*

Once again, God poured hope into areas where hopelessness was depleting me, and grace into areas where condemnation and shame were crushing me. With hope came joy and strength, and with grace came confidence: "If God believes in me, why shouldn't I?"

I believe the Lord made this so public because He was not only meeting my need for encouragement and validation for that time alone, but He was also affirming me and equipping me for the time ahead where my parenting capacity and reputation were going to be on the line and put to the test.

## Becoming a Foster Carer

After six months of ongoing assessments and rigorous scrutiny I was approved to become a therapeutic foster carer. I was truly blessed to be admitted into a private organization with very high standards and some of the best results in England. That meant I had access to ongoing, specialized training and this became a season in which I experienced great inner growth. I was given tools, and ample opportunity to apply them, to improve my self-awareness and my understanding of the way I emotionally process, so I could walk alongside somebody else and model it well.

A few weeks after I was approved, Lily became part of our family. She was fourteen at the time. Lily was, and is, beautiful, bright and able to learn and pick up new things quickly. She liked watching films and reading books which told real life stories and she carried a few interesting and challenging stories of her own. Daniel was thrilled to have a sister, someone other than mum in the house, and I was excited with the prospect of making a difference in someone else's life. We just didn't realize how much this experience was going to impact us and how it wasn't just going to be about what we gave to Lily, but what Lily was going to give to us too.

In spite of all the training I had already gone through, I still had some misconceptions about fostering. I thought I was going to 'save' a child who needed me and welcomed my help with open arms. I soon found out that wasn't always the case and I was stretched in more ways than I care to admit. Lily could be lovely, lively and bubbly. There were times when she loved chatting and seemed to enjoy moments conducive to connection, however, on many occasions she would become quiet, withdraw into her room, into her own world, and willingly choose disconnection, from myself and from Daniel.

For my son, this alternative connection, which he welcomed at first, was not always stable or easy to manage and, as time went by, this affected my relationship with Daniel too. The frailties in our own connection became more visible, as a painful evidence that my parenting style was not wholesome. The realization that I needed to grow as an individual so I could grow as a parent, became clearer and louder as the first weeks and months went by.

There were so many control issues each one of us carried on our own, I'm absolutely convinced that, even before I fully knew what I was doing, God was holding my hand and safely guiding me through what could otherwise have been a very dangerous and destructive emotional minefield. There are so many stories of 'broken-down placements' in the fostering system, but by the grace of God it did not happen to us.

We can never truly give away what we don't possess, so I ended up spending a lot of time digging holes in this 'desert' to find wells where I could drink from and invite others to drink with me. To grow meant to spiritually and therapeutically 'sort myself out', so I could become a secure base for someone who desperately needed, but didn't know how to deal with consistency, healthy boundaries, gradual empowerment, responsibility, and selfless love[76].

In time I grew in the understanding of what it meant to deal with complex issues connected to developmental trauma and attachment disorder. This tested and enlarged my capacity to forgive, to extend grace and genuine empathy, and to choose connection, even when rejection and abuse were being thrown at me. I began to empower, by believing, encouraging and

> *I began to empower my children by believing in them, encouraging them and giving them opportunities to step up.*

giving opportunities for my children to step up. In this new parenting context, where there was no room for punishment, the concept of taking ownership was a foundational one. Choices were encouraged and

---

[76] This was the time I also came across curricula like KYLO (Keep Your Love On) and LOP (Loving your Children on Purpose) by Danny Silk.

expected, messes were cleaned up in a constructive, formative way, and every little progress or success was celebrated.

It was not an easy road to travel but it was a very rewarding one. I would do it again. To this day I stay in contact with Lily, she still calls me Mum and tells everyone that ours is a success story. Our bond is real and meaningful, and I will always consider her as a daughter.

## The Lowest Valley

"You don't know Jesus is all you need until Jesus is all you have" (Tim Keller)

In the following summer we travelled to Portugal, as we habitually did during summer holidays, and Daniel decided not to travel back to England with us because he wanted to live with his dad. Not being empowering as a parent had created a lot of unnecessary friction and disconnection between us, but those bridges were being mended and I knew it was no longer about that. He was very unhappy at school and because of his negative relational experiences there, he got more and more isolated. Although he was a 'people person', he was a very lonely teenager and he had no significant friendships at that point. We also lived in a very feminine bubble. I had no male friends and all my female friends had female daughters. Daniel was growing up and craving for a different type of camaraderie and male bonding I couldn't offer. In Portugal he had his father and his grandfather (with whom he always had a very strong bond) living next door to each other, and he was ready to individuate and 'hang out with the guys'.

I could have made him return to England with me, his father was outspoken about letting me decide on this, but I knew in my heart, it wouldn't have been the right decision: I would be physically taking my son with me, but emotionally I would be inflicting serious foundational cracks in our connection which could be very costly, damaging and even irreparable. So, still engulfed by the pain of rejection, I decided to love him, respect his reasons and his decision, and empower him in a way I had never been able to do before. Letting him go was one of the hardest things I've ever done, and in the days ahead I went on to face one of the toughest seasons of my life.

That painful summer, when I returned to England with Lily and an empty seat on the plane, I was heartbroken and emotionally numb. I went on doing life like that for about a month. I was functional on the surface, but I was trying really hard to avoid the pain of mourning the loss of my son. I was afraid if I started crying I wouldn't be able to stop.

I had also lost myself. The last layer of my constructed identity had been finally stripped off. My labels, one by one had been removed by process of elimination: no longer a wife, no longer a ministry leader, no longer a career-focused professional, no longer Daniel's mother. All of those labels gave me a purpose and an identity and now I felt like I was at the end of myself, in the deepest valley of my life. And what a great place to be, isn't it?...

*The bigger the valley, the greater the flood it can contain.*

To be completely honest, I didn't really think that at first, but in time I found out that those who mourn will be comforted and the bigger the valley, the greater the flood it can contain - the Holy Spirit told me this and led me through it. This was the point in my life when I turned to Jesus as my only Source, my eyes were opened and what I saw and tasted changed the course of my life forever. This was when I had the "Heavenly Wolverine" encounter.

### *My Heavenly Wolverine!*

My journals are my most prized possession because in them I have recorded my history with God. I record prophetic words, prophetic dreams, inspired words and revelation, and life-changing encounters like the one I'm about to share with you.

Journal entry:

*I was having a very tough day and I felt so disappointed with myself again that I totally 'switched off'. I couldn't deal with fretting over my failures and shortcomings again. I was tired of feeling crushed by guilt and shame so I decided to withdraw from everything and everyone, and just vegetate. Watching a film seemed like a good idea and I was drawn to watch "The Wolverine"[77], because he is my favorite superhero.*

*In this attempt to escape from reality, I ended up watching the film three times in a row. I just couldn't stop watching it. Every time I watched it, my heart was getting tighter and tighter, like something was seizing it with the firmest of grips. I could feel myself investing tremendously in the story, especially in the main character. I started questioning my motives: "What is wrong with you woman? Is it because he's hot? Have you been on your own for so long that you can't handle watching an attractive, bulky guy without being seduced by his physical attributes?" No. I knew it wasn't just that. There was a genuinely deep emotional investment happening. My heart was deeply moved as I felt close to him, felt his pain and rejoiced in his victories. I tried to reason: "That's the way good films are made. Their purpose is to create empathy, connect you with the characters and draw inner investment and attachment out of you." That made sense, but I couldn't shake off the fact that I felt compelled by something stronger and deeper...something that even felt spiritual!*

*I didn't really have a clue about what was happening to me, and incapable of extending grace to myself, I defaulted to the familiar judgmental self-*

---

[77] "The Wolverine", directed by James Mangold, filmed in Japan, released in July 2013.

*talk. I made the decision that "I was a nutcase, a pervert, lusting for a muscular man, so needy that I would attach to a fictional character!" These were painful thoughts and I tried to dismiss them by completing house chores. All the while, a battle was raging inside of me and eventually I couldn't take it any longer. I ran upstairs to my room, fell on my knees and with tears streaming I poured out my heart and soul to the Lord. I asked for His forgiveness for having shunned Him away again and again instead of inviting Him to awake me from my numbness. I cried for His help as I confessed that I didn't really feel like a normal person. I felt like I was losing my mind. I felt confused, restless, emotionally overwhelmed, and intrinsically desperate.*

*The things I wanted to do I didn't, and the things I didn't want to do, I kept doing them! I asked for His help because I didn't want to feel that way anymore. Immediately, the Holy Spirit told me to "grab the bible and open it." No specific verse was given, as God had done so many times before, but my bible opened in the exact spot God intended it to open, Isaiah 43.*

Don't be afraid. I've redeemed you. I've called your name. You're mine. When you're in over your head, I'll be there with you. When you're in rough waters you will not go down. When you're between a rock and a hard place it won't be a dead end - because I am God, your personal God, the Holy of [Ana], your Savior. I paid a huge price for you ...That's how much you mean to me! That's how much I love you! I'd sell off the whole world to get you back, trade the creation just for you... So don't be afraid; I'm with you. Yes, I personally formed you and created you for my Glory.[78]

*As I read His Word for me, my heart just melted. I could feel God's presence and warm love washing over me. As soon as I read the first line, God spoke to me about redemption. He reminded me that my flesh and sinful nature had been nailed to the cross and are now where Jesus left them. When Jesus rose, He rose victorious and I rose with Him!*

---

[78] Paraphrase of verses 1 to 7 from the MSG translation.

*Then God drew on my experience to help me understand my situation. He reminded me how certain children who want to usurp authority will try to intimidate adults with violent, aggressive and loud behavior and how they will have a foothold if you give in to that intimidation. He showed me that was the way I had handled flesh and sin. They are no longer powerful. Their tyranny is over, their weapons have been made obsolete and all they can do now is bluff. If I believe they have a grip or any kind of authority over me then I empower them by opening a door and creating spiritual room for them. My beliefs shape my spiritual reality and I empower what I believe.*

*At the same time that God was renewing my mind with His perspective, He was also showing me a 'film' featuring Jesus when He went to hell and won the final victory! And what an amazing film it was. My words are inadequate to describe what I saw and experienced next, but I will do my best: There He was, a mighty, fierce warrior, the Lion of Judah! Roaring, brandishing His sword and kicking butt! Right there and then I understood why my heart was drawn to the character of Wolverine. It was a shadow of the One I had desired and longed for my entire life: kind, generous, merciful, with a tender, caring heart moved by the needs of the weak and vulnerable; passionate about His cause, not giving up, not getting tired or crushed until He achieved what had been set before Him. Powerful and majestic, a fierce Lion Warrior who will tear to pieces any power or principality of darkness which tries to stand between Him and his beloved.*

*I was no longer beholding a shadow, my eyes were now locked on the One true Savior. Besotted by that glorious vision I realized I was in the presence of my one true Love. My champion! The greatest passion of my life. In my bedroom I fell on my knees, but in my vision I ran to Him, embraced Him tightly, kissed His cheeks repeatedly and declared my love for Him. I thanked him for his patience and for his love beyond understanding, for the Truth that crushes the lies and for the seal upon my heart and arm[79]. There was no part of me that was not His, my Savior, Protector and always present*

---

[79] Song of Solomon 8:6

*Lover. Glad to have me back, He calmed me with His Love and delighted me with His song[80].*

*I cannot describe with words what happened between me and my Beloved. It was a pure, love-making moment, one I had been longing and waiting for all of my life. I felt deeply loved, cherished, embraced, kissed, held tenderly and dearly. I couldn't do anything else but enjoy His presence, receive and be fully satisfied by His perfect love, as I whispered, over and over and over: "You, it's you I've been waiting for all along."*

*When the encounter was over I thanked God with all my heart for all the doors which had been closed, and all the experiences with outcomes below my expectations, because if they had been fulfilling I would have been prone to settle down, be content and stop searching for what would truly quench me to the core: His intimate presence.*

*From that day onwards my relationship with God changed deeply and because of that my life was never the same again. Nothing will do if I'm not intimately connected to Him.*

*A few days later I came across the song "Unstoppable Love" by Kim and Skyler Smith[81]. I couldn't believe my ears! I cried and laughed at the same time (and produced copious amounts of snot) as I listened to a song that described everything I had seen, felt and tasted in that encounter.*

---

[80] Zephaniah 3:17

[81] https://video.search.yahoo.com/search/video?fr=mcafee&p=kim+walker+smith+song+from+home+album+champion#id=2&vid=02e31d04c4b547f1f1d849621cd29cfa&action=view

## "Unstoppable Love"

Try to stop Your love and You would wage a war

Try to take the very thing You gave Your life for

And you would come running

Tear down every wall

All the while shouting

"My Love, you're worth it all"


God you pursue me with power and glory

Unstoppable Love that never ends

You're unrelenting with passion and mercy

Unstoppable Love that never ends


You broke into the silence and sang your song of hope

A melody resounding in the deep of my soul

You have come running

You tore down every wall

All the while shouting,

"My Love you're worth it all"


No sin, no shame

No past, no pain

Can separate me from Your love

No height, no depth

No fear, no death

Can separate me from Your love


God you pursue me with power and glory

Unstoppable Love that never ends

You're unrelenting with passion and mercy

Unstoppable Love that never ends.


## Deep Wells in the Desert

A few weeks later, while I was browsing on YouTube, looking for inspirational teachings, I came across one of Bill Johnson's podcasts. Its title, "The Resting Place"[82]. To be completely honest, at the time I knew nothing about Bill Johnson, Bethel music or Bethel church. I was drawn by the comment written underneath: "very powerful." When I finished listening to this sermon, I was so deeply moved I started weeping profusely. I couldn't stop crying for the next couple of hours.

My awareness of the presence of the Holy Spirit was so heightened that God became more tangible and real than anything else around me. My emotional loss, and all the other circumstances which had been weighing

---

[82] https://www.youtube.com/watch?v=lsQmLuG-Exo

on me, paled into insignificance in the presence of a God without measure, who lavishly poured out a love, a peace and a joy so real and so profound it filled me to overflowing.

In what felt like the biggest, deepest valley I had ever been in, God's presence rushed in like a mighty flood and He revealed Himself faithful and big enough. I knew then, experientially, what it really means to have a God for whom no mountain is too high, and no valley is too low. Instead of being focused on myself and all that I still wasn't and didn't have, being focused on Him and all He is, realigned me with the truth that not only

> *Being focused on all God is, realigned me with the truth and set me on the right course.*

set me free, but built up my faith and set me on the right course towards the 'promised land': the place where God's promises for a happy family and a meaningful and purposeful marriage were going to come to pass.

Not all of us will need to go through ten years of digging in the desert to tap into such deep wells. Not all of us will go around the same mountains the same number of times. As I said before, your journey and your wilderness don't have to look like mine. However, regardless of how it looks, or how long it takes you, I pray that there will come a time when you too will experience the tension between being content while trusting God for your daily manna, and being hopeful and faith-filled as you keep your eyes on the horizon in expectation for the promised land. This will happen when you truly believe God is not only real, but He is also a good Father[83], and a rewarder of those who seek Him[84]. When I was finally reunited with the Father and established in the cornerstone of His unshakeable goodness, that revelation changed everything for me.

---

[83] Luke 11:11-13

[84] Hebrews 11:6

**Home**

A deep hunger for the tangible presence of God had been awaken in me and I started avidly listening to more podcasts from different pastors, evangelists and teachers in the Bethel environment or connected with the Revival Alliance. A fire had been ignited within, a passion and a hunger for the more of God. In the following year, I listened to hundreds of hours of teaching, read more books, written more songs, and filled more journals than I had throughout the entirety of my former Christian life. What I am about to share with you is again a journal entry where I recorded another life-changing encounter, this time with the Father.

Journal entry:

*Today I listened to a sermon by Bill Johnson entitled "Why did Jesus come to Earth?"[85] In it Bill explains how Jesus' main mission was to reveal the Father's heart. As he led me through some of the episodes narrated in the gospels through a father's perspective, and shared some of his personal testimonies as a son of a good God, perfect, attentive and kind Father, I had a revelation of the Father's heart as I had never had before. I realized He is so good He cares about the little details of our lives, pays attention to our desires, longs to answer our prayers and is invested in making our joint dreams come true. I realized God wants us to dream with Him and in the process manifest His glory on the Earth as His face shines upon us and His blessings are manifested in our lives. Suddenly, everything became so clear. My eyes were wide open to see the goodness of God in all of its*

---

[85] https://www.youtube.com/watch?v=cS5INotE_-o

*unquestionable, glorious, beautiful perfection. I remember crying like a baby for hours, again!*

*In this encounter, my wonderful, good Father restored my identity as a daughter: fully approved, fully accepted and fully loved. I saw myself as a playful, joyful, confident little girl ridding on His big, steady shoulders. I felt like a new life had just begun. I could see life from a higher place, as a daughter of the most high but also the most kind God. Amidst streams of tears and deep sobs I declared "From this day onwards I am going to walk in the presence of my Father." When I painfully realized how much I had missed out because of my mistrust, the time of intimate communion with Him I had lost, He told me "He redeems time and He will make up for all I have missed out until now" (the "vineyard workers full payment story"[86] came to mind).*

*My wonderful Father! I can't stop laughing! I've never felt so happy. I'm home! This was the best day of my life! I'm reunited with my Father!*

> *The major cornerstone of my faith has since been the goodness of God.*

I still cry every time I read this entry and am transported to that beautiful, life changing moment. From that day forward the major cornerstone of my faith and my life has been the unquestionable, unshakeable, eternal goodness of God. He has been faithful even in the way He has redeemed time. The next two years I experienced tremendous acceleration and entered an "and suddenly" season where I finally said goodbye to this desert. My favorite gift in this new season of my life was a God-loving, kind, sweet and amazing husband... but that is another story.

---

[86] Matthew 20:1-16

# Q & A

## M y s e l f  &  G o d

- Can you identify expressions of God's goodness in your life journey (circumstances, people, provision, learning outcomes, etc.)?

- Start making a list of those 'Expressions of God's Goodness' (If you feel like you are stuck, ask the Holy Spirit to refresh your memory).

- After contemplating His goodness do you believe He is attentive to your needs?

- Make a list of your personal needs. Discuss the list with the Lord, and ask Him if there are any deep needs you haven't identified yet.

- Suggestion[87]: Listen to the podcast "Why did Jesus come to Earth?"[88]

- Write down characteristics or aspects of the Father which stood out (while reading this chapter or listening to the podcast), but you hadn't seen or considered before.

- Write down a small paragraph of what you are passionate about, the deep desires of your heart and the dreams it harbors (alive or dormant, silly or outrageous, small or impossibly big).

- Have a conversation with God about it. Ask the Holy Spirit to show you how you are wired, and what are the dreams in which God wants to partner with you to shine His glory and make His Face known on the Earth.

---

[87] This is not the only good resource out there you can access about the goodness of God, but it is one which genuinely impacted my life, therefore I believe it can impact yours too.

[88] https://www.youtube.com/watch?v=lsQmLuG-Exo

- In what way has this exercise impacted you?

# T o g e t h e r

*(For those who want to work towards the restoration or improvement of their marriage)*

❏ Please, share with your spouse what the Holy Spirit revealed to you in your personal time with God.

- If you both listened to the podcast, compare notes.

- Discuss your lists of:

    - The expressions of God's goodness in your lives;
    - Your personal needs.

- Can you contribute, in any way, to meet some of the needs your spouse has listed?

- Read your paragraphs about passions and dreams to each other and share what the Holy Spirit has highlighted. (Be intentional in receiving your spouse's dreams with an encouraging, faith-filled outlook, remembering that "all things are possible to the one who believes" - Mark 9:23).

✦ Draw/paint/compose two creative posters, a "Thanksgiving" one with the most impacting expressions of God's goodness in your life, and an "Ask and it shall be given" one with the dreams you are going to consistently pray for.

- Display them in a prominent, visible area of your home.

# LifeLine

Revelation & Transformation log          ____/____/____

"Let perseverance finish its work so that you may be **mature** and complete, **not lacking anything.**"

(James 1:4)

# 7 SUFFERING, GROWTH & TRANSFORMATION

"The strongest principle of growth lies in the human choice."

(George Eliot)

You just have to flick through some of the pages in each of the previous chapters to find evidence that God had been revealing Himself as a good Father from the very beginning of my journey with Him, but my fear and inability to trust Him blurred my vision for a long time. During this time, I was still connecting the dots, unable to see the bigger picture: Love. He didn't love and pursue me relentlessly because that's what He does, but because that's who He is.

When I was finally reunited with the Father and my eyes were wide open to contemplate, in wonder and awe, His intrinsic, perfect, glorious, beautiful goodness, I no longer had doubts about His parenting. It all became so clear. Jesus explained it so well: the best father on earth doesn't come close to our God! Observe the best parents, the ones who really do a good job at it, and remember they still fall short of the glory and goodness our perfect, heavenly Father longs to express as He parents us[89].

## Acceleration

How did this revelation tangibly impact my life from thereon? It deeply affected the way I approach and interact with God and other people.

God had already chosen me and called me to Himself to be His daughter, even before the creation of the world[90], but now I had willingly chosen Him as my Father. Many of us who attend church Sunday after Sunday, year after year, have not yet had a personal encounter with our heavenly Father, and because of that we still approach God with some reservations. It all changed for me when I fully embraced His goodness. As I turned to the Lord, the veil was taken away[91]. I didn't have it all figured out yet but there was no awkward distance between us anymore, no unspoken suspicions regarding His motives, no hidden doubts. There was full-on eye contact as I felt completely safe and secure in His presence, relaxed to be fully myself, no longer afraid to be fully known and no longer afraid to fully know Him. It is in this place of deep, vulnerable intimacy that genuine transformation

---

[89] Matthew 7:9-11

[90] Ephesians 1:3-14

[91] 2 Corinthians 3:16

and growth happen. We open our hearts to become gradually and increasingly more like the glorious One we behold:

And we all, with unveiled faces reflecting the glory of the Lord, are being transformed into the same image from one degree of glory to another, which is from the Lord, who is the Spirit. (2 Corinthians 3:18 - NET)

I didn't get it right all the time, but I could see things beginning to shift in my heart as I opened up to God's voice of correction and discipline. That is a fundamental aspect of healthy parenting. It got easier and easier to break the deceitful fear of being exposed. This fear rose up every time I thought about going through scrutiny of some kind. Having someone exposing or commenting on my shortcomings and mistakes made me want to run and hide. However, I knew this was not just any *someone*, this was, and is, my Heavenly Daddy! I began to experience, in deeper ways, how His perfect love and rock-solid goodness really do cast away all fear[92], cancel shame and create an optimal learning environment.

This closer, more intimate relationship with God also affected the way I approach and relate to other people. It brought with it a higher calling

*The higher calling of revealing the Father to those around us.*

to reveal the Father to the ones around me, not for my sake but for their sake. There was an increasing awareness of deeper levels of wisdom, kindness and generosity God demonstrated to me as we did life together. The way He continued to instruct me, correct me, forgive me, inspire me, believe in me and empower me: I knew I was meant to bring those

---

[92] 1 John 4:18

ingredients to the table whenever I relate to others too. It also meant that there were other ingredients which needed to be taken off the table.

Where the Spirit of the Lord is there is freedom[93] and there is no room for control, manipulation and unkindness. That became easier to embrace and put into practice because fear did not have central stage anymore. I had already experienced this before, to a certain degree, in the way I engaged with my ex-husband during my journey of forgiveness and inner healing (especially through the process of separation and divorce), but this heightened awareness of God's relational attributes and Heaven's relational dynamics took it to a higher level for me. Any thought or action which degraded, demoted, disqualified and dishonored anyone I related to, was a misrepresentation of the heart of the Father and of His Spirit dwelling in me. To this day this realization brings the *Fear of the Lord* into my relational conduct: a reverent and weighty conviction to consider and look at others the way the Father does, and to be intentional in not becoming a stumbling block which will prevent them from turning their hearts to the Lord.

I didn't know it at the time, but this would be pivotal for the next season of my life because this realignment of my heart posture was one of the main shifts which needed to happen so God could entrust me with one of his precious sons to be my life companion. "You don't honor who you think you can control"[94], and understanding that the other person is a son of God, created to be free and powerful, was foundational. It became like a trusted compass which helped me to identify familiar thought patterns aimed at constricting and conforming others to my desired image of them. It also set the foundation for addressing others with a respectful and honoring recognition of their unique wiring, giftings and purpose.

When I got married again, I was amazed how this awareness impacted our relationship so profoundly. We have truly benefited from the positive and

---

[93] 2 Corinthians 3:17

[94] Danny Silk in Loving On Purpose Academy, course "People Helping People", lesson 3.

constructive way freedom and honor have released us to become more authentic and more assertive. It hasn't always been easy, but by being consistent at it we have created room for both of us to fully show up. This has solidified our alliance because it has developed and sharpened our capacity to communicate effectively and empowered us to continue to improve and grow, individually and as a couple. To fully know and be fully known and deeply connected is our goal and we're convinced we are on the right track because we're not doing it our way, but God's way.

## Brave Communication

If our goal is deeper connection we must be available to communicate openly and honestly about everything. This is possible when we are not only focused on what we are communicating but especially on how we are communicating it. We tend to adopt the models we have observed around us but we need to align those with the Kingdom values. The fruits of the Spirit empower us to be kind and exercise self-control but true transformation also requires a renewal of the mind, which comes from learning what to do and what not to do, and deciding to apply that knowledge.

*Brave communication*[95] is amazing when done properly, but it can be very dangerous ground if our hearts are not in the right place and our souls are not aligned with the Gospel of truth. We can easily fall off a cliff if we don't have the right map, the right compass or the right guide. What was initially intended to bring us closer can end up creating greater distance, and distance is not our goal but a more meaningful connection. Therefore it is very important that you become available to really listen, to get to know the other person's needs and heartbeat, but also to fully show up so they

---

[95] https://bssm2ndyearnotes.wordpress.com/tag/brave-communication/ and

https://www.happyandhealthy.co/blog/brave-communication-for-the-real-world/

get to know yours. The secret is to not tackle it leaning on our own rookie understanding but to learn how to do it[96] and ask for help if we need it. We can draw on the wisdom and knowledge of people who have weathered experiences similar to ours, and use the tools they have successfully tested.

Those people can be therapists, marriage counselors, church leaders or the couple down the road that has a tremendous testimony of restoration. Whatever degree of proximity you share, from the direct interaction to DVD sessions or books, make sure you are accessing content which teaches truth inspired by the Holy Spirit, anchored in the Scriptures, and turns your heart completely to God as your primary source of wisdom, inspiration, comfort and strength.

He is not a distant, empty-worded God. Do you invite Him to speak into your life and relationships? Do you take time to listen to what He has to say? What value do you have for His voice? His words will bring tangible light and life to whichever aspects of your relational experiences that are obscure, confusing or even hopeless. His words have the power to impact your circumstances and create a new reality, but He won't just barge into your private affairs. Remember, He is at the door knocking, waiting for you to open your heart and invite Him in[97].

*Conversations with God were never meant to be a collection of isolated events.*

I have discovered that if I want to see Heaven impact and reshape my life on Earth, I have to be intentionally aware of God's presence and be available and willing to listen to His voice in my everyday life. Conversations with God were never meant to be a collection of isolated events, instead they are meant to be a lifestyle. I believe that's what Paul was talking about

---

[96] https://shop.bethel.com/products/brave-communication (Empowering Skills that transform relationships by Dann Farrelly - MP3)

[97] Revelation 3:20

when he urged God's children to pray without ceasing[98]. Our God is a relational God who wants to be experienced, known and trusted as a Father on a daily basis.

In this catalytic season of my life, there was a shift and a development of my spiritual 'conversational skills' in such a way that I was no longer expecting to hear God's voice in the secret place alone, but I was attentive to what He was saying in, about and through everyday life events and circumstances. What I wasn't expecting was to get to know Him more deeply, not just by what He says, but by the way He says it. God's voice, together with His ways, reveal fascinating, mysterious aspects of His nature.

## His Voice Together with His Ways

The story I'm about to tell you might seem at first long and unrelated to your circumstances but, before you decide it has nothing to add or contribute to your personal experience and growth, I invite you to remain in the picture until it is fully painted. If you do, I guarantee you will be rewarded with a greater understanding of how God moves, talks, relates to, and develops us through the most mundane things.

In the months following my first Bill Johnson's podcast, I became more and more curious about the school of ministry at Bethel church. The more I listened and read content being taught at BSSM[99] and the more I prayed about it, the more the desire to attend this ministry school increased. Eventually, there was a day in the secret place when I knew it was God's will for my life: "It is official, I am going to BSSM!" Although there was a big list of impossibilities between my current circumstances and the fulfilment of that dream, I had no doubt I was heading to Redding, California at some

---

[98] 1 Thessalonians 5:17

[99] Bethel School of Supernatural Ministry

point in the future. I was certain that God was going to make a way for it to happen and I started to think, plan and prepare for that.

While helping a friend who, having lived many years in England, was getting ready to return to Australia, I realized when the time came for me to move to America I would be completely overwhelmed with the logistics of it all. So I decided to start preparing in advance. Part of that preparation involved moving to a new house. I set out to find a new rental property because I wanted one already furnished. The plan was to get rid of all the bigger, hard to move items and be a lot lighter and freer to depart whenever God opened that door.

I looked and looked in all the right places and there were no furnished houses for rent within my geographical boundaries. I continued to pray about it, but after three months of intensive searching without being successful, I 'put it on a shelve' and just carried on with life as normal.

A few months went by. The time for Lily to leave school was approaching so I started to consider moving to a house closer to her future college. The problem was that the college she had applied for was located in a highly sought after area. The average rents were not cheap, and it was very hard to find available rental properties, so when I saw an advert for one I immediately called the agency and asked them to put my name down. It was a very old house, but affordable and perfectly located. I was willing to turn another old house into a home if it meant less time in the car and a better quality of life.

When I went to the agency I found out that there was an extremely long list of applicants for that property and my name was not even in the top 10. When the lady behind the counter saw the disappointment on my face, she suggested I should take a look at their display because there were other options in a nearby area. After going over all the options, only one stood out but it was a fully furnished house. When I further enquired about it, the lady promptly answered: "Yes, it's furnished. It's a shame. It's such a nice house that it would have been rented long ago if it wasn't furnished." I left, even more disappointed.

I remember walking to the car and hearing the Holy Spirit say: "Isn't this what you were praying for, a furnished house?" I stopped and exclaimed out loud: "Yes, it is!" With the passing of the months and the busyness of life, it had completely slipped my mind. I went back into the agency, and the rest is history. The normal procedures, which included a couple of visits and all the necessary paperwork, and that property became our new home.

But why am I telling you all this? Because of what happened next. The following somewhat bizarre turn of events became a landmark on my journey of learning how to listen to, and trust, God's voice, while growing in self-awareness too.

I visited the house with Lily twice. No issues after the first visit. She liked the house, especially her new room, so I moved forward with the rental process. After the second visit something strange happened. I was no longer happy with my decision. I couldn't completely explain what was going on in my heart and my mind, but it felt like somebody had suddenly put a new pair of glasses on me and through those new lenses all I could see was what was wrong with the house. It was the weirdest of experiences, because although there weren't many negative aspects to notice, my excitement about living there was totally gone, to the point I didn't want to go through with it anymore.

I knew better than to make the decision on my own, so I prayed about it with the genuine intention of following God's counsel. He gave me a clear 'yes' to the house. Again I thought this was going to make it easier, but it only made it worse. Although I knew God's will was for me to go ahead with it, in my own eyes the house was becoming more and more unattractive. Before, it was just an impression, now I was completely sure that I did not want to live there anymore.

The Holy Spirit kept affirming that was the best decision, and He kept reminding me how much easier it would be to 'fly away' when the time came to depart to America. Going against my will, my understanding, and a sense of overwhelming apprehension I couldn't rationally explain, I decided to trust God's will and I finally signed the rental agreement. This was a history-making moment in my friendship with God. First because my absolute trust in Him was tangibly enacted, and second because *I collected spiritual and emotional memories from that experience* which, unbeknownst to me at the time, were going to operate as another trusted compass in the near future (as you follow the other avenues in this narrative, it is important you keep this in mind).

> *This was a history-making moment in my friendship with God.*

The time came to prepare for the move. After leaving Portugal, this was my second big moment of letting go of things in spite of the emotions attached to them. I kept telling myself, "At the end of the day, it's just stuff", but it's easier said than done. I remember putting worship music on and a load of 'meaty' podcasts to sustain me with encouragement, hope and joy and usher in the presence of God.

And He did come, and brought with Him such an indescribable peace that what happened next defies reason and goes beyond my ability to fully articulate it with mere words. God's presence around me was so thick it felt like I was floating on a cloud, and His presence within me was so exhilarating, I felt like I was joyfully inebriated most of the time, almost oblivious to the practical shores at hand. Especially when it was time to dismantle Daniel's room. I had left it exactly as it was when he decided to stay in Portugal. The following excerpt is taken from a journal entry I wrote that night:

*Sorting, bagging, packing and stacking things all day. 'Not the most exciting of days', I thought, until God's presence flooded in. I struggled to keep my balance most of the time because His anointing was so powerful. It was awesome! He kept my eyes, my ears, my heart set on Him all the time. He shared His heart with me, He revealed secrets about my future. What a great day! What a great God!*

The reason I include this entry is because, although it was meant to be the conclusive paragraph for that day, it really wasn't. A small arrow on the bottom right of the page points to a later addendum, on the next page, which I wrote just before going to sleep:

*Just realized this was the day I 'dismantled' Daniel's room and the Holy Spirit completely distracted me from that fact!!! God, you are SO good, so caring, so beautiful!*

This is exactly what happened. He held me so close I just floated through what had the potential to be a very heartbreaking experience. In His infinite grace, God was leading me on a relational, learning journey where I was fine-tuning my capacity to focus on Him and listen to His voice no matter the circumstances around me and the perceptions inside me. But He didn't stop there.

*A fine-tuning experience where I learned to focus on His voice no matter my circumstances or perceptions.*

Finally, moving day arrived. The whole process was permeated with peace, grace and favor. It went smoothly because I had all the help I needed and a special extra three day period to complete the move. I wasn't charged for those days and the extra time allowed me to do everything without feeling pressured. The fun part of it was the way my perspective started to change as we were getting settled in our new home.

Two days into the move and I became fully aware that the 'negative glasses' I was wearing before, had been removed. I felt as if I was being filled with increasing joy and enthusiasm. The more I cleaned, organized and decorated, the more my heart was happy, and my soul was convinced it was the perfect home for that season of my life. Day after day I kept unveiling one more positive aspect after another, until I realized that house ticked every single box and had every single feature I had listed when I started house hunting and praying, many months before. Again, I was in awe of God's goodness, thankful for the way He looked after me, and really moved by the tenderness He revealed in His attention to detail, giving me not only what I needed but what I really desired (like a fireplace, a conservatory, a breakfast bar, a large built-in wardrobe, beautiful wooden floors, etc.). I could go on for a while, it was a long list.

After a few weeks, I remember thinking that there was something very mysterious about the sudden, inexplicable change of perspective I had gone through initially, which continued to elude me for quite a while. I kept thanking the Lord for guiding my steps when I couldn't see clearly, because I was blinded by negativity and fear, but only future events would fully reveal the importance of this experience where I was equipped and prepared to recognize God's voice and trust His wise counsel, even when it seemed and felt contrary to my understanding and my perception.

Why did God let me go through this uncomfortable experience of self-denial? Why didn't He just tell me and show me clearly, from the beginning, what I was able to eventually see in the end? Isn't He a good Father? Didn't He know what was going on in my soul and my heart? Was there a good enough reason for Him to let me endure such an unpleasant and unsettling process?

*God's goodness is also expressed in the way He teaches and trains us.*

You do not yet possess full knowledge of how this story unfolds, but when you do[100], you will see that God's goodness is also expressed in the way He teaches and trains us. He doesn't just want to control us, or nurture us into an aimless life. He is an invested Father, committed to grow and develop us so we can be deployed into our destiny and fulfill our purpose. He loves us too much to let us stay where we are and He knows the 'much more' there is ahead, because He has prepared it for us[101]. Maturity is the goal, a relational learning process is the road.

## What does it mean to be Mature in the Kingdom of God?

If parents didn't teach their children how to do basic tasks and they reached adulthood depending on them to be fed, cleaned and clothed, there would be some serious developmental issues which would need to be addressed, in order for those individuals to reach their full potential. It would most certainly involve allowing those people to become more autonomous and proficient in a particular skill set needed to progress. The

*God wants His children to grow into Christ and become proficient in abundant life.*

goal would be to make these individuals more able or capable so they could become more independent. This seems logical and good. However, in the Kingdom of God increasing autonomy isn't necessarily a synonym of growth. In God's Kingdom, increased capacity, which is an indicator of growth, is not meant to lead us to independence.

As men and women in relationship with our Father and Creator, God, being dependent on Him to become more able to embody and express His nature and His ways is actually evidence we are mature sons and daughters.

---

[100] It will be fully disclosed in the next chapter

[101] Ephesians 2:10

Maturity in the kingdom doesn't mean self-sufficiency and self-reliance, but it doesn't mean incapability or powerlessness either. God wants His children to grow into Christ and become proficient in abundant life.

Using the initial analogy, it means we still depend on Him for the food, the clothes, resources in general and guidance and instruction on how to use them well. As we receive and learn from Him, we become equipped, empowered and resourced to make better decisions and act not only on our behalf but on behalf of our *neighbors*. In other words, maturity can be seen in the tangible ways we choose to steward His counsel and His gifts, according to His will, not just for our own benefit, but for the benefit of those around us. This is a game changer. I am not just focused on buttoning up my own shirt, I am teaching someone else how to do it. I am not just concerned with eating the food on my own plate, but I am cooking enough food for myself and others.

Only God's love poured into our hearts by His Spirit, together with the mind of Christ, can empower us to lay down our lives and prefer others to ourselves[102]. It's a lost race if we try to do it in our own strength and lean on our own understanding. His perfect, selfless love is indispensable if our desire is to build relationships where we can connect intimately and sacrificially with the ones doing life with us.

*His perfect, selfless love is indispensable.*

## Where are you at?

I believe that you have acknowledged, or you're in the process of acknowledging, that to do this on your own is probably not the best way to go about it. Are you willing to trust God, depend on Him completely and do things His way?

---

[102] Philippians 2:3

When an adult son and daughter willingly choose dependence, it goes against what's logical and expected in this world, but it makes perfect sense in the Kingdom of God. It underpins a relational journey which requires humility, trust, increasing closeness and willingness to let go of past experiences to step into newness and keep expanding while learning on the go: like an inquisitive child living in a house filled with hidden treasures, always asking, always seeking, always knocking expectantly, longing to find out what is behind the closed, promising, golden doors[103].

Therefore, in this process faith is, and will always be, foundational. But faith is not blind, it is visionary:

"Whatever you rehearse in your mind becomes your reality. Because we renew our minds with whatever we consistently believe in, we can't believe in something different from our past experiences if we can't see or envision something different."[104]

So, how can we envision something different and therefore alien to our known experience? Through the mind of Christ.

At the center of our relationship with God, there is also *a sound mind,* and this is an extremely important part of the process. A sound mind is a mind which has been willingly and consistently fed with the truth and engaged in its practical application. Effective learning only takes place when you decide to be actively engaged in the learning process. It's an act of the will. It will always involve

> *God's intention is not to control but to bring us into a voluntary partnership with Him.*

---

[103] Matthew 7:7-12

[104] Wendy and Steve Backlund, sermon at Mountain Chapel, Weaverville, December 2018

choice and it will always involve action and outcome. Through an active, personal learning experience we can *taste and see,* and acknowledge that His ways are better and higher than our ways. It's a liberating, empowering, transformational journey where we are invited, in every decision and choice we make, to trust Him with our hearts and see our identity and purpose through His eyes.

God did not create robots. He created us in His image, creative sons and daughters with free will, because His desire, above everything, is to be truly and intimately loved. You can't force anyone to love. Love will always be a voluntary offering of the heart. In other words, God's intention is never to control us, but to bring us into a voluntary partnership with Him.

When we partner with Him we are empowered and equipped to become responsible, mature, kind and generous stewards of our freedom. As we tap into the mind of Christ, submit to His perfect will and emulate His perfect ways, we find out how much He is invested in empowering us to become more like Him, so we can freely make good decisions, to live a good life while bringing Heaven to Earth within the communities and the spheres of influence we move in. What an amazing, generous and brilliant God! What a beautiful, empowering Father!

## Jesus, our Forerunner

Jesus is our role model, the one who set the standard for us to follow, so let's look more closely at His life. Did you know that the Bible says "Jesus *learned* trusting obedience"?

Because He [Jesus] honored God, God answered Him. Though He was God's Son, He learned trusting-obedience by what He suffered, just as we do. Then, having arrived at the full stature of His maturity and having been announced by God as High Priest in the order of Melchizedek, He became the source of eternal salvation to all who believingly obey Him (Hebrews 5:7-10 MSG).

While I was spending time in the secret place, the Holy Spirit gave me this verse of the Bible. As I read it, over and over again, I became aware of what was going on inside of me. I knew that in the past my intellect would have been stuck as soon as I encountered the word 'suffering'. Filled with doubts about God's goodness I would most likely have resented Him for setting a path where I could only achieve growth through suffering. I would have eaten, and been killed by the fruit of the 'Tree of Knowledge'. However, my story with God had led me to a place where His goodness and wisdom were no longer in question. From that place of faith (right believing), I was able to see, run to, pick and eat the fruit of the 'Tree of Life', which opened my eyes not to my nakedness, limitations and inabilities - like my dislike or fear of suffering - but to the unsurpassing wisdom of God, which I knew was rooted in perfect and complete Love. From this vantage point I was able to see more clearly how my heavenly Father was teaching and demonstrating how to learn and develop maturity in His Kingdom.

As I read the verse again, and proceeded to read the whole chapter, I was fascinated with the idea that Jesus himself had gone through a learning process. I started wondering: "If He learned obedience, does that mean He was once disobedient? If He needed to be perfected, or 'made perfect' (as it reads in the NIV), does that mean there was a time when He was not perfect?"

*Every time Jesus followed His Father's guidance, He learned how to be a victorious man led by the Spirit.*

I went back to the Word of God and read the context carefully, as you do. While I was reading, the Holy Spirit started to show me snapshots of different episodes narrated in the gospels: "the long litany of hostility He plowed through"[105]. I saw Jesus miraculously moving past irate mobs and escaping certain death. I saw

---

[105] Hebrews 12:5 MSG

Him performing miracles which brought provision to individuals and life-saving sustenance to crowds. I saw Him literally and figuratively navigating through storms and persecutions sent to destroy Him and His disciples or to bring doubt and confusion regarding His identity, divine purpose and destiny. Every hurdle, every challenge, every struggle, every battle was an opportunity to involve the Father and invite Him to be in charge and in control. Jesus only did what He saw the Father do[106]. Every time He followed His Father's guidance He learned more about who He was and what He could do as a victorious man led by the Spirit. He was fully God, and therefore perfect, but He was also fully man, which was a new journey, a process involving discovery and learning. He had been appointed as the first of many and His destiny, amongst other things, was to become our Great High Priest, able to empathize with our weaknesses, but also able to represent us victorious and righteous, without sin, so we could approach God's throne of grace with confidence[107].

Recently I came across a *Word Lab* by John Piper where he brilliantly explains this verse through a careful study of its context:

> "Perfection here can be thought of in terms of completeness (Hebrews 2:10). As Jesus moves through life, He is not moving from disobedience to obedience or from sinful imperfection to sinless perfection, but He is moving from unfitness to fitness. His obedience as a man filled with the Holy Spirit hadn't yet been fully tested, tried and proven. He wasn't complete in his fitness to be our perfect sacrifice and our perfect High Priest. Through suffering He was fully tested, and He passed the test with flying colors. If we could become perfectly obedient and fit on our own, we wouldn't need a Savior. When we believe in Christ and we put our trust in Him, all He achieved, including His perfection, is counted as ours and He becomes our perfectly obedient, perfectly complete source of eternal salvation."[108]

---

[106] John 5:19

[107] Hebrews 4:14-16

[108] https://www.desiringgod.org/labs/how-did-jesus-learn-obedience

This powerful revelation sheds light on the enormity of Jesus' commitment and faithfulness to His mission, and to all of us as beneficiaries of His immeasurable investment. Thank you Lord Jesus for enduring it all, for us, till the end! This revelation also put a whole different spin on how I view my journey through life, not just because I have had to navigate my way through perfectionism, but because of the way suffering gained meaningfulness. Suffering in itself isn't good (of course not!), but whatever places us in a position where we are required to deal with challenges, fear, intimidation, loss, lack, opposition, persecution, etc., which causes us to suffer, it also becomes an opportunity for us, like Jesus did, to depend on our Father's intervention. It makes room for Him to show off His glory, His redemptive power, His goodness and His love for us[109]. The more we know Him and experience Him as a good, faithful, powerful, loving, glorious Father, the more our trust in Him grows, the closer we draw to Him, and the more we partner with Him (doing things His way) in everything life throws at us.

> *The more we know our Father, the more we know who we are as a new creation.*

Also, the more we learn who we are now, as a new creation, and what it means to do life with Christ, the hope of glory, dwelling in us, comforting us and empowering us to be partakers of His nature and His absolute victory.

---

[109] As I mentioned before, I don't believe God is the one who steals, kills and destroys, but when we are faced with hardship and opposition He is the one who wants to flood our circumstances with abundant life and make all things work together for the good of those who love Him (John 10:10 and Romans 8:28).

## Be Encouraged

For those who are going through difficult and painful relational processes, I would like to remind you once again that yours is not a senseless suffering experience if it becomes one from which you can learn from. Jesus persevered and kept moving forward, towards the completion of His mission. He never gave up and he showed us how a completed experience will make us, in the end, perfectly equipped: "Let perseverance finish its work so that you may be mature and complete, not lacking anything" (James 1:4). In the process, our suffering must be confronted and addressed by the truth of the Word and the power of the Holy Spirit of God, not only indwelling but reigning in us and flowing through us. We are the ones who decide to acknowledge and enthrone Him, and follow in His footsteps, or not. I pray you do.

Keep your eyes on Jesus, who both began and finished this race we're in. Study how He did it. Because He never lost sight of where He was headed - that exhilarating finish in and with God - He could put up with anything along the way: cross, shame, whatever. And now He's there, in the place of honor, right alongside God. When you find yourself flagging in your faith, go over that story again, item by item, that long litany of hostility He plowed through. That will shoot adrenaline into your souls! (Hebrews 12:2-5 MSG).

# Q & A

## M y s e l f  &  G o d

❑ Answer these questions with honesty. The more authentic you are, the more you are inviting the Holy Spirit to guide you into all truth:

- Do you already believe that God is a good, perfect Father? Do you trust Him completely?

- Can you honestly say that you believe He is a rewarder of those who seek Him? Make a list of ten ways He's rewarded you as you've sought Him, and give thanks.

- Ask the Holy Spirit to reveal how your heart is positioned towards God the Father:

- Can you see yourself as an accepted and chosen son/daughter of a good Father?

    a) If you do, you have found your identity! List ten benefits of being a child of God, and give thanks for each of them. This will edify your faith and glorify God.
    b) If you don't, I pray that you decide to continue to seek the truth, because those who seek will find[110].

- Read 1 Corinthians 13:1-13. He is Love, therefore you can get a clearer picture of Him when you consider this description of perfect love.

- Have a conversation with the Holy Spirit and ask Him to show you in what ways you have grown while going through experiences that brought you suffering (take notes).

---

[110] Matthew 7:7 and Jeremiah 29:13 (You will seek me and find me when you seek me with all your heart)

- As you went through those experiences, did you invite Jesus to reign in your circumstances? If so, how did He impact your life in those moments?

- If you haven't, why not invite Him now?

# T o g e t h e r
*(For those who want to work towards the restoration or improvement of their marriage)*

- 1 Corinthians 13:1-13. Share together what you noticed in this passage, how it impacted you and the way you see God.

- Has this passage also impacted the way you consider your love for each other? (If it did, be specific about it).

- Can you see other people (including your spouse or ex-spouse) as a free and powerful son/daughter of God? How could that impact your relationship?

- Share the notes you have taken regarding your growth during times of suffering.

- If you have just now invited Jesus to reign over your circumstances, share that with your spouse and together invite Jesus to reign in every area of your marriage.

- Compose a poster with a nice photo/drawing/portrait of your spouse with the title: Son/Daughter of God. Include his/her attributes as a free and powerful individual created in the image of God.

- Leave room in the poster for a section where your spouse can add how freedom and power are going to be demonstrated in the way he/she relates to God and to you. (Stuck about what to write? When in doubt, always ask the Holy Spirit).

# LifeLine

Revelation & Transformation log     ____/____/____

**"Every good and perfect gift** is from above, coming down **from the Father** of the heavenly lights, who does not change like shifting shadows."

(James 1:17)

# 8 A MATCH MADE IN HEAVEN: MY DARLING MATTHEW ☺

"We do not behold the beauty of God merely in His work of creation, but more so in the stupendous one of redemption."

(William Scott Downey)

In this chapter I tell the story of how Mat and I got together and how God orchestrated everything. When it finally happened I knew we were getting together not out of need but out of purpose. Answers to prayers, prophetic words, dealing with overwhelming relational insecurities, God timing, miraculous provision for our wedding, getting ready for ministry school and moving to Redding, California, to do BSSM, are all part of the amazing redemption God brought into our lives in the form of a beautiful, out of the box love story. Ours is really a match made in heaven.

Why might this cascade of biographical episodes be relevant to you? Once again I share my processes, the way I connected with God by seeking His counsel and paying attention to what He communicates not only through words but also through the way He moves: how He can be seen, heard and known in the way He orchestrates or unfolds particular circumstances around us.

There are also other ingredients like fun, beauty, joy and hope while we tackle difficult challenges with a joyful, creative, even artistic approach. And last, but not least, I unveil details of my story which prove God listens and answers to our prayers, and fulfills His promises and the desires of our hearts with perfect timing. I sincerely hope, while you are reading this chapter, you stop many times to have a laugh, take a deep, heartfelt sigh, or with a heart filled with faith say a prayer: "Do it again, Lord, do it again!"

## Do you still look at the stars?

As the years went by, I continued to be trained in the 'art of living in tension': being content and enjoying my love story with the Lord in the 'here and now', and at the same time, being hopeful that my dreams, regarding a husband and a family, would one day come true. I eventually understood those were two different but complementary ways to express my love for God: to delight myself in Him (being fully satisfied in doing so) and to trust His integrity (holding firm to His promises). These two aspects of my relational journey with the Lord were very important.

My amazing God had shown Himself faithful time after time in this long journey through the 'wilderness', so I kept remembering His feats and telling myself He was, and is, worthy of my trust. In the meantime, He rewarded my trust with prophetic words and pictures about my destiny and purpose as His daughter, but also as a wife and a mother. Those were given to me directly by the Holy Spirit in the secret place (in times of intimate conversation and fellowship, which sprang from prayer and inspired Bible reading). Reliable people in various contexts, at different times, approached me with prophetic words and pictures which confirmed and complemented what God had already revealed personally. I also had night dreams which brought confirmation and unfolded other dimensions of the prophetic messages I had received. I stewarded them all faithfully and not only did I record them in my journals but I compiled them in a small booklet I carried with me so I could read it whenever my faith needed to be uplifted and my strength renewed. They spoke to me like the stars spoke to Abraham:

"Yes, the stars spoke to Abraham. Perhaps for a while, the voice of the stars haunted him as he would go out night after night staring into the realm of the impossible. But somewhere along the way, something changed. Did the circumstances change? No, well not yet at least. What changed then? Abraham, like the rest of us, went from mentally assessing to heart believing. Somehow God's dream steeped into Abraham's heart. After many trials and tests and errors, Abraham reached a point when He went out at night and rejoiced when he looked up! 'Yes, there is a promise! Yes, that one is for me! That star is declaring that God's word will come true! ...The promises of God are 'yes and amen'!"

(James W. Goll)[111]

No matter what point of the journey you are at, whether you have been waiting for a godly spouse, or whether you have tried again and again, and things broke down (or are at breaking point), it is crucial you believe our God has never left you or forsaken you. He is powerful to change your circumstances, He is for you not against you, He rewards those who seek Him and in His goodness He is working all things together for your good

---

[111] James W. Goll (Foreword in "Dreaming with God" by Bill Johnson)

because you love Him, but most importantly, because He loves you[112] and His love never fails[113]. Just *turn aside*, change your line of sight to contemplate the truth[114]. Your eyes will be opened, your perspective will be shifted from the gravel to the stars above, hope will rise, and your dreams will be fanned back to life.

When we can see Him as a powerful God, the Creator of the Universe, we will have no doubts about His size and capacity. He is bigger than any of our circumstances or mistakes and there is nothing beyond the redemptive power of Jesus' blood. In this place of trust and rest, our ability to hear His still, small voice increases. What is He saying to you right now? Which promises does He want to revive? You can trust His words, He doesn't lie[115].

> *The Creator of the Universe is bigger than our circumstances and our mistakes.*

In the times when I was discouraged and disheartened because of the waiting, and my neck didn't have the strength to lift my head up to look at the stars, God's words were like a lamp to my feet[116]. I couldn't see the horizon, but I always had enough light to keep moving forward, putting one foot in front of the other. Those were also times where my awareness of His closeness was very tender and, as I kept pressing forward, the Truth which illuminated my footpath kept shining brighter and brighter until I felt like His hand was pulling my chin upwards so I could see Him face to face, in my spirit, and hear Him speak words of life and promise over my present and my future. Great clarity and hope came with those encounters. I was

---

[112] Deuteronomy 31:6/ Hebrews 11:6/ Romans 8:28 / John 3:16

[113] 1 Corinthians 13:8
[114] Deuteronomy 28:14

[115] Numbers 23:19

[116] Psalm 119:105

reminded that every good gift comes from Him[117] and the right timing is also an expression of His perfect wisdom and goodness. I was also spurred on to aim for the stars again. There is nothing more beautiful, exhilarating, delightful and expansive than God's presence. When we delight ourselves in the Lord there is shifting, transformation and preparation for our capacity to be enlarged without stumbling over it. It enables us to thrive when the time comes for Him to give us the desires of our hearts[118], because we have come to the realization that the source of true joy is not the gift but the Giver.

> *Timing is also an expression of God's perfect wisdom and goodness.*

## Don't Undermine the Value of your Process

The passing of time can be disheartening and even disorientating if we keep our eyes solely in the horizon and forget to be present in what is going on in our lives in the here and now. We tend to want to escape painful and long winded processes. We just want to put an end to it and move on. We just want God to fix it, and many times when He doesn't do it straight away we decide to fix it ourselves in whatever way we can. When we do this, we miss an opportunity to lock eyes and arms with our God and find out what is the best way to go about it, the way which will produce much fruit and lead us closer into His heart, to become more like Him.

In the Kingdom of God all essential issues are issues of the heart, so in the end it is not about what we get but it is about who we are becoming. The development of a particular skill set can be very helpful, but the development of character is foundational if we are to sustain and manage

---

[117] James 1:17

[118] Psalm 37:4

(in other words, steward) the blessings well. Good stewardship will eventually bring growth, increase and added value, but in Heaven's economy those take place from the inside out.

> *In Heaven's economy, growth, increase and added value take place from the inside out.*

God transcends time and He knows what lies in our future. He can already see the fulness of who we are becoming and everything we need to fulfill the good works He has purposed us for[119]. As a good, diligent and committed parent He wants to prepare, equip and launch us for success, and if we let Him, He will use our 'environment' as a training ground.

I believe that in this dispensation of grace, testing is not about God finding out what we are made of. He is not an examiner. He doesn't need to investigate something He already knows (He is omniscient), and the appointed time for judgement is yet to come. Instead, testing is meant to develop us and to sharpen our vision. It reveals our need for Him but also reveals and asserts hidden or unrealized growth and capacity, and it increases our understanding of the potential growth available when we don't give up and keep moving forward and upward with Him: precept upon precept, from glory to glory[120].

There have been several catalytic moments in my journey of restoration where I was unaware I had been upgraded, and the condition of my heart was tested to reveal that a particular upgrade had already taken place. These were also moments which preceded displacement, and an accelerated movement towards *the promised land*. I have already shared a few of these with you, let me show you how God kept raising the bar.

---

[119] Ephesians 2:10

[120] 2 Corinthians 3:18

## Marriage: Another Way to get to Know and Reveal God

When you think about your closest relationships, are you all in or are you holding back? Are you still afraid of getting it wrong, or getting hurt? When you think of marriage, are you focused on what you can get, or do you consider what you can give? These questions are hard to tackle, but when we are vulnerable and honest before the Lord He will not let us stay on our own in the places where we face fear, doubt, insecurity or inadequacy. Our Helper, the Holy Spirit, will make sure we know the mind of Christ, so we can stop endlessly circling the same mountains, and continue to move forward, towards our destiny. I know this to be true because it has happened to me. You are about to watch me grow taller, get closer and closer to the firmament laid out before me, jump up, stretch my hands and grab me some stars. Figuratively speaking, of course.

I am about to let you in on one of the most peculiar learning episodes I have gone through with the Lord, and one of the most decisive ones. I believe it unlocked something in the spiritual realm and jettisoned me towards my destiny, which is, first and foremost, to reveal the heart of the Father in the way I relate to others.

It all started while I was browsing on YouTube and I came across a Q&A panel where a group of passionate revivalists were doing a very good job at answering difficult questions about the Gospel with insight, wisdom and sound biblical backing. One of them stood out to me and, as I was listening to him talk, a question bubbled up in my spirit: "Would you like to marry him?" I immediately said, "Yes!". I had watched some of his podcasts before and I knew about his incredible testimony and his burning passion for God and the people. He was inspiring and his passion was contagious. "Yes! I have always longed to be united with someone who is as passionate about God as I am, in this case even more!"

I googled his profile and browsed the web for information about him. There was a lot to plod through and although I did a thorough search, I couldn't find any information regarding his marital status. No photos or footage with a woman, nothing to suggest there was a life partner in the picture. All the while, in the back of my mind, I kept thinking this was too good to be true, and again more questions bubbled up: "Would you marry him? Why would you pick him?"

I took a deep breath, considered what I knew about him and found myself listing a series of attributes and lifestyle options which would completely stretch and challenge me. As I was doing this, I realized I was going down a very self-centered road and I immediately stopped myself because I didn't want to remain on that self-serving track: "No, this is not just about me, it's about him too." And another question immediately popped up: "What are you willing to give?" This time I found myself listing the different ways I could serve this man, support him, bring him growth, pleasure, delight and added value. With this frame of mind and heart, I began to believe that this crazy, adventurous possibility could actually work out well for both of us, even if I was required to sacrifice some of my personal dreams to support this man's ministry.

> *I no longer viewed marriage from a self-serving perspective.*

There were three other moments in the following hours when the Holy Spirit led me to pray about this. The first two times I was prompted to make declarations and proclamations about being part of a "godly union, for the glory of God." As I made these declarations, I felt so much power being released with every single word that I started shaking. The third time, the Holy Spirit said: "It will be like a rope with three strands, the three of us will be as one"[121]. As soon as I heard this, my memory transported me to the moment I had the greatest revelation of my life: My God is my most exceedingly great reward![122] There and then, I realized that marriage was going to be another way to get to know Him more intimately; to find out about His nature and heartbeat as I learn how to love like He loves and in

---

[121] Ecclesiastes 4:12

[122] Genesis 15:1

the process become a tangible expression of Him and His committed, selfless love. I grabbed a previous journal to look for the entry I wrote when I first saw this in the Scriptures, and I noticed I had penned down Paul's passionate desire. While reading it, I uttered it as my own prayer:

*In everything I go through, may it be an opportunity to know you Jesus, "to progressively become more deeply acquainted with you, perceiving, recognizing and understanding the wonders of your person more strongly and more clearly." So, yes Lord, may I embrace marriage with another laid-down lover with the same heart and mind-frame: "to step further, deeper, higher, wider into the possession of the priceless privilege (the overwhelming preciousness, the surpassing worth and supreme advantage) of knowing Christ Jesus my Lord"[123], amen!*

> *My God is my most exceedingly great reward!*

That night, I finished my journal entry with the sentence "I finally got it!". I knew in my spirit and in my soul this was a mountain I had conquered and would not have to go around again. God had tested my heart and the testing revealed that I was no longer a taker. I had become secure enough in my identity as a daughter of a good Father who takes care of me, and because of that I had become a willing giver. When I fell asleep, I had a dream with the same man. In the dream, he was passing by, amidst a large group of people and I looked at him and said: "There he is!". At that moment I heard a voice say twice: "That is covenant." As I heard those words, I felt a sudden surge of energy, like an electric voltage, going through my body. I started shaking so violently that I flipped sides on my bed and went from fetal position to being laid on my back, arms wide open. With my eyes still closed I saw a split-second flash of encompassing light. When that flash was gone I could see, against a pitch black backdrop, millions of blinking eyes, made of light. Again, God's Spirit spoke: "The eyes

---

[123] Philippians 3:8-10

of the Lord are searching the Earth for covenant people. When they see the love they will know. It's the covenant, the covenant will display Me."

When I opened my eyes I was determined to find the bible verse evoked in the dream:

For the eyes of the Lord run to and fro throughout the whole Earth to show Himself strong in behalf of those whose hearts are blameless toward Him. (2 Chronicles 16:9 - AMP)

My heart was full of gratitude and praise when I realized God longed to "show himself strong on my behalf". He was the One who initiated this new covenant and He is willing to empower us to sustain it and display it. I thanked Him for the glorious destiny He was inviting me into and declared that, although it

> *The eyes of the Lord are searching the Earth for covenant people, to empower them to sustain and display it.*

seemed impossible to my mind, I believed in my spirit He could make a way for unlikely, unreasonable, unmerited things to happen to me.

The next day, as I did one final browse, with great disappointment I found out, very quickly, an enormous amount of information related to this man's spouse and family. When I went to bed that night, I had a bunch of questions bombarding my mind and burning my heart: Why couldn't I find any of this information yesterday? Was I purposely blinded to it? Why did you let me believe this could even be possible? Why did you initiate this dialogue when you knew he is married? What about the dream? Your presence in my bedroom was real and powerful; What is the meaning of all of this? Why did my prayers and declarations felt like they were in agreement with your will? Was this not from you God? Is this all in my head? After all we have experienced together, am I no longer able to discern your presence and your voice clearly? How did I get this SO wrong?...

These questions weighed me down and it was with a heavy heart I eventually fell asleep, only to be awakened, a few hours later, in the middle of the night, by the Holy Spirit. I could hear God speak clearly, within my spirit. This is what He said, and I repeated out loud so I could record it in my phone:

"When you speak that which you truly believe in your heart, you release power and authority through your declarations and decrees. The words become spirit, which means they invade the spiritual realm. That which had no

*Just repent, instead of feeling crushed because you got it wrong.*

substance before it was uttered, becomes real and alive, spirit and truth. That is why when you proclaimed, declared and decreed you felt power rise from within. That happens when you believe and you activate your faith. Faith is creative and liberating: it creates and releases! Remember, you are created in My image. When you come to knowledge you didn't have before, regarding the legitimacy and lawfulness of such declarations, and you find that they are actually unlawful, then you just need to turn aside and repent instead of feeling crushed because you got it wrong."

I laid there in my bed reflecting on these words, humbled and honored by the way God Himself, in the person of the Holy Spirit, had listened to my questions and taken the time to bring wisdom, clarity and affirmation. I still cringed at the thought that "I could get it wrong" but in the stillness of the night, enveloped in God's peace, I began to ponder how I was going to apply this revelation in the way I prayed or dared to declare and proclaim my dreams in the future, and I heard in my spirit "Ecclesiastes 5:7". Our conversation about this wasn't over yet. I had no idea what this verse was about so I quickly opened my bible (in the Message translation) and read:

But against all illusion and fantasy and empty talk there is always this rock foundation: Fear God!

As I read these words the Holy Spirit pointed out how He had eventually brought light and truth to what was "illusion and fantasy", and how I could always trust Him to guide my steps and keep me safe from deception. If I examine my heart, and whatever I do and say is grounded in love, reverence, awe, respect and yieldedness to God, then I won't grieve Him because He knows my motives and He will always guide my steps towards the truth. This assurance also empowers me to not quench the Holy Spirit. If I *fear* God this way, I don't need to fear deception, I don't need to shrink because of the fear of failure or the fear of men: "The fear of the Lord is the beginning of wisdom, and knowledge of the Holy One is understanding" (Proverbs 9:10).

That's why being freed from the fear of making mistakes also means not choosing to limit God's limitlessness by lowering my expectations in the name of good sense. There is wisdom waiting to be harvested in our 'trial and error' journeys. The 'spiritual laws of connection and communication' between both realms shouldn't be doubted or questioned because we don't get every single detail right all the time. It's not our accuracy which is tested and approved, but the motives of the heart. As we keep moving forward with a humble and teachable heart, trusting Him to guide our steps, improvement will happen and accuracy will increase.

As I continued this conversation with the Lord in the following days, it became clear His focus was to give me opportunity and permission to believe that something outrageous and extravagant could happen to me. This belief was anchored in a tremendous change in the way I perceived my personal value. He wanted to open my eyes so I could see how far I had come. There are no limits for our heavenly Father, anything can happen to a son or daughter of

> *There are no limits for what can happen to a son or daughter of God, when He is the One guiding our steps.*

God when He is the One guiding our steps: I had started to believe this for myself. The Holy Spirit had been expanding my soul to comprehend bigger dreams, and enlarging my heart to make room for selfless love, a love with which I could prefer others and love them well because I'd had the opportunity to experience it myself first[124].

But the fun part is yet to be revealed. I didn't tell you everything about the night dream. There was a moment which I chose to ignore at first, because I thought it was the fruit of some subconscious glitch. Mat was there, sitting on an impressive high chair which looked like a throne. Observing, he sat on the sidelines of the dream, calmly waiting. We hadn't been in touch for years so I quickly turned my attention away from that unexpected appearance and gave it no further thought, until the time God made sure I could no longer ignore him.

God tested my heart and showed me I was ready and willing to honor, to bless, to give. He could send a precious, tender-hearted son my way because He knew I would be careful with his heart and I would not try to get something from him which only God Himself can give me. One year later and I was married to the one who was patiently waiting for me to reign in life at his side. I believe now I have married a man with the same passionate, extravagant, wild and kind heart as the man who was initially visible enough to draw my attention.

## Motivated by Purpose, not by Need

As the waiting season progressed, my life got better and better, especially during the two years prior to my second marriage. For the first time in many years I felt comfortable on my own. I still missed my son a lot but I knew he was well and thriving, so I had finally reached a place in my journey where I had time to breathe deeply and the opportunity to enjoy life at a slower and more fulfilling pace. Lily still kept me on my toes but she had come a

---

[124] Mark 12:30-31

long way and our relationship had a much more solid foundation. I had emotional stability, professional stability and financial stability too. I was a pretty content lady. I felt I had been given a very delicious cake and I was starting to savor it. The desire to have a partner was still there, in the back of my mind, but it was no longer an all-consuming priority, it was no longer the cake but it could very well be the cherry on the top.

That was when Mr. Matthew Redding reconnected with me. We had met eight years prior to that, just when I had moved to England. He attended the same church and worked in the same school I did. We were both coming out of broken marriages and going through divorces we really didn't want. We both believed there was still hope for our marriages, and we both walked the road of having partners who didn't.

When we first met we were still very broken and very lost. We became good friends but our friendship was not sustainable as each one of us came into the relationship with different expectations. We approached each other out of need, not out of purpose and neither of us were ready to build something healthy because we weren't healthy ourselves. In the process he held back, I got hurt and we ended up drifting apart and losing sight of each other for almost seven years.

After this experience I remained very single. I didn't want to risk being hurt again and I really didn't want to have to deal with any relational issues when I was still dealing with my own issues.

Mat's experience was different from mine and, as he kept searching for relational fulfillment, he eventually got seriously involved and entered into a relationship which ended up being abusive and unstable. That was a season of his life where it seemed like he had lost his way again. He went through a lot of pain and hardship and he had to journey a wilderness of his own where he didn't always feel close to God. He did not want to go through another relational breakdown and he tried, the best he could, to help mend the broken pieces of himself and his partner only to realize it was beyond his capacity.

Single again, Mat worked on getting healthy, in spirit, mind and body. He drew near to God and God drew near to him[125]. As he rediscovered the wholeness which flows from walking in righteousness, and delved deeper into God's love and peace, he found himself and found his way. He started exercising and deliberately trying new things. God's grace and joy permeated

*We reconnected when each of us was motivated by purpose rather than need.*

every area of his life and as he embraced life to the fullest he became a very happy and content chap. It was at this point in our lives, when neither of us was motivated by need and both of us were motivated by purpose, that God made sure our paths would cross again.

## Matthew, a Gift from God?...

Ever since his divorce, Mat had struggled to trust God with his relationships and to submit his relational aspirations and decisions into His hands, but now this had changed. His close relationship with the Lord restored Mat's trust in God's goodness and wisdom, and brought him to a place of complete surrender in an area of his life he had kept separate from God for many years.

It was during a Sunday service that the stage was set for our beautiful, God-orchestrated romance to lift off. During worship, Mat was having a great time in God's presence. With his heart bursting with thanksgiving for all the blessings and the transformation God had brought into his life, he made a special, earnest prayer regarding a future partnership: "Thank you God for everything but can you direct me on this, please. I just want to know what's going to happen?" Mat immediately heard the Lord reply: "That is the

---

[125] James 4:8

woman you are going to marry." He looked down and he knew straight away that the Holy Spirit was referring to me.

Mat's first reaction was not very positive, the history between us didn't make things easy for him. He was quite pleased he had already approached me on a previous occasion to rebuild burned bridges. The Lord had been moving so deeply in his heart that, a few months earlier, he felt the desire to approach me and ask forgiveness for the way he had hurt me in the past. I acknowledged both of us made mistakes and we forgave each other, hugged each other but still went our separate ways. This was different now, and Mat told the Lord: "You're going to have to tell her Lord, because I won't." He eventually did, but he had a lot of help from the Holy Trinity.

Every Sunday he made sure he would come and say "hi" to me. Sometimes I would speak to him for a few minutes, other times I would politely return his greeting but continued chatting with others completely overlooking his presence. This went on for months. Mat was very patient, persistent and committed. He was holding on to a word given by God Himself so he didn't give up, even when I did not respond to his attempts to reconnect. Eventually the penny dropped and I realized his interest in me was beyond friendship, but I was happy and content and every time I thought of Mat Redding I only saw the man I used to know eight years before, which made me even more determined to keep away from him, and by doing so, keep away from potential trouble and heartache.

Nevertheless, the more I purposefully looked down on this man and did my best to justify my stinking attitude towards him, the more my relationship with the Lord was directly affected by it. The best way I can explain it is what happens when you have a very close and intimate friend, the type of friend who doesn't even need to talk and you can sense and know what he or she is thinking, and suddenly something is awkward and off between you. That's how it felt. For weeks I wrestled with the Lord because of the way I considered Mat's tentative approaches and the way I judged his heart and intentions. For weeks the Holy Spirit filled me with conviction and the fear of the Lord regarding my lofty heart towards this son of His, whom He loved and pled for. He told me "not to shut this door" and I found out later that Mat was being guided "not to force or push the door."

## The House Episode Strikes Again

God had performed such extensive heart surgery on me during the ten years I was on my own, I thought I was all sorted, with nothing left to mend. That is, until I was faced with the possibility of engaging in a romantic relationship with a man again.

I started going out with Mat as a friend. We had some nice meals, went for walks and hikes in the beautiful English countryside and I began to enjoy spending time with him, but every time I thought about the relationship going to another level I froze. I had no idea how emotionally guarded I still was until Mat's gentle approaches triggered giant walls which erupted from the ground up and towered over me to keep me out of reach, safe from harm. They also kept me isolated, hidden and unknown.

I didn't know those gigantic walls were still hidden in the depths of my heart, but God did. He knew I would experience irrational fear and inability to move forward and take the risk to entrust my heart to a man. He also knew I wouldn't be able to fully articulate or make sense of my emotional responses so He prepared the way by taking me through an experience where I learned to trust Him without fully understanding what was really going on.

"The entire supernatural lifestyle is constantly filled with the nutrients needed for the next situation."

This was a line that jumped at me while listening to a series of teachings about "The Renewed Mind", by Bill Johnson[126]. In this series he dissects several episodes when the disciples did not understand what was

---

[126] https://www.youtube.com/watch?v=gx-elRUpmIQ

happening in the moment because they hadn't opened their hearts to the pedagogic opportunities encased in their previous experiences. Do you still remember the 'house episode'? I came to realize that through this particular experience God had provided all the 'spiritual nutrients' I needed to equip me for a defining segment of my journey ahead.

I continued journaling throughout this uncharted territory and I'm glad I did because it really helped me make sense of what seemed to be a very convoluted process at first. The following narrative is one of the journal entries I wrote at the time:

*I am struggling to open my heart to Mat. Everything in my flesh and my soul is screaming "keep away! Run for the hills!" I can't understand why I'm reacting in this irrational fashion. Where does this repulsion and this inexplicable fear come from?...*

*My spirit is telling me a different thing. I honestly believe this is a moment of testing: Shall I follow my natural inclination and lean on my own understanding, or do I trust what the Lord is telling me to do? He keeps telling me "to not shut any doors, to not turn away from Mat Redding and to totally believe that He is all wise, always good and that He knows what's best for me." This really feels like the 'house move situation' all over again.*

*The stakes are much higher now, but I remember back then having a strong sense that I was being prepared for something. I remember my sudden change of heart, how I could only see the disadvantages, the downside, the less likable aspects and how I only signed the contract because God was in it. I knew in my heart I had stumbled upon this opportunity by divine appointment and as I moved forward I knew God was orchestrating everything. I just stepped into what He was inviting me to do: to trust in Him completely and to totally ignore my limited, short-sighted, fearful reasonings and perceptions. There and then I felt tested too, and my connection with God was significantly strengthened after I chose to trust Him, in spite of my initial doubts.*

*Once settled in the house, my eyes were suddenly opened to see all of its potential and today I love living here. When my friends visit me their reaction is always the same, they marvel at it. It's the perfect house for our family in this season of our lives, and it meets every little desire of my heart. I sense that there is something prophetic in this parallel metaphor: I'm heading towards something amazing but I can't clearly see it yet. Is Mat, like the house, harboring a bunch of hidden treasures, which will meet the desires of my heart, but are not yet visible to the naked eye? As I walk in obedience, will the Lord adjust the lenses I am looking through and suddenly I will see the gold, and it's going to be wonderful?!...*

Later that week, in one of the many moments of doubt and exasperation regarding this matter, as I was asking the Lord to guide my steps and realign my heart with His, the Holy Spirit instructed me to pray for Mat, calling to the surface, speaking into existence, the hidden gold nuggets; not only the ones I couldn't yet see but the ones he couldn't see himself. I should do it with no hidden agenda and with a pure and devoted heart, as a friend, with no guarantee that anything would be in it for me in the end. I heard God's instructions and answered with a prayer: "So be it, as I consider Your commands, focus on Your words of life and remember Your goodness God, my heart settles and I feel empowered to continue to step further into this journey where I am required to walk without always knowing exactly where I'm going, trusting in your guidance completely and relinquishing control with a joyful and expectant heart. So be it."

*Pray selflessly, with no hidden or self-serving agenda.*

## Answers to Prayers

During the following months, our friendship kept getting stronger and my trust in Mat increased. We had come a long way from the first time we engaged in a deeper conversation and I made sure he knew straight away that in the near future I was heading to California to attend BSSM. I was certain after that revelation he would lose interest in me and move on. I was wrong. He told me later that during this waiting period his love for me kept growing. As he fell more in love with me, his persistence, kindness, patience and generosity were not loud but were consistent and purposeful. It was as if he was silently walking around the giant walls, getting ready for the moment when he just had to shout the truth and they would come crumbling down. That day finally arrived. It didn't happen in Jericho but it happened in Bulkington, England, in a beautiful and picturesque pub called "The Blue Pig".

After a nice afternoon spent hiking, chatting, laughing and appreciating the beautiful Wolvey landscapes we were ready to go indoors. It was cold so we were ready for a hot plate of homemade food and a nice cup of tea, sitting by the fire. In that cozy, nurturing and neutral environment I felt safe and relaxed to open my heart to Mat and share all my fears and insecurities. I was completely honest with him and warned him that I could easily back out and he could end up being seriously hurt by me.

He listened in silence, looked me straight in the eyes, like he wanted me to know he meant what he was about to say, and without any hesitation in his voice he replied: "I am willing to take the risk." Those words penetrated all defenses and pierced me straight to the heart. To this day they remain there and every time I recollect that defining moment, my heart is still impacted and deeply moved by the courage and selfless love Mat displayed.

Later in the evening, just before going home, I dared to ask another difficult but crucial question: What about BSSM? I knew he had been researching the school, the teachers, the curriculum, and he had been praying for that dream, which was my dream, to become his dream too. I didn't know if he had reached any conclusion yet, but again he was quick, firm and reassuring in the way he answered my question: "I am ready to embark on this great adventure with you."

Although we had a great breakthrough and our hearts were now on a collision course, I wasn't able to give any definitive answers to Mat and when we left the pub we were still just friends.

That night I had another life changing conversation with God. As I rehearsed those events in my mind, and chatted with the Holy Spirit about what had happened, a million thoughts exploded in my head. I had so many questions about my future with this man, I felt so overwhelmed and still so riddled with fear. There were so many things which could go wrong.

*Do you want a real man/woman?*

I continued arguing with the Lord: "I thought I was going to the school of ministry and there I would find a husband, someone who wants to serve you too." The Holy Spirit was firm and concise: "Do you want a real man?" Wow! I realized I had a real man right in front of me who I couldn't see because I was still fantasizing about what might happen. Right there and then my eyes were opened to the reality that God had answered my prayers!

I had been praying for many years for a partner who was in love, or ready to fall head over heels in love with God. Someone who would be willing to consecrate his life to the spreading of the Gospel, who would be willing to do ministry school and go from there to the nations. And here was Mat, a real man, highlighted by God, willing and excited to embark on this crazy God adventure with me! I couldn't wrestle with God about this anymore.

I was reminded again that every good gift comes from God[127] and I decided to say 'yes' to Him: "Lord, I don't really want to marry this man, I have so many doubts, but if you say He is the one for me than I trust you. I say 'yes'

---

[127] James 1:17

to your choice and I believe he is a gift from you and you always give the best." As I said this, a thick, enveloping presence descended on my room; a shower of liquid love, so tangible and tastable that I knew it was God's way to show me how pleased He was with my decision to trust Him regarding Mat.

At the same time, I felt like a dam had burst in my heart. A shower of certainty was released and my deep affections were turned to this man. I became fully aware there was a love erupting from within, from the depths of my being, which wasn't there before! It was being supernaturally poured out and it flooded my heart to the point I felt like I was about to burst.

In the midst of this most unusual and extraordinary experience, I had another epiphany. I remembered the way I had been praying for the past ten years: "Lord, when the time comes for you to give me a husband, please do it in a way that I am 100% sure he is your choice, because if I have any doubt I will not give him the time of day, I will not even look his way." That had been my prayer time and time again, and God had answered it in detail. After what I had just experienced I had no shadow of doubt regarding God's endorsement, as He had orchestrated it in such a way I knew that I knew Mat Redding was the man God had chosen to be my husband. What a brilliant God!

I must stress that this was my personal experience, yours doesn't have to look like mine. No one should use it as a formula or an excuse to marry someone they don't really love. There are many nuances in my story which sprung from years of consistent relationship and ongoing dialogue with God. When the time came for our wedding vows to be made there was no confusion, I had a clear word from God and a deep love for the man who was going to be my future husband. Seek God's guidance, listen to His voice, His freshly

*God's freshly spoken word will guide your steps towards purpose and away from confusion.*

spoken word over you and your circumstances, submit to His will and He will guide your steps towards purpose and away from confusion.

When these events took place, Christmas was just around the corner and we went our separate ways to spend the festive season with family. During that time we texted each other every day, consistently. Our soul and heart connection was exponentially deepened as we exchanged silly, but also profound, tender, heart-melting, encouraging and even prophetic messages.

The following is an excerpt of one of the journal entries I wrote during that first week:

*It has been a twofold divine process. God has been unlocking the deep fears of my own heart, as I find myself still dealing with pain, sorrow, fear of failure, disappointment and loss, and in return He is pouring His explosive river of perfect love which permeates my whole being and affects the way I see, the way I think, and the way I feel.*

*A joint plot!*

*Mat has shared with me that in this time of waiting where he was required to trust, believe for the impossible and not push the door, something happened to his heart and to his soul too. He realized God had changed him and he completely acknowledges he needed to change to be able to love like Him. This change is so evident in the way we communicate and connect now. Mat's words are like sharp arrows aimed straight at my heart and they pierce deep and become a part of me. I melt to the core and I can recognize my heavenly Beloved's heart and words behind it all - a joint plot to get me!*

*How wonderful to feel every step of the way that our love story is mixed and entwined with God's love story. We have now openly declared our love for each other, and will be meeting next Friday. Can't wait to see him and I find it hard to believe how much I miss him. It's getting more serious by the text.*

## The First Kiss: When Desire is Awakened.

I love the sight of my beloved:

Her hair cascading onto her shoulders,

A dark fountain of glorious promise;

Her skin glowing from the light

Of passionate inner spirit;

Her touch on my hands

Caressing love through all my being;

And her lips, oh those lips of sweet honey taste,

How can I describe their fire?...[128]

The time came for our first date. I had pictured a long, heartfelt embrace topped with a tender but passionate kiss. I had been waiting for this kiss for many, many years. When I got to the restaurant I was ten minutes late so Mat was already inside waiting for me. I knew I wouldn't be able to demonstrate the depth of my affection in front of all those people so I called him and asked him to meet me in the parking lot. A few minutes later there he was with a smile on his face, as usual. We embraced each other tightly like we wanted to breathe each other in, and we kissed tenderly and passionately.

---

[128] A poem Mat wrote for me.

Mat was surprised and joyful. He knew something had changed tremendously within me but now it was far beyond words as he got to taste the intensity of my feelings for him. It was a beautiful moment.

After a lovely fruit cocktail we headed to the Bull's Head pub/restaurant in Meriden. When I was thinking about our date, earlier in the day, I had a picture of us sitting in a cozy setting by a lovely fire. When we got there the pub was jam-packed but still we managed to get a two seat cozy settee by a beautiful, warm and crackling fireplace! God was literally orchestrating every detail. It was a wonderful evening. We acted and looked like two teenagers in love.

The sweetest revelation of the night was Mat confessing that when I asked him to meet me by the car he was completely clueless about my intentions. He thought there was something wrong with me, that I didn't want to go in after all. He proceeded to share how that was one of the biggest changes the Holy Spirit had made in him. Like my desire for intimate connection, his desire for intimate connection was now rooted in matters of the heart and no longer geared towards, or inflamed by, sensual appetites. We realized that we both longed for intimacy at all levels, but it wasn't just about the two of us anymore.

Journal entry:

*There are five of us now. Our relationship with God is central, vital, essential. We want our hearts and our hands to remain pure before the Lord because we don't want to hinder our intimacy with Him and risk not being able to see His face[129]. Nothing to do with the religious fear of being punished but everything to do with the reverent fear of compromising our*

> "I love you, and I want you, but I love you more than I want you."

---

[129] Psalm 24:4/Matthew 5:8

*intimate relationship with God. His presence, His voice, His counsel, His closeness are not secondary, but the foundation where we want to build our covenant. To jeopardize that foundation could seriously damage our ability to build a healthy and wholesome marriage, so that is not an option. "I love you, and I want you, but I love you more than I want you" is what Mat told me the other day while we were discussing this. This has become our motto for this season where we know we are so close to collecting the prize. We know that being honest about this with each other and God has positioned our hearts in a place to continue to walk closely with the Lord, and to receive from Him glorious resolution and divinely inspired resolve. We wait for that longed-for prize with trust, prudence, anticipation, deep breaths and speed walking in the cold air.*

## A Lady and a Gent

A lady of Latin descent

Loved an idiosyncratic gent

Forever and after

The sound of their laughter

Made a pleasing and heavenward scent


There once was a girl from Lisboa

Who always got lost going nowhere

She was given a chap

Who could read a map

Now they'll go to the ends of the Earth

She wanted him as her lover

With marriage preceding the other

But when their lips kissed

A beat her heart missed

And her body it trembled all over[130]

## Heading to Redding in more ways than one

In the space of a week we were talking about marriage and two weeks after our first date it was official, we knew we were getting married. I wasn't looking for a boyfriend and Mat wasn't looking for a girlfriend. We were both praying for a spouse. We spoke with our family and one month after our first date we were officially engaged and I had a beautiful ring to prove it.

The perfect ring, representing oneness, a white gold open circle with five small diamonds holding together the extremities of the circle. How we found this ring is a story of its own but the short version is: we asked God to guide us to find what we wanted and could afford and He answered our prayers. He guided our steps and the day we set aside for 'ring hunting', we found the perfect ring, for the perfect price, very quickly. Even in that we could see and taste the favor of God on our lives and our union.

---

[130] Limericks Mat composed about our story.

One of the most beautiful things which happened on the night of our first date was the fact that once we held hands, Mat was not prepared to let go of my hand anymore. We drove through main roads, back roads and countryside lanes with him using only one hand to steer the wheel. It was not an automatic car so we just slotted the gear stick together. I was relaxed, learning to follow his lead, he was decisive and assertive, holding my hand with a firm grip at times and caressing it tenderly at others.

*The final destination is to love like He loves.*

It was such a meaningful experience that the next morning when I was thinking about it I could feel God's presence fill the room and in my spirit I heard God say: "The natural precedes the spiritual; remember I use the natural things to help you understand the things of the Kingdom. That is the perfect metaphor to illustrate our love journey. Once you gave me your hand, I never let go. As you learn to trust and rest in me I will firmly hold on to you and guide you - I will drive you to your destination and you will know and understand what it means to love like I love."

## And the Fear of the Future was Gone

Perfect love was, and is, our destination but that is not as ethereal as some people may think it is. As Heidi Baker says, "love looks like something." It is visible in words and deeds, choices and decisions. In the process of planning and preparing a wedding, and sharing a home, many logistic and relational challenges arose. We had lived on our own for many years, we were both self-sufficient and very set in our own ways, and we approached and tackled those challenges differently, because we are very different people. Although I knew these challenges were a great training ground, whenever I considered God's standard of selfless, sacrificial love, I was not always happy with the way they revealed how far I still was from it.

When worry tried to creep up, I remember asking the Lord, "What say you about this my King?" and He replied, "Keep your eyes on the things above, take them off the ground and the gravel. Look up and keep flying." And that was what we kept doing. God gave me songs which gravitated around this message, and Mat wrote inspired poems and sent me daily messages which brought beauty, fun and a hopeful perspective.


Mat- I long for my love. She is tattooed on my heart

Her voice is Spring blossoms of new life.

Her kindness and goodness are legendary

Our souls fit together like all the pieces of a jigsaw puzzle,

And the picture is beautiful.


Ana- Good morning, my poetic flamboyant lover.

Busy with packing and sorting 'bits and bobs',

but stopped in my tracks by your honey-dripping words…

It's like a wave of peace, goodness, sweetness and tender love

is washing over me and suddenly I'm positioned on high places

again, with a clear view of the one thing that really matters,

True Love[131].

---

[131] Excerpt from a chat on Messenger

I got more and more excited about the future, and I did not panic or feel overwhelmed with the massive changes ahead, simply because I knew with all my heart that my wonderful, perfect, loving, good and powerful God was orchestrating and sustaining it all. I knew His goodness and grace were all we needed for success. "It will not be easy, but in the end it will be glorious. Hard work but no strife, blessing

*"Hard work but no strife, blessing without sorrow."*

without sorrow[132], that is what it means to walk in the will of the Lord": this is what I wrote in my journal, together with another passage of the Scriptures which the Holy Spirit prompted me to look up. These verses infused me with tremendous hope and peace, and my sincere desire is that they do the same for you:

The steps of the God-pursuing ones follow firmly in the steps of the Lord. And God delights in every step they take to follow Him. If they stumble badly they will survive, for the Lord lifts them up with His hands! I was once young but now I'm old. Not once have I found a lover of God forsaken by Him... (King David - Psalm 37:23-25).

**The first week**[133]

I watched as my beloved sang to the Lord

And she was beautiful

From afar I observed her worship

---

[132] Proverbs 10:20

[133] A poem Mat wrote which narrates the first week of our love story

And I admired her

Under the cool Winter sun I knew her peacefulness

As she rested in you my king

In the moonlight her compassion rose

Like a wave to engulf me in mercy

By the burning fire the passionate heart of my love

Smoldered with joy and desire

You are my delight, I long for you

My heart for your heart.

# Q & A

## M y s e l f  &  G o d

- Are there any 'mountains' in your own journey which you have been endlessly circling? (If you are not sure, ask the Holy Spirit).

- If the answer is yes, ask the Holy Spirit what is keeping you from moving past those mountains.

- When you relate with others, are there any situations which trigger 'walls of protection' to suddenly rise up?

- If yes, what are your fears? (Make a list).

- What would it look like to face those mountains and fears with the mind of Christ? (Complete your list with what the Holy Spirit is showing you; seek an answer for every fear you have previously listed).

- What do you need to feel safe enough to share those insecurities with the relevant people in your life? (The ones you want to connect more intimately with.)

- Imagine you are sharing your fears and insecurities with them and rehearse that conversation (make sure you use 'I statements'[134]).

- Are there any 'spiritual nutrients' you have gained from past experiences with the Lord (even in the most mundane contexts), which you think will be important for the days ahead? (If you are not sure, ask the Holy Spirit and write them down).

- 

---

[134] https://www.goodtherapy.org/blog/psychpedia/i-message

- Were there any moments of my story which brought you hope? What is He saying to you right now? Which promises does He

- want to revive? (Make a list of what dreams were brought back to life and what you were filled with hope for).

- Do you believe God answers prayers? What are you praying for? What are you going to pray for? (Suggestion: get a prayer journal and keep track of your prayers).

# T o g e t h e r

*(For those who want to work towards the restoration or improvement of their marriage)*

❏ This session has a very high emphasis on sharing what you have been working through in your individual reflective time with God.

- Share with your spouse what you need to feel safe, so you are able to be vulnerable and discuss the insecurities which trigger 'walls of protection' to rise up in your heart (consider your spouse's needs seriously and be committed to provide him/her with the safest environment possible).

- Share your fears and insecurities with each other (Don't forget to use 'I statements').

- Share the answers the Holy Spirit gave you (make sure you take more time with this, the solution, than with the problem).

- Share with each other the list of spiritual nutrients the Holy Spirit has highlighted.

- Share with each other what dreams were brought back to life and what you were filled with hope for.

- Share with your spouse what you are praying for.

- Write a list with 5 to 10 prayer points you will be praying for each other and for you as a couple.

✴ Suggestion: If you like to write, sing, dance, paint, do wood or metalwork, crafts, sewing, knitting, photography, culinary arts (or whatever creative activity fills you with joy and delight), create a work of art dedicated to bring beauty, fun and a hopeful perspective to a difficult situation you are dealing with as a couple.

# LifeLine

Revelation & Transformation log ____/____/____

"So I will **restore** to you the **years** that the swarming locust has eaten …"

(Joel 2:25 - NKJV).

# 9 A SUCCESS STORY

"Most great people have attained their greatest success just one step beyond their greatest failure."

(Napoleon Hill)

At first glance it might seem that our story is not one of success because our first marriages eventually broke down and we ended up getting divorced, but this is far from the truth. In our weakness, His strength was, and is, made perfect. It's time to look at people who weather divorce and come out on the other side closer to God, in a different, kind and honorable way.

## The original truth

Allow me to start with a question everyone has asked, is asking or will eventually ask, regarding the biblical legitimacy of divorce:

→ *Apart from adultery, are there any other reasons which legitimize divorce in God's eyes?*

I am the first in line to answer "NO".

My assertive reply might come as a surprise to you, especially because it seems to contradict my own personal experience: "Where does that leave you, then? Have you not been divorced yourself? Do you mean you are living outside God's will?..."

Before you judge me, I kindly ask you to take the time to judge what I am attempting to explain, by being patient and reading till the end. Then, you are welcome to make your mind up. I do not wish to cunningly persuade you of anything, but my intention is to bring information and revelation which have brought clarity to my understanding of this topic. I hope it brings clarity to you too. The final thing I ask is that you approach this with an open mind and an open heart. My prayer is that you include the Holy Spirit in this journey and whatever conclusion you reach, your heart may be attentive to His inner testimony.

The premise, which is valid because it's biblical, is that "no one should separate what God has joined"[135]. These words have extra weight because they were uttered by Jesus Himself. Let's go over the context. Jesus was in Judea, under the jurisdiction of Herod Antipas, the one who had John the Baptist beheaded over challenging his divorce. The Pharisees, true to their usual *modus operandi*, publicly asked Jesus a testing question: "Is it lawful

---

[135] Matthew 19:1-8 / Mark 10:9

for a man to divorce his wife?" They were attempting to get Jesus to say something which could get Him arrested and killed by Herod, or to trap Him by getting Him to say something against Moses, their venerated historical leader.

Their question was based on Jewish divorce law[136] and it was asked in the context of an ongoing debate between two schools of rabbinical thought. The liberal view (Rabbi Hillel's) said that divorce could be made on any grounds, called "Any Matter" divorce, while the conservative viewpoint (Rabbi Shammai's) believed that divorce was only legal on the grounds of adultery[137].

When they pressed Jesus for the interpretation of this law He went back to the beginning, to the Garden of Eden, where the creative and relational heart of God was expressed and brought into physical existence when His masterpiece[138], created in His image, received His breath of life. Jesus changed the focus of that discussion. It was no longer a matter of deciding which perspective was the best but instead He introduced and asserted God's original perspective. He reminded them that, after being created, man and woman were joined together as one flesh (a physical expression of a spiritual reality), before God[139]. Therefore, because it was a divinely designed and ordained union, no one should dissolve it.

*Jesus changed the focus of that discussion and asserted God's original perspective.*

---

[136] Deuteronomy 24:1

[137] Dr Brian Simmons, notations for Matthew 19:1-8 and Mark 10:9, The Passion Translation Bible

[138] Ephesians 2:10

[139] Genesis 2:24

I find it interesting that in this context Jesus spoke specifically to the men: "everyone who divorces his wife"[140]. He never addressed the women directly regarding this subject[141]. He explained that the allowances granted in the law of Moses were a response to their hard heartedness. The law of Moses was enforced to prevent or mitigate disputes and quarrels which arose from the male-dominated nuptial culture of the time. I am certain that not all men were wicked, abusive or unappreciative of their wives, but the way men viewed women, within God's chosen nation at that time, had completely drifted away from Adam's original view: "You are bone of my bone and flesh of my flesh." As Paul explains, reflecting about marriage in Ephesians 5:28, "no one ever hated his own flesh but nourishes and cherishes it."

On the contrary, these men were brought up in a culture which regarded women as inferior individuals who had little influence or say in public life, and whose sole purpose was to accommodate men's every desire, do manual work, bear children (who better be sons!), and look after the household without having a voice or making many waves.

Some of those expectations were not unreasonable, partnership always involves service and dedication, but in this specific cultural and historical context the inequality was staggering. Men could do basically everything women couldn't. They had complete control over their wife, and their daughter until she got married, and women could not inherit. This ancient synagogue prayer speaks for itself regarding the way women were demoted in men's eyes: "Blessed art thou, O Lord God, king of the universe, who hast not made me a woman"[142].

---

[140] Matthew 5:32

[141] And when he addressed the woman at the well, who had gone through multiple divorces, He still approached her with kindness and grace (John 4:4-42)

[142] https://www.bible-history.com/jesus/jesusThe_Role_of_Women.htm

The way many men devalued, replaced and discarded women when they didn't meet their needs and expectations was selfish, self-serving and heartless at times. A repudiated woman would be shamed for not being able to please her husband, which meant she would have to carry the pain of rejection together with the shame of inadequacy and insufficiency, in what became the ultimate segregation.

Jesus hit the nail hard on the head by bringing back into the picture, as He always did, the motives of their hearts and the carnality of their beliefs and skewed perspectives. Jesus only did what He saw the Father do, so He only said what He heard the Father say[143]. In that particular context, His counter-cultural perspective was an expression of the Father's heart and desire to protect, value and promote women. In those days, divorce did not promote or liberated women but disempowered and degraded them.

Fast forward to the present social and cultural reality, where gender inequality is still experienced in different ways, depending on the geographical location, and this issue, together with many other questions around the legitimacy of divorce, take on new contours which continue to raise other reasonable and pertinent questions: What about families who have to deal with destructive addictions, recurrent gambling debts, abuse, domestic violence or severe neglect? What about spouses who have to deal with possessive jealousy or unfounded chronic mistrust, emotional, verbal and sexual abuse, violence or constant intimidation? Is God detached from such realities? Does He not care?

And when we cried to the Lord, the God of our fathers, the Lord heard our voice and looked on our affliction and our labor and our [cruel] oppression; And the Lord brought us forth out of Egypt with a mighty hand and with an outstretched arm, and with great (awesome) power and with signs and wonders; And He brought us into this place and gave us this land, a land flowing with milk and honey (Deuteronomy 26:7-9 AMP).

---

[143] John 5:19 / John 8:28 / John 14:8-11

This is my story in a nutshell. This is who God is: a good Father who hears our cries with a compassionate heart, a rescuer, a restorer and a redeemer who not only makes wrong things right but makes right things abundant, beautiful and glorious.

During times of brokenness and hardship God is committed to shine His light and restore His eternal, life-infusing truth in every area of our lives. My deepest belief is that there is nothing which God can't restore and redeem, and that is true for both realities: building a solid and healthy marriage and rebuilding a life devastated by divorce.

At this point I can almost hear you question: "Are you saying that God is okay with us choosing divorce, after all? The answer is still "no". Jesus justified Moses' law in the light of a fallen reality, but apart from the exception of adultery (which tangibly defiles covenantal oneness), He was very firm about the definitive nature of marriage. You see, opinions, man's ways and man-made circumstances do not invalidate or change God's original truth and wisdom. His ways are higher than our ways but we are instructed to renew our minds with His thoughts and trust in the power of His Spirit within us, so we can think like He does and act accordingly.

> *Whether we're building a marriage or rebuilding a life after divorce, there is nothing God can't restore and redeem.*

It is important, before we go any further in this chapter, I reaffirm what I believe with all my heart: marriage is a covenant designed by God to join two hearts, souls and bodies with Himself as one. This oneness becomes deeper, stronger and more meaningful with the passing of the years. It is not meant for mindless experimentation but for consolidation and revelation of love, unfolded during a lifetime. Therefore, I do not consider the subject of divorce lightheartedly.

During my personal journey in a difficult marriage of thirteen years, I always believed there was nothing beyond God's redemption. Till the end, and even after the legal end of my marriage, I believed God had the power to mend our brokenness, and to empower and equip us to live a meaningful, fulfilling and purposeful life as a couple. However, I was only one part of the covenant and my individual beliefs and desires cannot annul or dismiss the other person's beliefs and desires. God himself doesn't override our free will, He gave it to us deliberately. In His sovereignty He has given us the dignity of freedom of choice, even knowing we would probably make some bad choices and some very wrong decisions. His integrity blows my mind.

I'm not an advocate for divorce. Divorce might be the easier option for some and the hardest for others, but it should never be the first option. When it happens, its consequences are never easy or simple. Two hearts who were meant to fuse are painfully torn apart, so there is never a clean break. Family members are deeply hurt, trust is broken, resources are wasted, children have their world turned upside down (and can be profoundly traumatized in the process). Each individual realizes with time that pieces of himself, or herself, were ripped out from within and are still stuck to the former partner somewhere in time, space or memory. There is great loss and brokenness which come with it, and people find themselves often having to mourn and grieve for the loss, and work hard on being put back together, before they can aspire to build any kind of healthy and hopeful future.

There is another aspect of divorce which, in my opinion, is even more significant for the children of God: the missed opportunity for God's love and nature to be revealed or made visible and known, and for His glory to be fully manifested in our story. Paul talks about the mystery of marriage[144] and how it is meant to be a reflection of the union, or oneness, of Christ and His Church. This was one of the consequences I was led by the Holy Spirit to repent and ask for God's forgiveness: for not inviting Him further

---

[144] Ephesians 3:32

into that process, and for not giving Him a fair chance or opportunity to do things His way, from the very beginning, so the restoration of my marriage could become a tangible testimony of His glory, power and perfect love.

*Why does God continue to bless people after divorce?*

So, as you can see, I'm not pro-divorce. Nevertheless, here I am as someone who went through divorce and came out on the other side with an extraordinary testimony which still reveals God's power, glory, goodness and love. How is this possible? If marriage is still a sacred covenant in His sight, why does God continue to bless people even after they make a big mess of their marriages and end up divorced?

You can argue it depends on whether there was adultery, which is the allowed exception (but doesn't have to be if you consider the "70x7" teaching when Jesus answered Peter's question about forgiveness[145]), or you can still argue it depends on whether one person has done everything they could to prevent divorce and, in the end, was left with no choice because the other spouse took the option of reconciliation out of the table[146].

What about unequal yokes? Even that is redeemed by the cross![147] Each case is different and the Word of God is always to be read and interpreted in context, and with the help of the Holy Spirit who brings sense to truth held in tension.

---

[145] Matthew 18:22

[146]"But if the unbelieving spouse wants a divorce, then let it be so. In this situation the believing spouse is not bound to the marriage, for God has called us to live in peace." (1 Corinthians 5:15 - TPT)

[147] "For the unbelieving husband has been made holy by his believing wife. And the unbelieving wife has been made holy by her believing husband *by virtue of his or her sacred union to a believer*." (1 Corinthians 5:12-14)

We could make a big list with other possible justifying reasons (some of them consensually accepted, others still rather controversial), but in our relationship with God the heart is always the starting point. When we draw near to Him with an open and sincere heart, He draws near to us[148] and His grace has the power to redeem everything!

## Amazing grace

But he said to me, "My grace is sufficient for you, for my power is made perfect in weakness." Therefore I will boast all the more gladly about my weaknesses, so that Christ's power may rest on me. (2 Corinthians 12:9)

Jesus' words about divorce were, and still are, a revelation of God's heart regarding the definitive and sacred nature of marital covenant. However, on this side of the cross, He has provided us with redemption whenever we fail and *fall short* of God's glorious designs[149].

As I was preparing to write this book I asked: "What is your angle about divorce in this book of ours, God?" He replied "Grace." He continued to tell

> "I don't see you as divorcees but as sons and daughters."

me: "There is nothing so broken my grace can't redeem and restore, not even a divorced heart, soul and body of a son and a daughter. I don't see you as divorcees but as sons and daughters. Remember, grace has nothing to do with you and everything to do with me. It's all about me."

---

[148] James 4:8

[149] Romans 3:23

For some, this may sound like a line coming from a very narcissistic God. I hear these words and I see mercy, freedom and unmerited favor. It's liberating to know that our success is not dependent on our best efforts on our best days, because even those are variable, circumstantial and limited, but our success is dependent on Him. He never changes[150] and He is an expansive God, without measure[151], who invites us into His ever increasing Kingdom and empowers us to expand and become like Him. What a beautiful, generous, good God!

The cross and resurrection changed everything. Through our belief in Jesus' complete work on the cross, forgiveness of sins is given freely because our loving Savior has paid the price, not only for us, but as us: in Him we died to sin and resurrected to a new life[152]. The blood of Jesus cleanses us from all sin and infuses us with heaven's DNA. In Him we become a new creation, with a clean slate: "the old things are gone and all is made new!"[153]

*There seems to be a double standard regarding divorce within the Church.*

This powerful reality appears to be forgotten when a heavy-weight topic like divorce is on the table. There seems to be a double standard regarding this subject within the Church. Most Christians believe the redemptive power of the blood of Jesus is sufficient to bring redemption and transformation to people from every walk of life dealing with all kinds of issues: addiction, emotional brokenness, demonic oppression, sexual immorality, experiences with the occult, etc. There is a long list of destructive or perverted behaviors which people display because of

---

[150] Malachi 3:6

[151] John 3:34

[152] Romans 6:8

[153] 2 Corinthians 5:17

broken, wounded and oppressed hearts, we believe God forgives and is powerful to redeem and restore.

However, the way many of us approach our brothers and sisters who are going, or have gone through divorce, seems to indicate this is an issue which goes beyond God's redemptive and restorative grace: "God can save you, redeem you and restore you, with Him you are going from glory to glory, except if you have gone or are going through divorce. Your life is now over because you messed it up so badly and made a mistake so terrible that not even God can fix it!" It sounds ridiculous when we say it out loud, doesn't it?

This underlying belief leaves people feeling like they are always going to be second rate Christians, never fully qualified, never completely accepted or good enough. The truth is we all make mistakes but some mistakes have greater impact on our lives than others.

Are you saying that getting married was, or is, a mistake? No. Marriage, as it was originally designed, is wonderful, but we live in a fallen world, and when we try to do it without being connected to and coached by the original Designer we can make many mistakes.

Some marriages, just like my first one, start with conflicting agendas or happen within the wrong timing. Some of us choose to share life with another without really knowing who we are ourselves and not being quite sure what we want in life. Some of us haven't even involved God in the important decision of choosing a life partner, or we have prayed about it and asked for His input, but deep down we had already made up our minds. Many of us have orphan hearts so we are in survival mode and are moved by need, not by purpose. I could go on.

So, now you are saying we can make mistakes in our marriages which God can't fix? No. If I was, it would still sound ridiculous. There is nothing beyond the redemptive power of Jesus' blood: "His divine power has given us everything we need for a godly life through our knowledge of Him who called us by His own glory and goodness."[154] He doesn't just want to fix it for us, He wants to fix it with us.

*Reconciliation is always lovingly spread on God's table.*

Our relationship with God is, and will always be, paramount in our journey to attain wholeness. We can only display His glory and goodness in our lives, and our marriages, when we get to know Him intimately and do life according to His ways. However, spouses are not always on the same page regarding this, which is expressed in words and actions not rooted in God's heart of reconciliation. Even then, that reconciliation is lovingly spread on His table of grace and when people come to their senses and repent of their sins, mistakes and wrong ways, the Father still runs with open arms to welcome them back into His lavish love banquet[155]. He is SO good!

"I'm not okay with exiling a third of the church to the ice castle of shame simply because they have failed in one area of life. It is our call and responsibility as the Body of Christ to redeem and restore into the fold anyone who has been through a divorce!"[156] (Kris Vallotton)

My heart longs for the day our brothers and sisters who are going, or have gone through divorce, feel church is a safe place for them. I don't like to generalize, so I will start by acknowledging the churches all over the world that are already doing this well. Thank you. You are a beacon of light in a broken society. Unfortunately, there are still many more which need to

---

[154] 2 Peter 1:3

[155] Luke 15:11-32 - The Parable of the Prodigal Son

[156] Kris Vallotton blog: "What God really thinks about divorce", 2019 (krisvallotton.com)

reconsider their dismissive, or critical and judgmental approach in the light of the Bible's teachings about grace.

In many religious circles, divorce (official or impending) is handled like a 'hot potato': we are convinced if we hold it long enough it will burn us. People in leadership are not always equipped to address this type of relational breakdown and many are fearful of "sending the wrong messages." If they are seen being supportive of any of the 'parts' involved they might send the message they are for one of the spouses and against the other or, even

> *In many religious circles divorce is handled like a 'hot potato'.*

worse, they might come across as being someone who encourages people to get a divorce instead of fighting for their marriages. Because it can become a controversial or divisive subject, this "hot potato" is left on the plate to cool down on its own.

In the meantime, families are going through real issues, facing real problems, experiencing heartache and pain, and often not knowing what positive or constructive steps to take next. They don't need judgement, they need grace.

What about the people who have been, or are being, reckless, neglectful, abusive, destructive or casual in the way they have conducted themselves in their marriage? What about those who broke the sacred vows of matrimony? And those who willingly choose, or chose, disconnection and separation? Yes, grace is available for all of those people too, because "if we confess our sins, He is faithful and just and will forgive us our sins and purify us from all unrighteousness"[157].

It can be very hard to embrace this message of grace and forgiveness especially when you have been the one wronged. Your spouse (or former spouse) was unfaithful, abusive or painfully disloyal and you feel you have

---

[157] 1 John 1:9

been defrauded at so many levels. Retribution seems to be the only way forward for you to get some sense of justice and closure: *It's not fair* the person who hurt you and hindered you so much is given a clean slate and a second chance because of grace. However, this is what our God is all about. The desire of His heart is that *all* men come to repentance and to the knowledge of the truth, so none will perish and *all* can be saved[158]. His priority is reconciliation. He came to bring salvation to *all* who believe, not condemnation[159], and "He gave us the ministry of reconciliation"[160]. Jesus explained (and demonstrated) that it is in the way we *love our enemies* (those who are wicked, those who wrong us or those who wish to harm us), we most clearly display our divine sonship and the heart of our Father:

But I tell you, love your enemies and pray for those who persecute you, that you may be children of your Father in heaven. He causes his sun to rise on the evil and the good and sends rain on the righteous and the unrighteous. (Matthew 5:44-45)

Do I take any pleasure in the death of the wicked? declares the Sovereign LORD. Rather, am I not pleased when they turn from their ways and live? (Ezekiel 18:23)

In the book of Habakkuk, the Lord explains how the wicked will eventually become prey of their wrongful doings. They will bring destruction upon themselves if they don't turn away from their wicked ways,

> *Our good God longs for those who are lost to be drawn back home, to Himself.*

however, they will not be left in the dark indefinitely because "the earth

---

[158]  2 Peter 3:9 and 1 Timothy 2:4
[159]  Matthew 3:17
[160]  2 Corinthians 5:18

will be filled with the knowledge of the glory of the Lord as the waters cover the sea"[161]. Our God is so good that He longs for those who are lost in their ungodly ways (that was you and me at some point) to find their way back home.

God isn't late with is promise as some measure lateness. He is restraining Himself on account of you, holding back the End because He doesn't want anyone lost. He's giving everyone space and time to change. (2 Peter 3:9 – MSG)

In this dispensation of grace there is a window of time granted for all who are blind to see the light and find their way back to Him. Who shines His light on the Earth? His children, you and me[162]. How will those who are lost see His Kingdom, His love, His forgiveness and welcoming acceptance, His light, if we don't let it shine?

*Who shines His light on Earth? God's children: you and me.*

Every time a lost 'sheep' is found, there is great joy and celebration in Heaven [163]. Will we humble ourselves and fully embrace God's grace, rooted in perfect love, for ourselves and our *neighbors,* or will we remain offended and refuse to party wholeheartedly every time a misbehaved prodigal finds His way back to the Father's arms?

Whether you have been wronged or you are the one who has wronged, when you turn aside from doing things your way and start moving in His direction, with a humble and surrendered heart, you will see that your

---

[161] Habakkuk 2:14
[162] Matthew 5:14 / Philippians 2:14
[163] Luke 15:6-7

heavenly Father longs to welcome you home and show you that you are accepted, restored and still fully qualified in Jesus to be His son/daughter.

## Offensive grace?!

From the world's point of view, God's grace may seem 'unfair' or even scandalous according to the human understanding of justice, but actually it is the only, truly fair measure we can find. It is never focused on individuals and circumstances, which can be limited and infinitely variable. It's focused on God Himself, infinitely invariable and invariably, completely available to everyone. I understood this on the day the Holy Spirit dropped an insightful pearl of wisdom while I was swimming. He said: "The same God, the same Kingdom with all His limitless resources is available to everyone, with no restrictions and no shadow of variation. This is true and absolute fairness. Nothing biased or circumstantial about it."

*Absolute fairness.*

As I reflected on His brilliant wisdom, an inevitable question arose: Then, why does it seem that some people land on their feet better than others, all the time?

"What has been fully given can never be earned, it can only be fully received by trust." (Graham Cooke)[164]

The source of grace continues to be unchangeable and fully available to all, but the way to access it requires faith, trust and surrender. Let's look together at "The parable of the Workers in the Vineyard"[165] so you can see this truth clearly illustrated:

---

[164] YouTube podcast: "Receiving the gift of unchanging presence"

[165] Matthew 20:1-16

For the kingdom of heaven is like a landowner who went out early in the morning to hire workers for his vineyard. He agreed to pay them a denarius[166] for the day and sent them into his vineyard. About nine in the morning he went out and saw others standing in the marketplace doing nothing. He told them, "You also go and work in my vineyard, and I will pay you whatever is right." So they went. He went out again about noon and about three in the afternoon and did the same thing. About five in the afternoon he went out and found still others standing around. He asked them, "Why have you been standing here all day long doing nothing?"

"Because no one has hired us," they answered.

He said to them, "You also go and work in my vineyard."

When evening came, the owner of the vineyard said to his foreman, "Call the workers and pay them their wages, beginning with the last ones hired and going on to the first." The workers who were hired about five in the afternoon came and each received a denarius. So when those came who were hired first, they expected to receive more. But each one of them also received a denarius. When they received it, they began to grumble against the landowner. "These who were hired last worked only one hour," they said, "and you have made them equal to us who have borne the burden of the work and the heat of the day." But he answered one of them, "I am not being unfair to you, friend. Didn't you agree to work for a denarius? Take your pay and go. I want to give the one who was hired last the same as I gave you. Don't

---

[166] A denarius was the usual daily wage of a day laborer.

I have the right to do what I want with my own money? Or are you envious because I am generous?"

So the last will be first, and the first will be last.

According to the world's perspective this story ends with injustice and inequality. If we read it without the insight and revelation given by the Holy Spirit (who unveils to us the heart of the Father and the mind of Christ), we will find ourselves feeling perplexed and even offended with the Master's apparently unfair behavior.

*What is God's perspective?*

We have that initial perception because we think the perspective of the first workers is valid: "the more I work, the more I deserve to be paid." Nothing wrong with that premise but, if we look closer, we will be able to discern entitlement based on seniority and performance: "I've been around for longer, I have accomplished more, I am more righteous, I deserve more."

The truth is that every single worker who was offered a job in the first hours was told in advance what their wages would be. Out of His goodness and mercy, the Master decided to pay the same to every single worker who accepted His job offer, independently of the time of day they were hired.

When the time came to give everyone their wages, the ones who had worked less hours and got the same salary didn't really take anything away from what was promised to the ones who worked for longer hours, but still, the long runners felt like they had been defrauded.

Their focus was on the hardness and length of their task and they were so jealous, envious and offended with the favor given to the late runners they were unable to acknowledge and celebrate the Master's kindness and generosity. They were also unable to recognize the fact that the recently arrived workers, who hadn't been promised a specific amount, took a risk and surrendered the right to expect or demand anything from the Master. In the end they were rewarded for their faith (or right belief), and their trust in the Master's words that "He would pay them whatever is right". And He did, and He always does.

> *They were so self-centred that they were unable to acknowledge the Master's kindness and generosity.*

Aren't you grateful that God's mercies are new every day? Aren't you grateful that "His divine power has [already] given us everything we need for a godly life through our knowledge of Him who called us by His own glory and goodness . . . and gave us His very great and precious promises, so that through them we might *participate in the divine nature!*"[167]

Those are His promises for all of us, no matter what 'time of the day' we have started. If we accept His invitation to know Him and become like Him, then our eyes will not be focused on our rights and privileges, status, seniority or performance levels, but we will be focused in everything which will unveil His nature and His ways. The greatest gift the 'late workers' were given was the revelation of their Master's goodness and with it a revelation of grace. They knew the reward they were given was the Master's idea and had nothing to do with their effort. They hadn't earned it and they didn't deserve it.

---

[167] Paraphrase of 2 Peter 1:3-4

Grace, the unmerited favor of God, is a gift[168] that no one deserves or can earn. We all have sinned and fall short of the glory of God[169] and there is nothing I can give, do or achieve which can make me more acceptable and worthy than my brothers and sisters. That would be unfair due to the inequality of people's backgrounds, opportunities and circumstances.

> *The greatest gift they were given was the revelation of their Master's goodness, and with it a revelation of grace.*

Instead we are only required to do one thing, which every single one of us can do: believe.

Believe that Jesus paid the full price and gave us full access to His Kingdom by inviting us into Himself as we invite Him into ourselves. Hidden in Him[170], one with Him, we are adopted into the heavenly family and can boldly approach the throne of grace in our time of need[171].

Whenever we find ourselves still trying to work it out on our own, striving to earn God's approval or favor (and demanding others to act the same way), then we have missed the point that *it is finished*, because through Christ, and Christ alone, all things have already been given to us in the heavenly places. We just need to believe and receive, like a child.

But because of his great love for us, God, who is rich in mercy, made us alive with Christ even when we were dead in transgressions - it is by grace you have been saved. And God raised us up with Christ and seated us with him in the heavenly realms in Christ Jesus, in order that in the coming ages

---

[168] Ephesians 2:8

[169] Romans 3:23

[170] Colossians 3:3

[171] Hebrews 4:16

he might show the incomparable riches of his grace, expressed in his kindness to us in Christ Jesus. For it is by grace you have been saved, through faith - and this is not from yourselves, it is the gift of God - not by works, so that no one can boast. (Ephesians 2:4-9)

Paul is talking to the saints, his brothers and sisters in the faith who believed Jesus was the Messiah, the Savior of the world. However, he was always addressing audiences which included a considerable number of people converted from

> *The revelation of God's grace will always result in a humble, liberated, hopeful and thankful heart.*

Judaism, who still incorporated in their practice religious rituals and traditions with the purpose of becoming more acceptable to God, and by doing so, were denying the need for a Savior and the absolute sufficiency found in Jesus.

If there was any other way we could be restored back to righteous sonship without the need for a perfect Savior, then the Father would have never sent Jesus to the cross. The cross, a symbol of shame and humiliation became, because of Jesus' triumphant resurrection, a symbol of victory and scandalous grace.

How does God show off the incomparable riches of His grace? By expressing His kindness to us through Jesus in us. His victories and accomplishments become our victories and accomplishments and His righteousness becomes our righteousness. Jesus really is "all in all"[172], which means that He is all in us too. It is a mind-blowing thought but one that is biblically legal. What an extraordinary gift! How can this be possible? The more we empty ourselves

---

[172] Colossians 3:11

of self-righteousness[173], which invalidates Jesus' complete work on the cross[174], the more room we make for God to, out of His kindness, pour Himself into us.

The revelation of God's grace will always result in a humble, liberated, expectant and thankful heart. Humble, because we become aware of our need, liberated because we know that we are not to rely upon ourselves but we can rely on "Christ, the hope of glory"[175], and therefore, hopeful and expectant of goodness and greatness, and thankful for who He is, all He has done and all He is about to do.

The revelation that both the fruits of our transformation, and the blessing of the works of our hands, don't come from our own effort and brilliance but as an outcome of Jesus' finished work, will be manifested in the way we extend grace to ourselves and others. In other words, in the way we express generosity, kindness and honor towards ourselves and our 'neighbors', especially when they don't deserve it.

## What is grace saying to me?

Not having grace for our brothers and sisters might be an indicator there are areas in our own lives where we don't believe God's grace is sufficient. We have believed the lie that our mistakes, problems or circumstances are bigger than Him, or beyond the reach of His perfect love. He can't, or He won't, fix them, so we keep a safe distance while we try to fix ourselves. In the process, when we fail we punish ourselves, and because we approach

---

[173] Biblically speaking, self-righteousness, which is related to legalism, is the idea that by our good works we can somehow generate, within ourselves, a righteousness that will be acceptable to God (Romans 3:10)

[174] Galatians 5:4

[175] Colossians 1:27

those around us with the same belief system, we feel that whenever they mess up we need to punish them too.

Not having grace for our brothers and sisters might also be an indicator we feel superior to them in some way. We look down on them because we have already achieved and improved so much that we feel more qualified, more acceptable and entitled to preferential treatment. This is a very dangerous place to be because "God opposes the proud but He shows favor or gives grace to the humble"[176]. But what does it mean to be humble in the Kingdom of God?

*Grace indicators.*

At BSSM we often heard teachers say "to be humble is not to think less of yourself, but to think of yourself less." There is great wisdom in this maxim. Our wonderful God places so much value on us that He gave His precious Son to bring us back to Himself and restore us as royal priests[177] and co-heirs with Christ[178]. He took off our former sinful rags and clothed us with splendor[179] and when we are before Him what we cast at His feet are our crowns[180]. You can't give what you don't have, so don't devalue, dishonor or disqualify what the Lord has gloriously restored in you.

On the other hand, if we forget that all we are and have comes from Him, is in Him, flows through Him and is to be consecrated to Him, for His glory[181], then we will be in danger of starting to believe that it's all about us and we are, or have to look like we are, "the best thing on this side of

---

[176] James 4:6

[177] 1 Peter 2:9

[178] Romans 8:17

[179] Zechariah 3:3

[180] Revelation 3:11 / 1 Thessalonians 2:19-20 / Revelations 4:10

[181] Romans 11:36

heaven." When we are focused on how great we are becoming and how high we can achieve we become so full of ourselves that not only do we lose the awareness of our needs and weaknesses, but we avoid them like the plague.

Longing to attain perfection and striving to maintain it without grace and love, has led, and is leading many to emotional, mental and even physical breakdown. Fear of failure and fear of men are again the great deceivers and destroyers that can be found at the root of this fallacy.

## In our weakness He is made strong

While I was reading Bill Johnson's book, "Face to Face with God," the Holy Spirit started showing me I don't need to be afraid of my weaknesses. I already knew by heart the verse which says "His power is made perfect in weakness"[182], but to be honest it was almost like a cliché I used without completely understanding how this exchange works. I don't presume to have it fully grasped yet, but what God revealed that day shed tremendous light on what was once a blurry subject to me. The following is what I wrote in my journal after that inspired teaching moment:

*When I approach my weaknesses without fear and with the conviction of love, I will stop being afraid to face them and, more importantly, I will no longer be afraid of facing God. The realization of my weakness will not only become the place of my awareness of need but it also becomes the place of possibility for love to be displayed and experienced. It will become the place*

*A fearless realisation of weakness opens up the possibility for His love to be experienced and displayed.*

---

[182] 2 Corinthians 12:9

*where I am going to be perfected in love because God is going to show up and the way He is going to strengthen and empower me to surpass and overcome that weakness is going to be another opportunity for Him to reveal Himself, His nature and His perfect love, to me and the world watching. I am not just perfected, I am perfected in love[183]. No longer a fearful awareness of need, it becomes a hopeful, expectant awareness of how need will be surely and lovingly met! In tears I prayed: "May I always be aware of my needs and, as David[184], long for and love your alignment and correction, as you come through with your life-giving, transformational, perfect love."*

The journey through separation and divorce is often experienced not only as a painful event but also a shameful one. We feel like we have made a complete mess of our lives and all the "shoulda, woulda, couldas" are staring us in the face, reminding us how inadequate, incapable and wrong we were. The judgmental voices inside of us and around us reinforce the destructive "blame & shame" speech, and we end up just wanting to be left alone and hide away from condescending and condemning words and looks.

It is wise to take cover when we don't feel covered but that is not the case in our relationship with God. He made sure we could come boldly, unafraid and unashamed, before the throne of grace, and exchange our weakness for His strength, our imperfections, for His perfection. It is in the awareness that my weakness is beyond my capacity to fix but not beyond His that I put my trust in God and invite Him to restore and redeem my mess. He is at the door knocking[185], He comes in because I invite Him to come in. He transforms because I invite Him to transform. He shows up in all His might

---

[183] 1 John 4:17-18

[184] Psalm 139:23-24

[185] Revelation 3:20

and all His strength because I hand Him the keys of my heart, fully opened, fully surrendered, with nothing hidden or withheld, and I present Him the good, the bad, and the ugly.

> *It's okay to be vulnerable before God. He welcomes our honesty and authenticity.*

It's okay to be vulnerable before God because He doesn't reject me but welcomes and embraces my honesty and authenticity. To hide my weaknesses is to take away His opportunity to manifest His glory in me and through me. In my weakness He shows up. In my weakness His presence is real. In my weakness there is room for His greatness. I no longer need to be afraid of my weakness because I don't need to be afraid of Him. Jesus has already taken upon Himself the punishment that brings me peace[186] and His perfect love dispels all fear[187] and washes away all shame.

I find it interesting that our weakness is also proof of our free will, that we are not puppets in His hands. It's proof we are not magically changed, or mechanically switched on and off. The transformation which God longs to produce in us, so we can step into the wholeness He has conquered for us, starts with a voluntary decision, an act of the will activated through relationship. As we walk with Him and we acknowledge the superiority of His wisdom, the perfection of His ways, and His beauty beyond description, we fall in love and long to become like Him, so we can experience more deeply the extraordinary mystery of being strong because we are becoming one with Him.

---

[186] Isaiah 53:3

[187] 1 John 4:18

## The Superiority of Grace

Does this mean I should just embrace weakness and be okay with it? No. Weakness is never the final destination, grace is. Wherever you find yourself in life at this moment – whether you're the one who has wronged someone or the one who was wronged – God's grace is still powerful, transforming, restorative and expansive. His grace is really enough to lead you into righteousness and abundant life. This is how Paul explains it:

So then, the law was introduced into God's plan to bring the reality of human sinfulness out of hiding. And yet, wherever sin increased, there was more than enough of God's grace to triumph all the more!

So what do we do, then? Do we persist in sin so that God's kindness and grace will increase? What a terrible thought! We have died to sin once and for all, as a dead man passes away from this life. So how could we live under sin's rule a moment longer?[188]

Paul makes sure that his readers are focused on the superiority and rulership of grace. Just because *grace superabounds where sin abounded*[189] is not a reason to give sin the center stage and perpetuate it so grace continues to be increasingly manifested. Grace is more fully manifested in the wholeness we display as a result of our union with Christ[190]. God's grace is enough, and superior, because it engulfs brokenness and transforms it into wholeness. The greater the brokenness, the greater is the grace and restoration power displayed.

---

[188] Romans 5:20 and 6:1-2 (TPT)

[189] Romans 5:20 (NKJV)
[190] Romans 6:11 (TPT)

> *Grace is more fully manifested in the wholeness we display as a result of our union with Christ.*

So, what is the right thing to do as a Christian, do I remain in my broken marriage and continue to believe for and invest into its restoration, or do I just walk away and trust that God's grace will eventually redeem it all?

As I said before, I strongly believe that divorce should be the very last resort, when every possible remedial avenue has been pursued and exhausted. Its consequences, which you can't always completely foresee, will significantly impact the rest of your life, and the lives of the ones closest to you. In both scenarios, messes need to be cleaned up and in the process people should be treated with respect, but beyond that, we should not generalize. The truth is that each case is different.

Whether we are seeking guidance for ourselves or we just want to counsel someone else wisely, the above question is one we must pose first to God. If we don't want to risk jumping into premature judgement of people and circumstances, or foolishly presume to fully know people's hearts and motives – as well as God's thoughts about their situation – the Holy Spirit must be our guide through every step of this very delicate process.

God alone knows all the ins and outs of a couple's journey and He alone knows the condition of each spouse's heart[191]. When we seek and hear His voice, His freshly spoken word, regarding a particular situation, and we proclaim it, we begin holding hands with heaven and preparing the way for miracles to happen: "Let the weak say I am strong"[192].

---

[191] Jeremiah 17:9-10

[192] Joel 3:10

What if one spouse has drifted away and wants nothing to do with God? We can still pray, intercede, declare words of life and reconciliation, and patiently wait for them to turn their hearts to the Lord. God

> *God alone knows the condition of the heart.*

in His great love and mercy will give them a window of opportunity and will give the other spouse the grace to endure and move forward: "I can do all things through Christ who strengthens me"[193], and "all things are possible to those who believe"[194].

In the meantime, freedom of choice continues to be granted (each spouse has the capacity to take this opportunity and choose either way), which leads us back to my initial premise: each case should be treated as unique and handled under the Holy Spirit's wise counsel.

In the Church, we have not always been wise or asked for the Holy Spirit's guidance on this. We have often judged people hastily and burned bridges for future reconnection, or we have been passive when vulnerable ones need care and protection. Telling vulnerable women to endure abusive marriages, when not only themselves but their children might be at risk, without doing anything to support

> *Are we misrepresenting the Father's heart for the most vulnerable?*

them and change their situation, is to misrepresent the Father's heart for the most vulnerable. He listens and He cares and His desire is to make all wrong things right[195], but when we are passive about people's plights in the name of religious legalism we lead them to believe that God cares more about rules and regulations than He cares about people. Nothing could be

---

[193] Philippians 4:13

[194] Mark 9:23

[195] Isaiah 61:1-3

further from the truth. Jesus' approach to the Sabbath[196] and to the law of Moses demonstrates something very different:

Teacher, which commandment in the law is the greatest? Jesus answered him, "Love the Lord your God with every passion of your heart, with all the energy of your being, and with every thought that is within you." This is the great and supreme commandment. And the second is like it in importance: "You must love your friend in the same way you love yourself." Contained within these commandments to love you will find all the meaning of the Law and the Prophets[197].

Jesus didn't come to eradicate the law but instead He came to fulfill it. However, He did it in a very different way than the religious authorities were expecting. When He completed His mission He fulfilled the Law because he made a way for the superior 'Law of Love' to be established: to love God, ourselves and our brothers and sisters, completely, not holding anything back or against anyone.

His grace is truly sufficient because His redemptive blood was, is and will always be truly sufficient. His arms continue to be wide open to those who repent from their wrong ways[198]. Remember that our heavenly Father adopted us into His family[199] when we received His Son and, although

---

[196] Matthew 12:11 / Luke 13:15 / Luke 14:5 - Then he asked them: "If one of you has a child or an ox that falls into a well on the Sabbath day, will you not immediately pull it out?"

[197] Matthew 2:36-40 TPT

[198] 1 Corinthians 16:23 MSG

[199] Ephesians 1:5

"religion celebrates perfection, family celebrates progress"[200]. Success in the Kingdom of God looks different to success in the world.

## A success story

"The primary message of this Covenant is the power of God's love to make us whole. The power of the authentic love of God transforms everything it touches"[201]. (Bill Johnson)

What is success in the Kingdom of God? In the Kingdom of God success equals wholeness. To be whole and wholesome means to be complete, mature, "lacking nothing."

Let perseverance finish its work so that you may be mature and complete, not lacking anything. (James 1:4)

To succeed is to not give up. To succeed is to persevere and continue to move forward towards the full stature of a son/daughter of God[202]. It's not

*In the Kingdom of God success equals wholeness.*

about becoming a doctor or a judge or a teacher or an artist or a pastor, or whatever other title you want to add to this simplified list. It's about

---

[200] (The first time I heard this pearl of wisdom was in a sermon by Steve Backlund).

[201] "Face to Face with God", p.209.

[202] Ephesians 4:13

becoming one with Christ, so we too can reveal the heart of the Father and be ambassadors of His Kingdom, because we approach life and relationships with the mind of Christ in whatever circle we move in. This is being successful.

It doesn't happen overnight but it is the result of a mind renewal process which will expose broken and weak places in our hearts, and lies or debilitating beliefs in our souls. Whenever this happens, the tendency is to be ashamed and try to hide it from other people around us and even from God (I know it sounds silly, because He can see everything, but we have all been there and done that). That's when we try to solve problems and tackle burdens on our own which were meant to be shared and relinquished.

How different would it be if we approached those challenges knowing God is for us, having shame washed away by the blood of Jesus, and being infused with the strength which springs from the joyful anticipation of increase?

If we go back to the beginning of chapter one of the book of James, he is telling his readers to be joyful when they face "trials of many kinds" because something good will come out of it. It's an opportunity for growth. We started with verse four but if we read the previous verses in order to grasp the context, we find out that "perseverance is produced by the testing of our faith" (v.3). Therefore, perseverance, which leads to maturity or full development, is not produced when all goes well but when we are confronted with situations which test our faith, in other words, test what we believe.

*Perseverance is produced when we go through situations which test our beliefs.*

What I find interesting about those testing circumstances, which are called "trials" (v.2), is that they are not selective. What do I mean by this? In the original Greek texts the word used here is *peirasmós* [203] which means temptation or test – both senses can apply simultaneously (depending on the context) [204]. In many translations they have opted to use the expression "trials of many or various kinds" or the words "troubles" or "problems." I believe this is significant because the different types, or kinds, of trials also point to different sources: life, God, the enemy of our souls and ourselves.

Life in general presents many challenges and obstacles and we are constantly required to solve all sorts of problems. Two people who face the exact same problem or challenging circumstances can have a completely different outcome depending on the way they approach it. The way I position my heart, when I respond or react to life's trials, is always going to impact my personal development. Therefore, there are some difficult circumstances in life which I believe God allows [205] so our hearts can be tested [206], our capacity enlarged (as we tackle things in partnership with Him), and our growth manifested in good and abundant fruit.

Then there is temptation, the enticement to sin, which doesn't come from God, but from "our own evil desires" [207] (the enemy of our souls works against us on this front too, but with Jesus in the picture we have been

---

[203] πειρασμός - Strong's Concordance 3986

[204] The positive sense "test" and negative sense "temptation" are functions of the context (not merely the words themselves).

[205] I do not include sickness here. Jesus is our model. He healed all the sick He encountered (Acts 10:38), He only did what He saw the Father do (John 5:19) and He never said sickness was from God. He is not the one who came to steal, kill and destroy but He came to give abundant life (John 10:10).

[206] "The refining pot is for silver, and the furnace for gold; but the Lord tests hearts." (Proverbs 17:3) - God brings trials into our lives not to hurt us but to reveal what's in our hearts so we can be developed.

[207] When tempted, no one should say, "God is tempting me." For God cannot be tempted by evil, nor does he tempt anyone; but each person is tempted when they are dragged away by their own evil desire and enticed. (James 1:13-14)

given the power and the freedom to make good or bad choices and decisions).

> *No distinction is made between the types of trials and their outcomes.*

What I find extremely significant is the fact that no distinction is made between the types of trials and their outcomes. All of the above can be used to test our faith and produce perseverance which will lead to maturity and wholeness. Even divorce? Yes, even divorce. How is this possible?[208] It is possible because of God's immutable grace. Whatever happens, God is the same. He never changes and He is committed to make all things work together for the good of those who love Him[209].

The goal is not perfection according to the world's perspective but according to God's perspective. In the Kingdom of God perfection has its foundation in loyal, faithful love.

Blessed is the man who perseveres under trial, because when he has stood the test, he will receive the crown of life that God has promised to those who love Him. (James 1:12)

What's going to be tested in the end? My heart's motives. What moved me? What kept me going? Was it my love for God and for my 'neighbor'?

---

[208] I recently heard a podcast from Graham Cooke where he explains the idea that "we are to see everyone and everything in the light of God's goodness and mercy, because all things, all trials, are challenging us to explore and discover another layer or dimension of the goodness of God." I was very blessed by this teaching and I believe you will be too, should you choose to listen to it. The title is "We are only challenged by goodness" - link: https://www.youtube.com/watch?v=BOZzx0CW8cM&feature=share&fbclid=IwAR0K7CgNI NKcY23EmWHimAG8YC6KpMZCHOumV0Clhnilpz_ohNFGWq-r4_o

[209] Romans 8:28

To persevere is first and foremost to not give up on God, even when things

---
*To persevere is to
not give up on God.*
---

don't happen the way we want, or when we want. To believe His ways are better and higher than our ways because He is always faithful and good. To draw near to Him, to seek His counsel and guidance, and to obey His commands and embrace His will because He has loved us first, fiercely, and in response we have grown to love Him and now we can't live without Him.

It all starts with surrender and humility. This is one of the recurrent messages in my story: to come before Him with a yielded, humble heart, repent from leaning on my own understanding and carry on seeking Him, trusting Him, obeying Him because I love Him more than I love His gifts, blessings and promises.

Our perseverance, through *thick and thin,* even when going through relational breakdown and divorce, speaks loudly of where our trust is anchored, who our Rock is, where our strength and hope come from. It is also a witness of our love for Him, a light shining in the darkness, an undisputable display of His glory. In the end, this devoted and tangible love is the only measure, the only standard, the only criterion mentioned for those who will be crowned with a "crown of life."

## Heading to a wedding

Mat and I got married seven months after we got engaged. The Holy Spirit continued to reveal more gold nuggets hidden in Mat, some kept surfacing and others were still to be mined in the years to come. Every one of those revelations was like a beautiful gift of peace and hope wrapped in joyful expectation.

God also continued encouraging us through affirming prophetic words about our future as a couple. Words which gave us a clearer vision of His plans for us, and emboldened us to believe, proclaim and speak them into existence, because we knew we were praying in agreement with Heaven. By doing so, we were pulling Heaven into Earth. And we saw His Kingdom come, and be tangibly manifested in the way every relational, financial and logistic need was provided for.

We started paying off credit cards and putting money aside to fund our future costs with BSSM so we had a very limited budget for our wedding. Nevertheless, God gave us wisdom to manage our resources wisely and we saw multiplication happen in front of our eyes. He also brought extraordinary people[210] who ran with us and helped us to put together a beautiful ceremony and a great reception. When the wedding day came nothing was missing.

From my beautiful dress, to the bridesmaids', flowers, rings, hairdresser, nails, make-up, wedding car, a beautifully decorated venue, photographers, videographers, amazing musicians, a top notch catering team and delicious food, we saw God's provision and favor come through in every detail in an amazing and abundant way. We even had someone lending us radio equipment and individual headsets so that all of our Portuguese guests were able to understand the ceremony which was fully translated into Portuguese[211].

Most importantly, we were surrounded by friends and family who loved us, cheered us, celebrated our story and our journey, and who got to be a part of the beautiful redemption paraded that day. God gave us ideas,

---

[210] A special thank you to Jim and Marie Morris and their brilliant catering team, to my mother for cooking great quantities of delicious Portuguese food, to Janelle Kingham for doing a cracking job as a project manager, decorator, fashion consultant, hairdresser (and organizer of a million other amazing logistic details), to Amber Semple for creating a beautiful, safe and creative area for the children, and to Sam, Emma, Erin and Noah Kelly for lending us their beautiful "Pebbles" to be our wedding transport. We will never forget how you were God-given and instrumental in making our special day happen the beautiful way it did.

[211] Thank you, Matt Cairns and Paula Ramos!

strategies, systems and teams who worked together to mobilize people and organize a monumental potluck provided by our guests.

We called it "our joint venture" and we wrote a heartfelt letter, which we attached to our wedding invitation, letting everyone know their presence was the most important gift they could bring and how they could help us make this happen. We had friends and family coming from various areas in the UK and different parts of the world, who were welcomed and hospitably accommodated, with the help of our family and the church community. In the end we had almost 400 guests sharing that glorious day with us.

Our heavenly Father got to show off his goodness that day in so many ways, at so many different levels. The week we got married it rained from morning to night every single

> *Our heavenly Father got to lavishly show off His goodness in our wedding day.*

day except the day of our wedding. That day the skies were blue and the sun was shining! (Even a greater miracle if you consider this was in England.) In all of these blessings we could see expressions of God's favor, like He was smiling on us, but it was when we started doing life together that we became increasingly aware of how His amazing grace had been, and kept on, sustaining and transforming us.

Coming out of a desert opens your eyes (and all your other senses) to the precious value of little things that you used to take for granted. A light breeze, a cool shade or a scarce and invaluable water droplet are regarded and received with a deep sense of gratitude.

With the passing of the days we both began to understand the tremendous growth and transformation we had gone through. The closeness to God, the determination to keep moving forward and not settling for anything that is not His best for us, the high value for deep connection and purpose, and the desire to prefer each other in love, were like ripe and prosperous fruits bursting forth in season.

While we had been waiting for each other, the Lord had prepared us and fashioned us for each other. When the door was finally opened, we knew we had been on a journey to become conformed to His image, empowered and equipped to love better, and to contain and handle colossal, weighty blessings without being crushed by them.

As soon as we got engaged, several people on different occasions approached us with words of hope, restoration and restitution. The one which kept recurring was "The Lord is going to give back to you the years that the locust has eaten"[212], and He did. We didn't have it all figured out but we soon started to taste what it really means to go from glory to glory. In different ways for each one

*Ripe and prosperous fruits bursting out in season.*

of us, there were so many things that had been defiled, stolen and destroyed with divorce, to which God brought so much redemption. My words are not enough to describe the depth of gratitude we started walking in.

In our usual daily relational dynamics there are so many simple, but precious, things which most of us don't even notice or just take for granted. Not us, the simplest things stood out and continue standing out. When you have been deprived of certain 'delicacies' for a long period of time, no matter how simple or small, if they are put back on the table you eat them with great satisfaction and profound gratitude, without wanting to take them for granted ever again. There was so much added value poured into our partnership which came from this heightened awareness and this different, grace-filled perspective on married life, that we soon realized the Lord had not only changed our lenses but He had given us new eyes along with upgraded hearts.

The following year we applied for BSSM, were accepted, prepared and got ready for the significant transitions ahead, and again and again saw God

---

[212] Joel 2:25

come through, with everything we needed falling into place at the appropriate time. Finally the Reddings moved to Redding, California. And a new and exciting episode of our lives began.

# Q & A

## M y s e l f  &  G o d

❑ Use the following blank lines to write the questions you still have about divorce (regarding your own situation or for counseling purposes); Make sure you take notes of God's answers.

- _____
  _____
  _____

- _____
  _____
  _____

- _____
  _____
  _____

- What is grace telling you? (If you don't know what this means, check this section of the chapter again).

- Ask the Holy Spirit if there is anything you need to repent for, or any mess you need to clean up; invite Him to lead you into all truth.

- With an open and vulnerable heart, ask the Holy Spirit if there are any weaknesses in which His strength can be made perfect.

- If the answer is yes, ask Him what is the next step towards restoration.

- What do you think has been, and is being, developed in you during this time of relational trial? Do you feel you have grown? In what way? (If nothing comes to mind, ask the Holy Spirit).

# T o g e t h e r

*(For those who want to work towards the restoration or improvement of their marriage)*

❏ This session has a very high emphasis on sharing what you have been working on in your individual reflective time with God. Some of these questions require you to be very vulnerable, so if you and your spouse haven't yet been able to develop communicative environment where you feel safe, secure and protected, then be honest about it and select the ones which are beneficial for the time being.

- Share with your spouse the questions this chapter raised for you and God's answers to those questions.

- Share with your spouse if there were any moments in this chapter which brought hope, joy or both. Why?

- Share with your partner if the Holy Spirit led you to repent and gave you instructions to clean up messes. Discuss what can happen (best or worst case scenario) and plan what is going to be your response (set up a deadline for this to be followed through so you can be accountable for it).

- Share with your spouse what the Holy Spirit revealed regarding your weaknesses and His instructions towards restoration.

- Share with your spouse the ways you think you have grown and what is being developed in you, and ask for his/her honest, constructive feedback.

- Do you celebrate progress? If not, how are you going to celebrate progress from now on? Decide together.

- What is God saying about the future of your partnership?

- What would you say to someone who has given up on God? Write a small but power-packed paragraph with the main reasons why He's worthy of our trust and perseverance; write it on a wallet size card and, if you can, laminate it so you can carry it around. (If possible, make and carry more than one so you can bless others).

# LifeLine

Revelation & Transformation log          ____/____/____

"Hope deferred makes the heart sick, but **a longing fulfilled is a tree of life.**"

(Proverbs 13:12)

# 10 LIFE AFTER SECOND MARRIAGE

"If you change the way you look at things, the things you look at will change."

(Unknown)

Have you heard any stories of people who find themselves in a second marriage and continue to struggle so much they begin to believe another relational breakdown is inevitable? Are you in the middle of a similar, painful story? The good news is, it doesn't have to be like that. God can, and is willing to help you change past scripts and recreate your love story, from the inside out. He always tells a better story.

I am not writing a book because I already have a 'perfect marriage'. It became very clear, as early as the honeymoon, that although God had already brought me through deep and extensive emotional healing and restoration, there were hurts caused by a man which, in my case, were supposed to be mended and healed through a godly man, filled with the Holy Spirit. I had to eventually face my fear to love and trust again, be honest about my attachment disorder and follow God's lead on how to embrace vulnerability.

## Who is driving?

After ten years of learning how to become more efficient as a single woman, I had created methods and systems to ensure I could get jobs done well, on my own, in every area of my life. I wasn't always successful in my own eyes, because I was usually spinning too many plates at a time and as a result I couldn't always complete tasks to the high standards I set for myself. Performance was a friend and a foe: a friend when I felt proud of my achievements and a foe when I felt like a failure. Therefore, successful self-sufficiency came with a high cost and its sweet and sour taste always lingered in my mouth as I ran through life trying to do as much as I could, being the best I could be. Amidst that 'rat race', God was committed to showing me a better way. He consistently challenged me to reposition my heart to trust in His perfect wisdom and rest in His faithfulness and grace.

*When the time came for me to share my life with a man again, I had no positive history to lean on.*

The two years prior to reconnecting with Mat were the ones where I saw greater breakthrough in this, because I completely let go of the reins of my destiny to follow God's will, allowing Him to lead the way. Nevertheless, when Mat came into the picture I realized a new type of challenge was around the corner. In my relationship with God, relinquishing control was an outcome of an ongoing relational history where a foundation of trust had been built, but when the time came for me to share my life with another person, and I had no positive history to lean on, I realized I needed to learn how to trust a man again.

The Lord knew I was very set in my own ways and He also knew how I would struggle with the idea of submitting my will and being accountable to a partner, not only regarding big life-changing decisions but also the ordinary, everyday ones. His approach to this condition of my heart was brilliant and very effective.

For a period of time I kept having a recurrent dream where I was driving through very narrow streets paved with cobblestones. It looked like I was trying to find my way around an ancient city like old Lisbon or Venice (which is definitely not car friendly!), and I kept going into dead ends, having to reverse or make nerve wracking U-turns while avoiding pedestrians, monuments, bridges, stairs and other vehicles. Many times I ended up getting stuck because the streets kept getting narrower and narrower until I couldn't squeeze the car in any further.

The impending possibility of crashing was overbearing and tiresome and I would wake up emotionally drained, filled with fear and anxiety, relieved it was all a dream and I had finally escaped what seemed to be a never ending road trip of torment and distress.

*The contrast was striking.*

I didn't understand why I kept having this dream until another dream put this one into perspective. In this dream, Mat was driving the car. As soon as I realized he was the one holding the wheel, the car flipped from one side of the road to the other and not only were we driving in the opposite direction but we were driving on a spacious motorway. No other cars in sight, we just moved forward, fast but not furious. The skies were deep blue, the sun shone brightly, Mat had a big smile from ear to ear, and the atmosphere was full of joy. There was no anxiety or fear in a journey which felt easy and peaceful. The contrast was striking.

I remember waking up, writing the dream in my journal and having an epiphany: "Mat is the one who is supposed to be driving!" I also remember being filled with the *fear of the Lord* regarding this, as I realized God was showing me something which was going to be foundational for a successful life and partnership.

I knew I had to share this with Mat and when I did he was able to connect some dots of his own. You see, he himself had a dream where he had let me drive the car and I had crashed. He thought nothing of it until I told him what I believed God was showing me and we both understood the Lord was sending a clear, illustrated message to both of us about the wisest and favored way to keep moving forward together, towards our destiny.

Mat was impressed by the way God had, once again, spoken to the two of us in tandem, but at the same time he didn't feel completely comfortable with the idea of being 'the wheel keeper'. He said "I am driving but you are the co-pilot, we are doing this together." And he was right, we are in this together, but I was not meant to hold the wheel nor determine the trajectory in this first leg of our journey.

Not long after that conversation, I had another dream where we were both in the car but I was driving. Again, the same exasperating saga. We were going across an old village and it looked like there were archaeological excavations and road works of all sorts happening everywhere. As I tried to plod my way through it all, I felt anxious, fearful and hopeless. Mat kept telling me where to go but I didn't always follow his advice. I got more and more frustrated. Eventually there was a point where I stopped the car because we had to go through a narrow passage between old stone walls and the road was blocked with several piles of building materials. Mat asked me why I had stopped and I replied, very annoyed: "The road is blocked! Can't you see the obstacles ahead?" He looked and with a startled expression he exclaimed: "There are no obstacles ahead!" When I looked again, the obstacles had vanished into thin air and I could move the car forward.

You can argue these dreams were God's way of asserting that "the wife is the one who submits", implying an inequality in the relationship, but I truly believe that, after the cross, both men and women are called to live in a partnership which is no longer under the curse following the fall, but is now fully redeemed by Jesus[213] to the original covenant where Adam saw Eve as his equal: "bone of my bone, flesh of my flesh"[214].

*A careful read of the "submission passage."*

If you read carefully the well-known "submission passage"[215], you will see her submission[216] is a response to a husband who loves her like Christ has loved the Church. How has Jesus loved the Church? He preferred her to Himself, gave His life for her, and He continues to be actively committed and invested in her restoration, growth and beautification. This selfless, sacrificial love, which lies at the foundation of this covenant where the husband is appointed as "the head"[217], doesn't give men permission to be tyrants who decide everything on their own and always have the last, selfish word, but actually brings with it great responsibility, devotion and service.

The purpose and responsibility of the head is to keep the body safe, functional and healthy. To ensure effective connection, because a body disconnected from the head cannot function, and to manage all systems, resources and opportunities to maximize growth and wellness of a unit which was never meant to exist separately but as one.

---

[213] Galatians 3:13; Galatians 3:26-28

[214] Genesis 2:23

[215] Ephesians 5:22-25

[216] Being submissive is an act of the will. Submission is only genuine as a voluntary response of the heart; that's how the church submits to Christ.

[217] Ephesians 5:23

I truly believe that, instead of asserting inequality of gender, which is the complete opposite of what Jesus did when He walked the Earth[218] (and He is the *exact representation* of the Father[219]), God in His goodness was giving us, in these dreams, clear instructions to tackle something we weren't yet aware of (and couldn't fully understand), but which had the potential to seriously hinder and compromise the prosperous future He had in mind for us[220].

> *We both had to make the decision to realign our perspective with God's.*

We both had to make a decision whether or not to realign our perspective with God's. I needed to embrace, encourage and respect Mat's leadership and Mat needed to grow in confidence and assertiveness in his God-ordained leadership. The way God spoke to us in our dreams brought vision, clarity and discernment of the times, and opened and prepared our hearts to obey a higher, wiser truth, even when we couldn't yet see, or fully understand, the bigger picture.

When life happened to us, throwing our way all the big and little things which are part of the logistics of living together, it became clearer and clearer why Mat was the one chosen to drive us into our destiny.

---

[218] Jesus's regard for women was much different than that of his contemporaries. He was openly countercultural in the way he regularly addressed women directly in public. Jesus valued women, their fellowship, prayers, service, financial support, testimony and witness. He honored women, taught women, and ministered to women in thoughtful ways. https://www.crossway.org/articles/how-jesus-viewed-and-valued-women/

[219] Hebrews 1:3

[220] Jeremiah 29:11

## Attachment disorder, me?!...

I knew nothing about "Attachment Disorder"[221] until my dear friend Rose started to educate me about it. She was driven by love and determined to make a real difference in the lives of children who were unable, because they did not know how, to form healthy emotional connections or attachments.

Doing life with Rose while she fostered, exposed me to many learning opportunities. Situations where she could see past the behavior for what it was - mere leaves on the tree - to dig into its possible roots of fear, want and mistrust, brought added understanding and empathy.

To become aware of what lies underneath a person's behavior is like having a window open into their souls and hearts so it's not an easy or simple task to accomplish. Rose's in-depth knowledge was acquired through extensive reading, research and plenty of real life opportunities for practical application and experimentation (because each unique individual's responses will stem from different attachment styles forged in distinct upbringing circumstances).

The time came when I became a foster carer myself. The organization I worked for provided therapeutic services and I went through continuous, extensive training which included a great deal of information on "Attachment Disorder". It was a season where I learned a lot and grew a lot, and realized I needed to address my own stuff if I wanted to provide any sort of valid therapeutic support to the children or young adults in my care.

---

[221]Attachment disorders occur when a child has been unable to consistently connect with a parent or primary caregiver. If a young child repeatedly feels abandoned, isolated, powerless, or uncared for—whatever the reason—they will learn that they can't depend on others and that the world is a dangerous and frightening place.

Attachment difficulties work on a spectrum. For some the effects are minimal, for others the effects are emotionally traumatic. The more I delved into this, the more I was able to identify patterns in my relational experiences and interactions which revealed some of my own difficulties in forming stable, healthy attachments.

As I said before, my parents did the best they knew and they didn't intentionally set out to hurt me, but I did grow up feeling there was something wrong with me. I was always striving to be loved and accepted but felt powerless to change anything. Comparison, ongoing criticism and conflicting messages about the conditional nature of their love left me confused, and afraid of connection.

These relational dynamics kept me trapped in toxic emotional cycles where the pain of rejection (self-rejection included) was experienced and rehearsed over and over. I used to lock myself up in the bathroom, put a towel in my mouth so no one could hear me, and ugly cry the pain away. Eventually someone gave me my first journal and writing down my frustration, sadness and offense became an outlet for my pain.

Many years later, when I was a teenager, I was prompted by the Holy Spirit to throw away that journal. I didn't know then but it was a prophetic act. It meant I was throwing away the bitterness and the resentment so I could forgive and forget, and willingly choose to look at my parents with different eyes, focused on what they were doing well and committed to love them well too.

*It became safer to feel nothing than to revisit the pain of rejection.*

There was great inner healing when I obeyed the Lord in this, and the way I saw and related to my parents changed significantly. However, when I had to deal with rejection during my first marriage, old wounds were prodded and poked and started to bleed again. Dealing with the pain of rejection not just on a daily basis but multiple times a day, turned into a very traumatic experience. Trauma is not a word I use lightly.

The reenactment of a relational script where inadequacy, powerlessness, and performance-based love and acceptance were constantly on the table, led me on a downward spiral into the belly of pain. Looking back, that's the best way I can describe it. The deep-seated pain of rejection had become a beast which kept devouring me, tearing my heart, my soul (and eventually my body) into pieces. It mauled me and crushed me until I had no joy, no hope and very little will to live left in me, so I did my best to regain power and control in order to escape its claws.

Over and over again I promised my heart I wouldn't put myself in a position where I could be so hurt again. I learned the 'art of emotional withdrawal' and vulnerability stopped being part of my vocabulary: "If I hold back my love for you, then I reduce your power to hurt me. I know you are going to eventually reject me, so I'll just reject you in advance." Those were my unspoken beliefs.

The 'only' problem with this was the deep desire to feel connected, which remained at the very core of my being. We have all been created and designed for connection, so when we try to fight it, we end up fighting and crippling ourselves.

In the previous chapters, you have watched from the front row how God loved me back to trust and tenderness of heart. How His unreasonable, unmerited grace melted my defenses and opened me up so I could hear His voice speaking abundance of life, liberating truth and restored value over me, until I was finally ready to take a calculated risk.

> *I was finally ready to take a calculated risk...*

You might ask, "What do you mean by calculated risk?" I mean I loved and trusted God with all my heart, but it was still very risky for me to trust and love a man with all my heart again. Therefore, I entered this second marriage stepping out on God's words (they were like a firm rock under my feet), but at the same time, being somewhat doubtful about the caliber of my husband's words and motives. In the unseen depths of my guarded heart I did not believe my husband loved me the way he said he did so, without even realizing it, I was always on the lookout for anything that could justify or substantiate those beliefs.

I know that when I love and give myself unreservedly, I do it in a deeply passionate and wholehearted way. The idea of becoming so vulnerable again, and being hurt, absolutely terrified me! As I was being held emotionally hostage by this conflict - the desire for intimacy as well as the fear of it - my emotional insecurities and my inability to form healthy, consistent attachments became a serious challenge to our connection.

We had more good moments than challenging ones, but occasionally, when faced with situations where communication became awkward, unclear or equivocal, I would quickly go into defensive/offensive mode and allow certain triggers to lead me into *Ambivalent*[222] or *Disorganized*[223] responses: "come here, go away", "I love you, I love you not".

---

[222] Ambivalently attached people have had caregivers who were *on again off again*, inconsistently tending and attuning to the child. Their object relation is "I can want but cannot have." You may observe that in ambivalent attachment styles there is a tendency to be chronically dissatisfied. First, there is a tendency to project their own familial history onto their relationship. Secondly if the other person becomes available, they become unavailable. Unaccustomed to receiving love, having it available doesn't fit their profile of "still wanting". Over time, partners of Ambivalent people can be discouraged by their love being dismissed and the loss of the relationship can be both, the feared and created outcome. (Adapted from https://dianepooleheller.com/attachment).

[223] A Disorganized Attachment style results when caregivers present double-binding messages to children. An example of this is a, "Come here, go away" message. Parents create situations for the child that are unsolvable and unwinnable. When exposed to these impossible-to-resolve situations over and over again the child develops a pattern of not solving problems. When parents set up these interactions that are frightening, disorienting, inherently disorganizing, and which sometimes involve violence, the parents become the source of fear. The disorganized pattern arises in the child when there is a desire to be close to the parent as an object of safety conflicting with a drive to detach from a dangerous and confusing caregiver. For the adult this may mean being held emotionally hostage by the conflict of the desire for intimacy as well as the fear of it. (Adapted from https://dianepooleheller.com/attachment).

At the slightest hint of rejection (or perception of rejection), I would shut down emotionally, willingly choose disconnection and set my "auto pilot" on numbness and apathy. It was safer to feel nothing than to risk revisiting the pain of rejection.

This familiar and dreaded pain evoked memories and feelings of hopelessness, despair and overbearing sadness. Years of recurrent negative experiences would pile up in one single moment and lend it an inexplicable, unreasonable, irrational, crushing weight. This is what trauma does. Suddenly you are back in the dark belly of the beast, torn to pieces again, and you can't even explain it rationally because most of the time the process escalates out of proportion, very quickly, on a subconscious level.

As we faced these relational challenges, the "driving dreams" started to make a lot more sense. I remembered how I drove through old cities and archeological excavation sites and how that actually pointed to revisiting or digging up the past. I had indeed experienced extensive inner healing in my love story with God but there were still deep, traumatic hurts I had experienced in the past, while journeying through life with a man who didn't love me and consistently rejected me, which remained dormant for many years because I didn't have to deal with them while living by myself.

Being in a partnership again meant revisiting and reliving some of those evocative scenarios, and I found out that, in my new story, God wanted to partner with a man filled with the Holy Spirit to bring complete healing and restoration to past hurts and desolation caused by another man.

*The past should not travel into the future with us unless it holds teaching value.*

Things from our past should not travel with us into our future unless they have a teaching value. If what we carry perpetuates cycles of torment and bondage or keeps us from moving forward, then something must be done to cut us loose from the past and propel us towards a different, prosperous future[224]. Attending a particular school of ministry together was a very good start.

## Then there was BSSM[225]

Our time as BSSM students was a very significant, life-changing part of our journey. First year was all about nurturing and establishing our identity in Christ. Mat loved every moment of it, I found it difficult and disconcerting at times, but also beautiful, disarming and full of promise.

I found out I had more inner layers than I thought, and the painful part was relinquishing control of each one of them as the Holy Spirit helped peel them off.

For quite a while I considered the level of vulnerability modeled a bit scary, but I couldn't deny how attractive and moving it was to see leaders, brothers and sisters I respected and honored, sharing their struggles and their processes in such honest, genuine, authentic ways. The power and glory released, the increase of hope and faith, as an effect of individual victories becoming corporate ones, was something I had never witnessed and experienced like this before. And I loved it!

The more I was exposed to it, the more I became profoundly moved and impacted by an atmosphere of grace which was conducive to genuineness and facilitated opportunities for deep healing and restorative, redemptive empowerment.

---

[224] Jeremiah 29:11

[225] Bethel School of Supernatural Ministry

*Do I perform from love and acceptance or for love and acceptance?*

Second year was all about being prepared and equipped for leadership and service and it provided multiple opportunities for a different type of growth. As we were encouraged and trained to move from knowing who we were to expressing our identity through ministry, in a school filled with amazing, gifted and skilled men and women from all over the world, we were constantly faced with the choices to either entertain comparison, or value and celebrate uniqueness and diversity. To perform from love and acceptance, or for love and acceptance.

As my mettle was put to the test and the insecurities which were still repressed started coming to the surface, I didn't like what I saw and, instead of embracing my shortcomings and limitations with a humble and childlike heart (inviting God's power to be made perfect in my weaknesses), I embraced shame, believed its poisoned lies, and found myself struggling with the fear of failure and the fear of man, again. There were more lessons to learn concerning these.

## An upward or downward spiral, what will it be?

I once heard someone bring a teaching on how we, as disciples of Jesus Christ, go through life in an ascending movement[226]. Once in a while we get to step into a lift which causes acceleration by carrying us a few floors above, but those are exceptional moments. What usually happens is a step by step upward movement, where we have the time and opportunity to

---

[226] "But the path of the righteous is like the light of dawn, that shines brighter and brighter until the full day."

(Proverbs 4:18 - NASB)

build and consolidate precept upon precept[227]. The most interesting aspect of this step-climbing analogy unfolded when we considered that we are not moving in a straight line but our ascending journey towards growth takes place on a *spiral staircase*.

I remembered what I had learned in university about the "Spiral Approach"[228] in language learning and it made a lot of sense to me. Repetition has a tremendous impact on our ability not only to acquire new information but to retain it and build on it, layer upon layer.

The only problem with this 'upward spiraling progression' can be the surrounding landscape. We keep envisaging familiar scenarios or circumstances, and sometimes we end up feeling discouraged, because once again we are tackling something we thought, or wished, we were already done with. We fall into this deception without realizing we have actually gone up a loop and

*Our ascending journey towards growth takes place on a spiral staircase.*

our perspective and capacity have been increased and strengthened so we can continue achieving higher levels of breakthrough, which will eventually lead us into the desired outcome of "lacking nothing"[229].

Don't be too hard on yourself when you realize you are reliving familiar relational scenarios or circumstances, but ask the Holy Spirit to give you eyes to see what you have already learnt and how much you have already grown. Your focus will change, your heart will be full of thanksgiving and

---

[227] Isaiah 28:10

[228] The *spiral approach* is a technique often used in teaching or textbooks where first the basic facts of a subject are learned, without worrying about details. Then as learning progresses, more and more details are introduced, while at the same time they are related to the basics which are reemphasized many times to help enter them into long-term memory.

[229] James 1:4

hope, and the stage will be set for you to step up and step into further growth.

I wish I had done that sooner than later. It would have saved me a lot of heartache and pain. Yes, I had experientially learned so much about God's unconditional love and unmerited grace, and in turn got increased freedom and significant inner healing, but there were still debilitating beliefs regarding self-worth, self-hatred and self-righteousness which were buried deep below consciousness and needed to be uprooted so I could continue to climb up.

The new challenges I was forced to face in this particular context exposed many of those beliefs, and at first I worked really hard to cover them up. I was still striving to "get it right once and for all!", so in a state of intermittent frustration, I started bringing judgement upon myself again. Although I did it on a milder level than I used to in the past, I was still trying to achieve on my own, isolated (hiding from scrutiny).

*When we are disconnected from God, we become easy prey to the lies of the enemy.*

These incursions into self-accusation, condemnation and self-righteousness kept me wandering further and further away from God's empowering grace. I felt disconnected from Him and instead of listening to His voice I fell prey to the lies of the enemy. Grace for myself was out of the picture so I wasn't able to extend it to my husband either. I began to entertain and rehearse self-centered, discouraging and hopeless thoughts, and I let offense dwell in and damage my heart again.

It came to a point when I was so consumed by this internal turmoil that I made the decision to go back to what was familiar to me: "I can't do this anymore so I'll just carry on married but I'll do my thing my way and he can do his thing, his way. I'm shutting down love because to love wholeheartedly is a liability I am not willing to embrace anymore!"

The problem was this contradicted everything I had learned and experienced about God's love. His extravagant love is selfless, passionate, relentless and all in. He holds nothing back, He is slow to anger, forgiving and kind[230]. How had I drifted so far away from this truth again?

This was a year where God was wooing us into greater and deeper intimacy with Him and with each other but my lenses got so warped that the more I encountered the perfect, selfless Love of God, the more I felt like I was miles away from being able to love like Him: "I can't love my husband well. I can't love myself well. I can't love you well God. I don't know how to be a good daughter, a good friend and a good leader. How can I be in the ministry and love and lead other people well?! This was all a big mistake. I can't do this. I'm going to give up school", blah, blah, blah...

There I was on that spiral staircase, looking down, dangerously close to the edge, considering whether the best thing to do would be to just throw myself down those stairs, even if it killed me, even if it compromised my calling, my marriage, my purpose and destiny. This was one of the darkest moments of my life. Looking back I know I was under great oppression. I remember I couldn't even think straight and it felt like I was trapped in a dark pit, with no light and no way out, all over again.

## Let there be light!

In that very dark pit, God came in and said "Let there be light!" and it was the beginning of something new. That's who He is and that's what He does: He brings life-giving truth and makes all things new[231].

---

[230] Nehemiah 9:31; Exodus 34:6; Numbers 14:18; Psalm 86:5; Psalm 86:15; Joel 2:13

[231] Revelations 21:1-8

I have set before you life and death, the blessing and the curse; therefore, you shall choose life in order that you may live, you and your descendants, by loving the Lord your God, by obeying His voice, and by holding closely to Him; for He is your life [your good life, your abundant life, your fulfillment]... (Deuteronomy 30:19-20a AMP).

It was Randy Clark's Healing Conference week. As I stood in the queue, waiting to enter the Redding Civic Auditorium, there were groups of other BSSM students praying and blessing the people standing in that long line. One of them approached me and started praying for me. I immediately sensed the presence of the Holy Spirit and I made a joke to let him know I acknowledged God's power in and on him: "The force is mighty with this one!" The truth is that I used humor as a shield, so I didn't have to engage seriously with what was happening, but it didn't work. He smiled, and as he continued to pray and lay his hands on my head, I started shaking under the power of the Holy Spirit.

As the shaking intensified I could clearly hear The Holy Spirit's instructions: "You need to start asking God for what you really want." Deep in my heart I knew what I really wanted. I was tired of feeling disconnected from Him, I missed closeness with Him and I knew I had been the one putting up barriers between us, so I just blurted it out: "I want to be fully surrendered to you! Heart, soul and body."

Immediately after I acknowledged this before the Lord, another student, who had also come to pray for me, gave me a prophetic word: "The Lord is telling me you are going to set the standards high." As soon as he said this I was 'zapped' by a wave of God's power so strongly that I was unable to stand up on my own. Until we got inside the building I had to have one person on each side in order to be able to walk, as I could barely coordinate my movements.

With every part of me experiencing the manifest presence of the Holy Spirit, I continued our inward dialogue. I started questioning my disgust toward my perfectionistic tendencies (as the source of all my unhealthy performance issues), and I enquired: "So, it seems there is nothing wrong with having high standards, and it seems I have been designed to set standards high?..." The Holy Spirit, who knew what was behind that question, replied: "It's not about setting high standards, it's about how you set them." It was clear I didn't know how to do it so I asked Him: "How do we set high standards, God?" "Lovingly and hopefully", He replied. "I don't have, and never had, one thought about you failing, Ana". And I was undone. I remember thinking: "If God believes in me and in my success, who am I to doubt Him and to doubt it?!"

> *"I never had one thought about you failing."*

He stooped down to lift me out of danger from the desolate pit I was in, out of the muddy mess I had fallen into. Now he's lifted me up into a firm, secure place and steadied me while I walk along His ascending path. (Psalm 40:2 - TPT)

The God who makes all things possible continued to pursue me and to reveal deeper layers of His limitless kindness and 'can do' love. Although I had been focused on the 'can't dos' (burdened with shame, consumed by self-reproach), He didn't give up on me. He was determined to snap me out of this afflicting and deceptive episode of 'temporary amnesia'. I had forgotten that our kind and good heavenly Father doesn't just want to do things in us and through us, but also for us and with us. I had to learn how to receive from Him and how to partner with Him. In this process, it has been really helpful to have a husband who is a man after God's heart.

## Washed by the Word

I remember one significant episode where, after a few days of disconnection and apparent apathy (while trying to ignore the underlying emotional and spiritual torment that came with it), I engaged in a conversation with my husband who had been relentless but gentle in the way he had grabbed every little opportunity to pursue me and restore our broken connection.

As a son of God, in close, intimate relationship with his Father, and with a beautiful story of redemption of his own, Mat became a carrier of extravagant hope and joy, and unreasonable kindness and generosity. In other words, he tasted, and has continued to taste God's grace in such a deep way he is able to extend that same grace to those around him.

My *ambivalent* and *disorganized* messages of "come here, go away" or "I love you, I love you not" did not faze him. I know I hurt him many times in the process but Mat was secure in his love: forgiving, determined, faithful and persistent in the way he continuously pursued connection, even when it was not the easiest or most convenient road. And that's why he was the one holding the wheel: no matter how bumpy the road, whenever he started driving we got unstuck and we always ended up moving forward and getting closer.

Journal entry:

*After a week of struggling to believe the best about my husband's heart motives and about the future of my marriage, feeling like we had been striving to communicate effectively for quite a while and not being very successful at it, we finally had a meaningful conversation. Mat initiated it and he made me feel at ease to share the thoughts and beliefs troubling my heart. It was not a perfect conversation but there was genuine listening. Misunderstandings were identified and picked apart and suggestions for ways we could connect throughout the week were made. My mind felt clearer and my heart felt lighter after that.*

*As I turned my attention to the Holy Spirit, the massive wall that had been there for the past 24 hours wasn't there anymore and I started asking the Lord to forgive me for my lack of faith. I asked His forgiveness for my unwillingness to believe for a higher reality, and for having allowed myself to remain stuck in beliefs rooted in fear, in lack and in doom. In His restorative, empowering presence I felt a cry erupt from within: "I am able to build healthy attachments! I was not created for attachment disorder, I was designed to build healthy attachments, I was designed for empathy and compassion! I was created to build healthy attachments!"*

*The Bible was open before me in the book of Ephesians and I started reading chapter 4 where Paul talks about unity in the Body of Christ: Be completely humble and gentle; be patient, bearing with one another in love (v2). Make every effort to keep the unity of the Spirit through the bond of peace (v3). He proceeds to remind us that "there is one body, one Spirit, one hopeful calling, one Lord, one faith, one baptism, one God and Father of all, who is over all and through all and in all" (v.4-6).*

*As I read this, I was reminded of how we were guided by the Holy Spirit to the shop which had the perfect engagement ring: white gold open circle, with both extremities brought and held together by five stones (five small diamonds). We knew this was to be a reminder that our covenant is one of*

When I shut my husband out, I am also shutting out the One who is one with him.

*oneness with each other and the Trinity (later I found out that five is also the number which symbolizes grace). I also remembered some of the lines the Holy Spirit inspired me to add to our wedding vows: "I will intently pursue oneness with God and with you, for you are God's gift to me and I am God's gift to you." In that moment, it became crystal clear that now, having entered into a covenant with this man, before God, I will never be* able to access the fullness of what God has prepared for me if my husband is not included. When I erect a defensive wall to shut him out, I am also shutting out the One who is one with him. That was and is a sobering thought.

> Being part of a covenant means that I will never be able to access the fulness of what God has prepared for me if my spouse is not included.

As I kept reading Ephesians, something else stood out, impressed my spirit and grabbed my soul: "Husbands, love your wives just as Christ loved the Church and gave Himself up for her to make her holy, **cleansing her by the washing with water through the word**..." (Eph 5:25-26). The Holy Spirit whispered "That's what Mat has been doing." I stopped, and suddenly the revelation hit me: "Yes, that's exactly what my husband has been doing, consistently!" He has been speaking truth into my life, calling forth a higher reality, proclaiming the Word over me, washing my heart and soul from the debris of past mistakes and disappointments with words picked from the tree of life. Bringing truth which sets me free, and correction which enables growth. Proclaiming words filled with faith: the substance of things that are not yet as if they were. Mat had been setting higher standards, lovingly and hopefully!

I thanked God with all my heart for giving me a godly husband, a man connected to His heart, and later I shared this revelatory encounter with Mat, and with tears rolling down my cheeks I thanked him for consistently speaking words of life over me, especially when I wasn't able to do it myself.

> God kept highlighting intimacy and deep connection.

Later at church, during the evening service, Bill Johnson talked about "Returning to our First Love". He taught, from personal experience, how to keep moving closer to God, how to keep making choices to leave stuff behind (not just bad *but unnecessary things too) to keep growing and increasing our capacity for more of Him. Where there is growth and increase there is always chaff, therefore, there is always pruning of what needs to be removed and burned out, so growth is not stunted. What was most interesting about what he said that evening, considering what I had experienced a few hours earlier, was that "being pruned, is actually a synonym of listening to God's words because the truth of His word, His counsel, washes us and enables fruitful intimacy":*

The words I have spoken over you have already cleansed (or pruned)[232] you. So you must remain in life-union with me (grafted into me), for I remain in life-union with you. For as a branch severed from the vine will not bear fruit, so your life will be fruitless unless you live your life intimately joined to mine. (John 15:3-4 TPT)

*At the end of the night, another student prayed for me in the prayer line, he suddenly grabbed my left hand and pointed to the finger with my engagement ring and wedding band and asked me: "Are you ready to go on a honeymoon?" Intimacy and deep connection, God kept highlighting them.*

## Vulnerability, the road to restore and deepen connection

"We cultivate love when we allow our most vulnerable and powerful selves to be deeply seen and known. Connection is the energy that is created between people when they feel seen, heard and valued - when they can give and receive without judgement." Brené Brown

In a day and age where people have almost unlimited access to information, in its many combined forms, there is the illusion we know

---

[232] The Passion Translation Bible: Inserted on the footnotes as a synonym.

certain individuals well, just because we see them and read about their lives regularly. Nothing could be further from the truth. Not even when we consider the most popular so called "reality shows".

These narratives are scripted and edited to include only the best or most engaging parts of the story. The goal is to broadcast a biased perspective and send a particular message to the viewers/readers to elicit certain emotions or reactions, and to influence the way they think about someone or something. These are deceptive and sometimes manipulative pieces of information, and this can only be pulled off because of the distance we have from the subject or subjects.

Proximity changes everything. However, geographical proximity isn't always synonymous with emotional proximity. We can live in the same house, eat at the same table and even sleep in the same bed and exist in separate inner worlds which never touch. Behind tall walls and securely locked doors, we can

> *Shame feeds on the fear of disconnection.*

hide from prying eyes, guard shameful or painful secrets and protect the tender, wounded and raw parts of our internal landscape.

That's why it takes a great deal of courage to give someone else the keys to those doors and let them into the depths of our under-construction-self. In her book "The Power of Vulnerability"[233], Brené Brown paints a brilliant picture of the priceless value we bring into our lives and the lives of those around us when we embrace vulnerability.

Shame feeds on the fear of disconnection, "If you knew the real me you would reject me", so we end up fabricating a persona and experiencing the illusion of connections which are unfulfilling, because they too are

---

[233] Book overview
https://i.pinimg.com/736x/22/2a/3a/222a3a115d2c5d75bdf58ce54c596816--the-power-of-vulnerability-brene-brown-quotes-vulnerability.jpg

fabricated and therefore unable to quench our deep need for intimate and meaningful relationships.

Healthy, intimate connections give purpose and meaning to our lives but in order for a genuine connection to happen we have to allow ourselves to be really seen. True connection happens as a result of authenticity, when I let go of a projected, interpreted or filtered representation of myself, to be the real me.

> *True connection happens as a result of authenticity.*

I'm aware there are environments which are not 'vulnerability friendly'. When we don't feel safe, or we feel like we are constantly under attack, we don't want to be seen. On the contrary, becoming invisible might be the best protection we have against potential hurtful, abusive and even traumatic interactions. When that is the case, it is wise to be prudent and mindful of the magnitude of the risks we face before stepping out on a frail limb.

However, even in safe environments, there is always an element of risk when we choose to be vulnerable. We can find the courage to step into it if the benefits outweigh the risks. I can't fully predict what someone's response will be when I reveal my real self and disclose my authentic memoirs, but I have a relational story with them which tells me they are kind and respectful. Our story also tells me that, not only they didn't reject me the last time I fully showed up, but we have grown closer and our connection became deeper and stronger.

I have experienced great breakthrough and growth as I have gradually invited my husband into all the previously locked rooms of my heart and my soul, and we have experienced deeper and stronger levels of connection in the process. However, my increased willingness to be vulnerable has been proportional to the relational equity he has gradually and consistently built during our partnership. Building trust is a fundamental part of this transaction. "All dysfunctional relationships are rooted in broken trust," [234] all attachment disorders and relational difficulties stem from experiences where the "cycle of trust"[235] has been broken.

*Building trust is a fundamental part of this transaction.*

We come into this world completely vulnerable and dependent on others for all our basic needs to be met. When we cry to express or communicate our needs, whether they are met, neglected or punished, we begin to interpret ourselves (self-worth perception) and the world around us according to the type of responses we get.

As we grow up, the messages which are more consistently reinforced in the way others interact with us and respond to our expressed needs will determine our beliefs about ourselves and others: whether we believe we can or can't trust others to meet our needs (no strings attached), whether we are valuable or good enough to receive other people's attention and support, and whether the world is a safe and nurturing place or a punitive and abusive one.

As adults, set in our own ways, we have adopted models of interaction and communication which have best suited us, for whatever reason. Our personal history is full of experiences that have shaped the way we communicate or conceal our needs, and the way we function to have them met.

You know enough of my personal story leading to my second marriage to understand why I had given up on vulnerability, but the next part of this story brings with it a delightful and glorious contrast which redeemed and changed my past familiar relational scripts.

---

[234] Danny Silk, "People Helping People" course, session 4 - LOP Academy

[235] https://medium.com/@danaecouturewoodall/the-trust-cycle-6e4d1e2d4115 (simple informative article about the cycle of trust)

From the very beginning of our marriage Mat has been invested in pursuing connection. He is intentional about it and his commitment has been consistently and tangibly expressed in the simple moments and things of life. The way he brews me a nice coffee (even though he is not a coffee drinker[236]), the way he opens doors for me (even the car door), the way he cooks a lovely meal or shares domestic chores with me, the way he carries bags for me, the way he makes shopping feel relaxed and fun, the way he hugs me, kisses me and holds my hand throughout the day, the way he is generous and passionate when we are physically intimate, the way he makes me laugh and the way he really listens.

> *Past, familiar relational scripts redeemed.*

At first, I found it really difficult to receive some of these practical gifts. I had never been loved this way, so well. I told him "he didn't have to do it, I could do it myself", but his answer was always the same disarming one: "I want to do this for you, I love you, let me show you I love you."

Day after day, I experienced his selfless love firstly in the way he was attentive and willing to meet my needs. Having the cycle of trust restored brought confidence and self-worth, assurance of love and the security to break off shame and choose authenticity.

"Each display of love, no matter how seemingly small, is a powerful act of spiritual warfare that removes anxiety from the environment, replaces it with freedom and safety, and invites each person to bring his or her best self forward in the relationship."[237]

The safer I felt, the more vulnerable and authentic I was able to be, which meant I was able to fully show up and freely express my needs or issues,

---

[236] I know...unbelievable! (For Mat "revival in a cup" can only happen with proper English tea).

[237] Danny Silk in "Keep Your Love On"

but also my dreams and desires. The more information Mat was given, the more intentional he could be in his responses to please me and meet even deeper needs.

> *Constructive communication and feedback became a key to fully know and to be fully known.*

Obviously this was not a one sided process. It worked both ways. Constructive, engaged communication and feedback became a key to fully know and be fully known. The fact I was carrying so much emotional baggage was not something clear or outspoken at first. It took many hours of difficult but rewarding dialogue, where the Holy Spirit was always welcomed to bring His wisdom and discernment, so that patterns could be identified, and fears, wrong beliefs and self-preserving motivations could be exposed and brought into the light.

It wasn't, and it isn't always easy, in fact it can be very uncomfortable and painful at times, but the more we do it the more it becomes natural and normal to us. The next journal entry is a perfect example of our process.

Journal entry:

*After a long conversation with Mat I realized that I am still acting in some ways like a powerless person, not being assertive because I'm afraid of being considered bossy or overbearing. I don't fully show up but then I end up blaming and resenting him and going into passive aggressive, proud, self-preserving mode.*

*Mat's ability to listen well and articulate some of those things in a language that is not offensive, but still not compromising of the truth, brings so much clarity. His pastoral heart has enlarged and his capacity and skill level has increased. I can see his assertiveness and his spiritual authority increasing too. The way he conducted himself in a conversation where a very hurt me was ready to argue and fight, was exemplary. His patience, kindness and insight completely disarmed me, helped me tidy my own thoughts, and calmed me down. I was able to listen to the Holy Spirit again and He led me to recollect the moments when I could have been clearer and more assertive, but instead I had chosen to embark on a familiar cycle of victimization. I thanked God for the insight and for the amazing husband he has given me, and once again I realized the significance of His wise counsel instructing me, from the beginning, to allow Mat to do the 'driving'.*

*I can understand now that my need to take the wheel was and is fear based. Self-reliance is birthed from the fear of trusting and being disappointed. I'm meant to drive too but only when I'm healthy, when I'm not just focused on firmly holding on to the wheel 'for dear life' but I can actually let go of perfection and celebrate progress. Then, I will enjoy the ride without losing sight of our destination. To hold on tight is still about control and therefore it is still selfish and self-centered, because it's rooted in self-preservation, which again is rooted in fear. Mat told me this is a giant I must run at.*

*Later when I was inspired to act as a powerful person, clear and assertive at all times, I told my husband jokingly: "I'm not sure you will like the powerful me...you have unleashed a monster." Without a moment of hesitation he looked me in the eyes and replied: "No I haven't." When he said that, once again the way he looked into my soul, spoke volumes.*

## Perspective Matters

The way my husband kept looking at me with kindness and faith, set a new standard and challenged me to change the way I saw myself. In the process, it has also impacted the way I look at him, and consider him. This gradual change of perspective has been something else I cannot take full credit for, not only because it has been initiated by Mat but, because its success is only possible through the empowering of the Holy Spirit.

His empowering presence is not just a good idea, an abstract philosophical or intellectual concept, or the outcome of some religious discipline. It's a reality experienced from the inside out, a precious gift partaken within a close and honest relationship which impacts and changes the way we think and approach the smallest, most practical things in our daily lives.

I remember one day feeling really annoyed with Mat because he had put the laundry in the dryer, did not tell me he had done it, and then forgot to take it out. Not really a big problem. It even sounds a bit silly when I explain it like this, but it really got to me. Efficiency makes my heart happy and I can't completely explain why, but I utterly detest even the idea of waste.

*His empowering presence impacts and changes the way we think about the most practical things in our daily lives.*

When we take the clothes out of the dryer straight away, fold them and hang them, they look fine and ready to wear. To have, as the final outcome, very creased clothes, made me feel like the whole process was a waste of time and electricity.

"This is SO annoying!", I blurted out. Nobody was in the room but I felt immediately convicted. I knew I was not meant to harbor those critical thoughts and negative, burdensome feelings about my husband. I also knew I couldn't change that mind frame on my own. I turned my attention to God and said: "I think I'm supposed to give this annoyance to you...You are the one who has offered to carry burdens. Can I just give this annoyance to you?" And He said "no"! He really got me by surprise. I wasn't expecting that answer but I felt in my spirit that He was enticing me to carry on with the conversation, and I did. "How am I supposed to do it, then?" The Holy Spirit proceeded to explain that it is an exchange. I don't just give the annoyance to Him, I'm supposed to ask Him "What do you give me in return?" When I did, He filled me straight away with love and patience, and with a nurturing, loving kindness for my husband.

I remember pondering on the fact that we all forget things, get things wrong, make mistakes, disappoint people: why was I being so hard on him because of something so insignificant? Thankfulness and empathy were back on the table as I thanked God for having given me a husband who willingly helps me with the house chores.

There and then, the Holy Spirit revealed the value and power of this exchange in every other area of my life, whenever I'm faced with situations or challenges which defy and undermine the mind of Christ, and His divine nature indwelling in me. As I grow in the knowledge of Him, such knowledge is supposed to impact and reshape the way I do life and relationships with practical, tangible displays of grace and peace[238].

As I remained in this conversation with God, I realized once again how it is very much about relinquishing control. I can't fix myself but I can trust that God has the power and the willingness to do it, and act accordingly. I just need to stop, invite Him into whatever is happening and open up my heart for this exchange, because I really can't work or strive for the fruits of the Spirit, they are a gift, not a reward.

> *I can't work or strive for the fruits of the Spirit, they're a gift, not a reward.*

In this exchange, we stop ourselves because we acknowledge that His will and His ways are so much better, so much higher, wiser and perfect. We remain grafted, connected and come to Him to say:

*"I give you this; This is not a fruit of the Spirit, this is a fruit of the flesh; This is not who I am, this is not what I have been made and designed for. I give you this, Lord. I am supposed to live by the Spirit and I want to see the fruits of the Spirit popping up on my branches, so, what do you have for me, Lord? What do you want to give me in return?"*

---

[238] 2 Peter 1:2-7

And then, believing that He really does give of Himself, I position my heart to receive. It's that simple, because He made it simple.

I've said it before and I'll keep on saying it, that's who He is, that's what He does: "He makes all things new"[239]. Ultimately, deep inner healing and full restoration are enabled and empowered by God's redemptive grace, freely given and available to be apprehended by faith.

What do you believe about God and about yourself? Because of His redemptive grace we can now see ourselves through the eyes of Jesus (and His eyes always reflect the eyes of the Father). If you can see it, you will believe it, be it and do it!

"Grace is the empowering presence of God that enables you to become the person that He sees when He looks at you." (Graham Cooke)

We keep coming back to this because it's really the heart of the matter. Can you see God for who He is: loving, good, kind, powerful, brilliant and perfect in all of His ways? In His brilliance He planned to save and restore humankind back to the original glory[240] in a way which allows Him to see Jesus when He looks at us![241] Can you see yourself through God's eyes? Can you see the people who share or shared life with you through God's eyes? If you can't, ask Him to perform 'spiritual eye surgery' on you. I guarantee it will not only change your perspective but it will change your life: it will heal your past, transform your present and lay a firm foundation to expand your creative potential to build a prosperous future.

**"When you look at a field of dandelions, you can either see a hundred weeds, or a thousand wishes."** [242]

---

[239] Isaiah 43:18–19; Revelation 21:5; Isaiah 65

[240] Isaiah 43:7; 2 Corinthians 3:18

[241] Colossians 3:3; Galatians 3:26-28

[242] Unknown author

# Q & A

## M y s e l f  &  G o d

❏ This time we are going to revisit some of the questions asked throughout this chapter.

● What do you think your predominant attachment style is? Open this link to find out: https://dianepooleheller.com/attachment-test/

● Remember, we are not locked-in to our original attachment patterns; God wants to heal and restore you. If this is the case, ask the Holy Spirit to show you what is preventing you from creating secure attachments and ask for His guidance in breaking those patterns or cycles. Take notes.

● Are you focused on the "cans" or the "can't dos"?

● If you're focused on the impossibilities ask the Holy Spirit to reveal the root of your perspective. Then, ask Him to give you His perspective. Take notes.

● Can you **see** yourself **through God's eyes**? Ask the Holy Spirit to open your heart and open your eyes. What do you see? Write it down.

● Can you **see** those who share or shared life with you **through God's eyes**? This time, pick from one to three close people (make sure you include your spouse/ex). Ask the Holy Spirit to open your heart and open your eyes. What do you see? Write it down.

● Have you experienced greater freedom and clarity in your mind and healing in your heart and soul while seeing through God's eyes?

- Make a list with the Holy Spirit of the new possibilities you can see in your personal and relational present and future circumstances.

# T o g e t h e r

*(For those who want to work towards the restoration or improvement of their marriage)*

❏ In this session you will be sharing with your spouse what you have realized and discovered in your individual reflective time with God.

- Share with your spouse what the Holy Spirit revealed to you regarding your attachment style.

- Share with your spouse what the Holy Spirit revealed to you regarding your "can/can't do" perspective and His perspective.

- Share with your spouse what God revealed when you looked at yourself and others (especially your spouse), through His eyes.

- Share with your spouse if (and how) you have experienced increased clarity and inner healing.

- Share with your spouse your God-inspired list of new possibilities.

✦ Draw, paint or graphically design your own "Tree of Life" and fill it with big fruits (big enough to be used as speech bubbles). In each fruit write God's words over your present and future, individually and as a couple).

# LifeLine

Revelation & Transformation log        ____/____/____

"A new commandment I give to you, that you love one another: **just as I have loved you, you also are to love one another.** By this all people will know that you are my disciples…"

(John 13:34-35)

# 11 Keys for Loving Well

## (Written by Mat Redding)

*"Husbands, love your wives, just as Christ loved the church and gave himself up for her"*

(Ephesians 5:25).

In this chapter, we'll be looking at practical ways we can love our partner well. For some it's immediate, right now advice. For others it's a testimony speaking to your future: the mistakes, hurts or failures of past relationships don't define the bright future ahead, where you love well, and are loved well. I haven't always known how to love other people well. I've gone on a gradual learning journey, and it's one I'm still on. Some of the painful parts of life, like divorce, may have been avoided if I'd done things differently, but the only reason to look back on life is not for regret or recrimination, but to

*Loving is more important than winning.*

learn to do things better in the future. Don't be consumed by hurt, by might-have-beens or by bitterness, rather be motivated to love someone else well in future. I enjoyed my first marriage, and didn't want it to end, but it did. Blaming my ex-wife, or blaming myself, are not going to change that. I learned that loving is more important than winning, especially in discussions with people I love.

To love anyone else really well, we start from a foundation of two things: understanding we are loved completely and unconditionally; and loving ourselves with kindness and grace. We are taught to "love your neighbor as yourself"[243], so loving ourselves is a prerequisite to loving others.

*Loving ourselves is a prerequisite to loving others.*

You are loved completely by God. His love and approval of you is there already, and when you do the right thing in response to His kindness and love, it doesn't

make Him love you more, as He loves you completely already. "But God demonstrates his own love for us in this: While we were still sinners, Christ died for us"[244]. A logical consequence of this is by our failings we can't decrease God's love for us either. We are, however, transformed further into His likeness when we experience further the kindness He has for us. His kindness brings us to repentance[245], which is a change of thinking, and

---

[243] Matt 22:39

[244] Rom 5:8

[245] Rom 2:4

we know we are transformed by the renewing of our mind[246], so any encounter with His kindness changes us irrevocably.

> ## Any encounter with His kindness changes us irrevocably.

I've learned to love myself better, which makes me better able to love my wife. I actually like myself now. When I succeed, or make progress, I celebrate myself, and consequently I'm not comparing so much. When I fail, I deliberately celebrate the times that week I got it right, not the time I got it wrong. This motivates me to do better in future, far more than trying to control myself using guilt and shame at my failings. I think it's a lot closer to how God looks at me, and the grace He has for me, since he put me into Christ[247]. If anyone is in Christ, that person is a new creation[248], and God isn't looking at the old one.

Love is characterized by two things: feelings and choices. I propose the deeper and more meaningful the love, the more it is led by choices, with feelings following them. More superficial kinds of love are characterized by feelings leading, and choices tagging along behind. Here are some keys for putting your choice to 'love well' above your feelings.

## "I want you, but I love you more than I want you"

I used this phrase many times in the months of our engagement. In previous times I hadn't done well in maintaining purity early in relationships, and with Ana I was determined I would honor her in this way as we prepared for our wedding. When my resolve was stretched it was helpful to acknowledge I desired my wife to be, had passion for her. But I wasn't focused on that, I had my eyes on something higher: my love was greater than my need or desire. When we are focused on an issue or a problem it

---

[246] Rom 12:2

[247] 2 Tim 1:9
[248] 2 Cor 5:17

can seem insurmountable, but when we focus our minds on the truth, on something higher, the solution or the breakthrough is no longer eclipsed. It's a practical application of "set your hearts on things above … set your minds on things above, not on earthly things."[249] Having a higher goal to set our mind on is far more powerful than focusing on avoiding temptation. The vision we have for the positives in our relationship will give us strength and purpose. If we don't have an end in mind, which we are aiming for, we will struggle[250].

## Keeping Your Beliefs On

Maintaining high beliefs, about myself and my wife, has been key to inculcating trust and consistency in our marriage. Allowing our beliefs to reduce when we are tired, disappointed, hurt or busy is not helpful in loving well. At these moments it is helpful to realize our judgment is affected by these things, so we aren't blaming someone else for normal bodily processes in ourselves. If you're getting 'hangry', eat something! If you're tired, take a break or plan to rest well.

We first have to really believe in ourselves, as it's impossible to consistently do what we don't believe we are. Saying out loud: "I have what it takes to be a great spouse" is a good start. I don't say it to convince anyone else, but to convince and encourage myself.

*Don't allow your past to limit your future.*

If we allow our past to put limits on what we believe about ourselves, we will likely repeat the same mistakes in our future. If we start to speak out something higher than we've experienced, we plant seeds for our future which will grow and bear fruit in time. It's a practical application

---

[249] Col 3:1-2

[250] Prov 29:18

of faith. Our aim is to have a high level of belief and faith in our partner, but we also need to have faith in ourselves. The belief we have in ourselves cannot be based in past experiences, otherwise the mistakes and shortcomings will kill it off. Our belief in ourselves has to be based in how God sees us and considers us. When he looks at us he sees us "in Christ"[251], and instead of viewing us through our failings, he longs to fill in the gaps where we don't look like Jesus yet, "complete in Christ"[252].

> *It's not our job to fix our spouse, but to love them and believe in them.*

"But when He, the Spirit of truth, comes, He will guide you into all the truth"[253]. Understanding it's not our job to fix our spouse, but to love them and believe in them, is an important revelation. Trusting the Holy Spirit to do that job can be uncomfortable, particularly if we're used to subtly using guilt to conform our partner's behavior to what we're expecting. If you do this to your partner then it's likely you do it to yourself too.

Really believing in someone we love can be scary at first, but it's always worthwhile. I had to believe I could get fitter and lose weight after an extended period of relative inactivity. Without a change in belief any effort I exerted would be of limited effectiveness. What works for us is also true in others: trying to change people's actions without helping them to change their beliefs won't bring lasting transformation.

---

[251] Col 3:3

[252] Col 1:28

[253] John 16:13

## Loving Through Disappointment

Relationships of all types usually go through a three-stage process: initially there is excitement, but in most relationships disappointment will occur at some stage. This is normal, but it's what we do at this critical juncture which defines the future of the relationship. Following any disappointment we can choose disengagement, or we can press in for growth and increased depth in the relationship. In our marriage I have been intentional about pressing in for connection during times when disengagement was the easy and habitual go-to we both would default to. Changing those habits takes time and perseverance, but above all intentionality. If we really want a deeply connected relationship, then it's during those uncomfortable times of disconnection we have to press in with kindness and love. In doing so consistently we create a new normal. It helped that we had agreed in our marriage vows to pursue oneness with God and with each other, so we knew what we were aiming for.

Getting my own motivation right was critical for creating a safe and nurturing environment for connection. If I tried to break through the wall of disconnection, but I was still harboring annoyance or frustration inside, it was unlikely to go well and build improved connection for the future. My role is to love, not to demonstrate I'm right. It's to break down a wall of silence not to build my own. It's in these moments we get to demonstrate something higher than we're feeling or experiencing. Our feeling of

*My role is to love, not to demonstrate I'm right.*

disappointment doesn't get to drive our actions or thoughts if we have a deliberate, higher purpose in mind. If we are concentrating on the feeling we would hope to overcome it's not terribly effective, but if we concentrate on the higher truth or purpose, usually love in some form, then we'll start to think, and do, something better.

## Choosing Engagement

You have a choice. In marriage we can't afford disengagement. I can put up with disengagement and distance in my marriage, sometimes it's easier than confronting the issues and pressing past

> *In marriage we can't afford disengagement.*

an emotional wall, in myself or my wife. It may be easier, or our habit, but it's not healthier. When Ana and I first married it wasn't long before some deep issues came to the surface for my wife, even as early as the honeymoon. I knew my comfortable, habitual reaction of ignoring the sense of disconnectedness until she sorted herself out, wasn't the best way forward. I gave her space but gently gave repeated opportunities for communication about how she was feeling and why. In the first few months these episodes of disconnection would last up to a week, but gradually they reduced in frequency and length. Now they are not so common, and we have developed ways to communicate so they are fleeting. The keys were:

- Believing in our connection, even when it was broken.
- Not blaming.
- Taking responsibility for repairing connection.
- Realizing fixing our connection and loving her doesn't equate to fixing her behavior.
- Being patient.
- Listening more than talking.
- Believing in my wife more than she believes in herself, being her greatest cheerleader.
- Speaking out the truth of who God says she is, what she's made for and capable of.

## Fostering a Sense of Togetherness

In the first year of our course at ministry school, we went with our revival group (a group of 65 students who have a dedicated pastor) to a high ropes course. We'd been married for just over a year by then, so we were still getting to know one another. The ropes course is on two levels, and we began on the lower level. As our group of about eight or ten students went across, doing team exercises and challenges, I had so much fun, leaping, jumping, bouncing and laughing the whole way. I was blissfully unaware of my wife's feelings. I had no idea she felt unsafe, exposed, nervous or disregarded by me in the process. As we finished the lower level of the ropes course we had a conversation about it, and I became increasingly aware, which didn't feel so blissful. She told me she wouldn't be doing the second level. It was clear she felt like a failure, inadequate and less than all the others who were continuing to the higher level. My encouragement at that point was ineffective, as I had unwittingly contributed to the problem. To be effective in our encouragement it is important to build trust. When trust is broken, encouragement is ineffective.

Over the next year there were many opportunities to build trust and understanding, and then an opportunity for redemption and healing presented itself. We were going back to the ropes course in second year! This time, encouragement and affirmation paid off, as my wife's initial "I'm not going" changed, with the assurance I'd be there and would remain at her side supporting her and believing in her the whole time. It wasn't about me the second time, how much fun I could have, or how much excitement I was going to get out of it, but it was a far more satisfying experience as I saw my wife get breakthrough and healing. Our connection was strengthened that day.

When Jesus said "And surely I am with you always, to the very end of the age,"[254] He was talking about those difficult times. When we allow Him in to share in those experiences, He doesn't disappoint us, but helps us to

---

[254] Matt 28:20

grow and to heal in them. I'd learned another way to love my wife as Christ loved the church, and it helped both of us.

## Learning to Love Without Conditions

I've been on a journey of learning to love my wife without conditions. I never set out to put conditions on my love, or to withhold affection in subtle ways when she didn't do what I wanted her to do. I look for times when I do that, and deliberately love, intentionally and on purpose. It started when I realized I was disconnecting emotionally when she did, in the early days of our marriage. It's easy to find reasons and justification for small actions and attitudes which withhold love in certain areas. I was giving her time and space, letting her sort herself out, or process her emotions. What I wasn't doing was loving in a connected, relational way. There will always be reasons to be offended at some point in a relationship. Learning to love unconditionally is a journey where we become less and less offendable. It's the way God loves us, and as we stay connected to Him, we demonstrate more of His nature. "Just as the Father has loved Me, I have also loved you; abide in My love." [255] [Note: I'm not saying we shouldn't have boundaries in our relationships, but they should be there to guard us against abusive behaviors. As our relationships become healthier less boundaries are necessary.]

> *Learning to love unconditionally is a journey where we become less and less offendable.*

---

[255] John 15:9

## Not Waiting for Perfection to Celebrate Progress and Growth

The nature of grace is to focus on progress and growth, not waiting for perfection before we celebrate people around us. More subtle, but even more important, is how we speak to, and encourage, ourselves. When we fail, how do we react on the inside? Look for your own progress and celebrate it, then you'll be able to celebrate the people closest to you. I've been approaching failures with this attitude, and it's been transformative. Instead of condemning myself for failing one day I deliberately celebrate succeeding on six days. If I'm starting from zero, I celebrate succeeding on just one day, because I'm progressing. Having a mindset of celebrating progress is powerful in removing condemnation and self-accusation from our thinking, including the pernicious thought, "I should have achieved more by now."

> *Grace doesn't wait for perfection to celebrate progress and growth.*

At the same time as deliberately celebrating my own progress, I've been doing the same for Ana. Often this emerges as I challenge her thinking when she is self-accusatory or condemnatory. I used to be uncomfortable whenever Ana said how much less she thought negatively about people or situations (she was considering her progress), in case she thought she was OK and didn't have to try to improve any more (I was focused on how much more change was needed for perfection). This wasn't very effective in encouraging change. Now I celebrate her progress and cheer her on. It's a powerful and empowering way of thinking.

## Deliberately Speaking with Kindness, on the Inside as well as Outwardly

Having begun to speak to myself with grace, I am enabled to not just treat other people with grace externally but to have grace internally. It's a transformation of our inner, first reactions, and it's growing. When something happens in my marriage, or in another relationship, and I notice I'm reacting on the inside with some impatience or annoyance, it gives me a great opportunity to upgrade the first reactions I have, to those of love, patience, kindness, etc. Once we have got in the habit of applying self-control to what we say outwardly, speaking kindly and without impatience or annoyance, it's time to go after what we are thinking in those very first reactions.

> *It's time to go after what we are thinking in our very first reactions.*

It is, after all, through the renewing of our mind that we are transformed[256]. We're kind, loving, and patient, it's our new nature in Christ, so we get to cultivate that fruit[257] in our thinking, and cooperate with the Holy Spirit as He prunes the vine of our internal reactions, "every branch that does bear fruit he prunes so that it will be even more fruitful"[258].

## Taking responsibility for my own attitudes and happiness

I was taking a flight recently and, as always, the safety instructions included the part about the oxygen masks, with the usual reminder to put on our own oxygen mask first before helping others. It's not unusual to have an attitude of trying to meet an expectation of making our partner happy, and putting this priority above our own happiness. After all, surely the definition of selfishness would be to prioritize my own happiness above my wife's? Yes, that is true, but it is not my wife's responsibility to make me happy, nor is it mine to make her

> *Happiness is an inside job.*

---

[256] Rom 12:2

[257] Gal 5:22

[258] John 15:2

happy. Happiness is an inside job, true joy isn't dictated by outside circumstances, which is why we can be joyful when circumstances are not conducive. When I took responsibility for my own happiness, mental well-being, and for my own attitude, it meant I wasn't so easily sidetracked from my own peace and contentment by other people's moods. If we realize we are powerful to control our own inner reactions then we become more reluctant to cede that power to others, or to circumstances. I'm not saying I don't care about my wife's, or other people's, happiness. Of course I do, but I recognize it's not my responsibility, but theirs, and my job is to help them maintain it, not to take on the pressure of keeping them happy at all times. Also I can't be a positive influence if I lose my own peace and joy in my concern for other people's. I have to put on my own oxygen mask first. [Note: I'm not saying we shouldn't be attentive and caring about others' happiness.]

## Transforming our inner attitudes

If we really want to learn to love at a higher level, it's helpful to go after our inner thoughts, not just the outward actions and words. "The mouth speaks what the heart is full of"[259]. We can try to hide our first reactions of annoyance or impatience, but some of those things will be evident to the listener, whether our words say it directly, or whether we restrain ourselves. It's great when we progress from reacting outwardly without much love, to the restraint of waiting until we are calm and can speak in a more loving manner. We celebrate that, it's a massive step forward. But don't think it's the final destination. Removing annoyance, impatience and offence from our inner reactions is the final goal. Realizing we're in training for patience, love, endurance, and even longsuffering, in every relationship,

*We're in training for patience.*

---

[259] Luke 6:45

but especially in covenant partnership, will transform the way we think as well as the way we speak.

It's one of the keys I've used in learning to love my wife well in my second marriage. Many of these keys I wish I had known years before in my first marriage. I didn't, and it's ok. We always need to extend grace to ourselves, and just do our best where we're at, to celebrate our progress when we make a step in the right direction, and not condemn ourselves when we stumble. When we can do that we're in a much better position to really extend grace to our partner. A divorced man is just a man God is in the process of restoring. [Note: I'm not saying we should wait for our inner attitudes to change before we exercise self-control in what we say or do outwardly.]

## The power of changing beliefs and making declarations

"The tongue has the power of life and death, and those who love it will eat its fruit"[260]. Many of us have experienced the destructive power of words spoken to us, by a teacher, a parent or a friend. More powerful still is the consistent affirmation and encouragement we can receive from positive words, words which carry the power of life in them. It's great when other people speak such words over us, but we don't have to wait for that to happen, we can declare words of life over ourselves, bringing our experience up higher by our words: "Let the weak say, 'I *am* strong'"[261].

*Our life-filled words bring transformation in our lives.*

It's not a denial, but speaking life into ourselves. "When we put bits into the mouths of horses to make them obey us, we can turn the whole animal.

---

[260] Prov 18:21

[261] Joel 3:10

Or take ships as an example. Although they are so large and are driven by strong winds, they are steered by a very small rudder wherever the pilot wants to go. Likewise, the tongue is a small part of the body, but it makes great boasts. Consider how a great forest is set on fire by a small spark"[262]. Our life-filled words are a spark setting a fire of renewal of our minds[263], which brings transformation in our lives. If we want to see transformation in ourselves and our relationships, we need to change what we think and believe, about ourselves and others. One way to accelerate this is by making declarations of the truth of who God says we are, and who he says those around us are too. [Note: I'm not saying we shouldn't be doing practical things to improve our situation alongside making declarations.]

Declarations to get Truth into me:

- I have what it takes to be a great spouse.
- I love myself really well.
- I love people around me well.
- I care for myself physically, emotionally, spiritually.
- I am able to respond with love no matter the circumstances.
- I am patient; kindness flows out of me.
- I'm increasingly learning to love unconditionally.

---

[262] James 3:3-5

[263] Rom 12:2

## Practical Wisdom

**Love languages**[264] - If you want to love someone well, it's very helpful to find out their love languages, and those things which you can do practically which mean a lot to them. It's not always a complicated thing: my wife feels really loved when I scratch her back, so I do it almost every day, whether I'm tired, or not. It makes her feel special and valued.

**Prioritize Important Relationships** - one way to work out how to do this well is by considering different people's closeness and access to us using 'circles of intimacy'[265]. This can be helpful in deciding how close we want to keep different people in our life, deliberately spending more quality, intimate time with some, but limiting the access others have in order to value and protect our relationships with those closest to us.

**Active Listening** - A skill used in coaching is active listening, but many aspects of it are very helpful in our closest relationships. In particular, it informs the types of questions we ask, and how we check we are understanding not only communication of information, but also feelings. There are several different models for active listening, but with practice it can enhance all our interactions, both personal and professional. My wife has already made mention of it in a previous chapter, and a quick web search will bring up useful articles and podcasts.

---

[264] www.5lovelanguages.com

[265] https://planinstitute.ca/wp-content/uploads/2017/03/Worksheet-4-Relationship-Circles.pdf

> *It takes deliberate practice to change your thinking habits.*

I hope you've found some helpful tools and ways of thinking here, to apply into your own life and relationships. Remember it takes deliberate practice to change your thinking habits, and it's really afterwards that lasting change will come in your actions and consequently in your relationships. Give yourself time and grace to change. As we see in Romans 12:2, we are "transformed by the renewing of your mind", and we take an active and ongoing role in this. The word translated as "transformed" means metamorphosis - the complete, total change which occurs in a caterpillar when it turns into a butterfly. The change which will occur in you as you wrap yourself in the cocoon of truth, what God says about you, how He looks at you with love, approval, and complete acceptance, will indeed transform you in a one-way, irrevocable process. It's impossible for the butterfly to go back to being a caterpillar, and it's the same for you. As this happens, you'll be increasingly empowered and motivated to love those around you at a higher level.

# Q & A

## M y s e l f  &  G o d

- Write down three things you've done well in a relationship. Celebrate yourself - cheer, give yourself a pat on the back, tell yourself well done! They might be ongoing successes or a one-off action. (If you can't think of anything, ask the Holy Spirit to show you.)

- Think of a relationship area you want to get better at. Imagine three ways you could do it well, turn these into declarations like the ones above and speak them out loud. Say them like you really mean them, with enthusiasm. Make these declarations every day for a month and see what happens.

- Pick one of the relationship skills which you identified you want to improve. What practical steps could you take to begin the process? [Example: if you wanted to improve your listening skills, you could read up on how to listen well, or listen to a podcast on active listening.]

- Read the list of fruits of the Spirit in Galatians 5:22-23. Pick three you've demonstrated more than you used to. Reflect, give thanks and celebrate. Pick one to deliberately practice. What beliefs and habits need to change to improve in this area?

# T o g e t h e r

*(For those who want to work towards the restoration or improvement of their marriage)*

- Share your three relationships successes. Celebrate each other. Think of one more thing to add to each other's list and celebrate that too.

- Talk about your declarations list, why you picked those particular ones, and what beliefs you are aiming to upgrade.

- Share what practical steps you identified for the relationship skill you want to work on. Ask your partner if they have any other ideas to do this. Can you think of a way you could support them, or they could support you, as you do this?

- Reread the list of fruits of the Spirit from Galatians 5:22-23. Write down, and then share, three examples which you've seen your partner demonstrate, what the situation was, and why you appreciate that about them.

- Create a special fruit bowl where you can display the fruits of the Spirit you are growing in (they can be replicas of real fruits with emoji stickers, or a new 'breed' of fruits cultivated and produced in the soil of your imagination).

# LifeLine

Revelation & Transformation log          ___/___/___

"I pray that the eyes of your heart may be enlightened in order **that you may know the hope to which he has called you**, the riches of his glorious inheritance in his holy people" (Ephesians 1:18).

# 12 To Be Continued...

"Never be afraid to trust an unknown future to a known God."

(Corrie Ten Boom)

**Tracking Together**

Welcome to the final chapter. It's so good to have you here! For the past eleven chapters you have been watching a condensed movie of my life: my mistakes, my doubts, my learning curves, my epiphanies, my victories and my ongoing relationship with God. The desire of my heart is that you haven't just been tracking with me but you have also been doing some tracking of your own, and have become increasingly aware of the ground you've already covered. Don't feel discouraged or condemned if it seems like you are not really tracking yet. If all you have right now is a clearer perspective and you feel more prepared and inspired to embark on a new joint venture with the Lord, then that is already a reason for celebration. I celebrate your hopeful heart. More importantly, our heavenly Father, the risen King and the brilliant Holy Spirit (together with hosts of angels) celebrate you and the glorious destiny you were created and redeemed for.

## A Tracking Map

I thought it would be helpful to compose a 'tracking map' of my journey with a clear, simple and visible outline of my progression: from where I started, through to all the major defining and transformational moments along the way. As you scroll through it, I would like you to make a mental note every time you can identify goals in your personal journey which may have something in common with mine. The purpose of this exercise is not to show you what you haven't attained yet, on the contrary, it's to help you build a clearer picture of your own progression, how far you have come, where you are positioned, and what possibilities and avenues are still available and open for you. It is really an invitation to envision and anticipate the more God has for you as you continue to track with Him.

> *An invitation to envision and anticipate the more God has for you as you continue to track with Him.*

In Revelations 19:10 it says "The Testimony of Jesus is the Spirit of prophecy", so when you see His miracles, signs and wonders in other people's stories you are being invited and given permission to believe it's available for you too and He wants, and is willing, to do it again. My prayer is that this blesses and encourages you, and builds your faith.

| From... 😔 | to... | 😊 |
|---|---|---|
| ⚠ being **suspicious** about God's motives and carrying an **orphan heart**... | ⇒ | ♡ discovering my **identity** as a loved and accepted **daughter of God**, with an experiential revelation of Him as a **good Father**. |
| ⚠ being dependent on others for value and affirmation, and making **others responsible for my happiness** and success... | ⇒ | ♡ **getting my value from God**, becoming increasingly aware such responsibility starts **within myself,** and becoming proactive about it. |
| ⚠ having a **victim** mentality... | ⇒ | ♡ being empowered and becoming a **powerful,** assertive, responsible and proactive person, a **leader** in my own life. |
| ⚠ being **self-sufficient** (trusting myself, and tentatively God, but not others) ... | ⇒ | ♡ being **dependent on God** and **able to trust** Him and others again. |
| ⚠ being **hidden**, edited and afraid... | ⇒ | ♡ being authentic, seen and **known**. |

| | | |
|---|---|---|
| ⚠ feeling **crushed by**, and crushing others with, **perfectionism** and unreasonable expectations... | ➡ | ♡ **celebrating progress** while still setting high standards lovingly and hopefully. |
| ⚠ being too quick to **judge** and **condemn** myself and others, riddled with **shame**, the **fear** of failure and the fear of man... | ➡ | ♡ **experiencing** the revelation of unmerited, redemptive, liberating, restorative, empowering **grace!** |
| ⚠ striving to **perform for love** and acceptance... | ➡ | ♡ resting in the sufficiency of God's unmerited grace and being able to **freely receive** His love and favor. |
| ⚠ being **disconnected**, or superficially connected... | ➡ | ♡ being meaningfully **connected**. |
| ⚠ being **adrift** through life... | ➡ | ♡ living with a **purpose and a destiny**. |
| ⚠ being **hopeless**... | ➡ | ♡ discovering the **HOPE** of glory within me! |

For all these things, THANK YOU, GOD!

> *If HOPE is your compass, you will keep moving towards your goals.*

Whatever tracking ground you have covered, whatever detour, bypass, mountain, river or valley you are facing in this leg of your spiritual, emotional and physical journey towards health and wholeness, if HOPE is your compass you will keep moving towards your goals. One of my favorite Steve Backlund's quotes is: "If you're believing something which has no hope, then there is a lie attached to it." It's time to demolish old strongholds and disempower destructive lies, believing that, in Jesus, God has made us more than conquerors[266]. Our hope is not just wishful thinking but "Christ in us, the hope of glory!" Whatever we don't know, He knows, whatever we can't, He can, and our story with Him isn't over.

## This is not the final chapter

No, I'm not contradicting myself. This is the final chapter of this book, but it is not the final chapter of my life, nor yours. We remember the past and reflect about the present so we can extract the learning value these narratives have to offer. Empirical[267] learning, passed on, creates legacy, as its value is found in the impact it will have in reshaping our future narratives; our own and our descendants'. There are a bunch of new life chapters God is waiting to write with me and with you.

I wrote this book during our third year of marriage. We loved each other more than we did in the beginning but the initial glamour was gone. In the previous two years, Mat and I had grown closer as a couple and had seen great improvement in the clarity of our communication and the depth of our connection, but not without facing a variety of challenges which arose from our different cultural and linguistic backgrounds, contrasting ways of

---

[266] Romans 8:37-39

[267] Originating in, or based on observation or experience (Merriam-Webster Online Dictionary)

dealing with our emotions and very distinct ways of treating and processing information.

There were also recurrent issues around my self-image which I struggled to openly discuss with my husband. They had been with me for a lifetime and had a great deal of shame and condemnation attached to them. That room of my heart was closed, I put up a sign on the door saying, "under construction", and then I locked it and threw away the key. Mat's intentionality in pursuing connection in a safe, kind, loving and patient way gave him access to that very vulnerable place through momentary windows of opportunity he didn't waste[268].

Through exploration, experimentation and application of the truths found in the Gospel, our relational dynamics gradually changed. Mistakes were made but they were totally worth it, because great progress was achieved. Some of the narratives in this book bear witness of those achievements, for this generation and the generations to come.

The assignment God gave me to write a book about my story was loaded with His goodness. He knew this story would not only be an inspiring, liberating and equipping tool for my readers but it would also become an empowering tool for me. Writing became a creative way to reflect, make sense and keep track of the journey, reminding me of important landmarks, answered prayers and promises fulfilled, and keeping awaited promises in my line of sight, alive and kicking! It enhanced my vision, raised my faith and hope incrementally, increased my joy and sharpened my blade.

Writing this book has also been a platform for encounter. A mental balcony, a higher place where I could look from a distance, no longer immersed in emotional turmoil, and contemplate the bigger picture of who God is, by remembering who He was, has been and continues to be for me, through me, with me and in me.

---

[268] This is a journey we are still on.

There were so many moments where I had to put my laptop down because my heart was so full of gratitude, wonder and awe. The only thing I could do was to cry and worship. New songs were birthed, new praises were uttered, new tears were shed, as my connection with the living God became deeper and stronger. You see, the main love story in this book is not Mat & Ana, but God & Ana and God & Mat. Those are the love stories which will continue to unfold throughout eternity. There are no last chapters in eternity.

*The knowledge of Him keeps us grounded in the promise of Him.*

When I am engaged in a love story with Love Himself, and I can see Him more clearly and know Him and His ways more deeply, every relationship in my life will be profoundly impacted. God's centrality and presence in our lives is, and will always be, THE foundation for a loving, healthy, prosperous and lasting partnership. The knowledge of Him[269] kept us, and keeps us grounded in the promise of Him: "He is our most exceedingly great reward"[270].

When we are convinced of this, we can overcome the temptation to make our spouse the source of our happiness. When we come into marriage believing our partner should be the one to make us happy, something which was meant to be an extraordinary but weighty blessing can turn into a curse. As we drift away from the real Source and compromise our empowering relationship with Him, we tend to crush our spouse under the weight of unrealistic expectations, which never originated in God's heart.

We were never meant to do this marriage thing (or any other thing) on our own. Happiness is an inside job and He lives inside of us. When we let Him rule in every area of our lives, His Kingdom comes and His will is done in our relationships as it is in Heaven. This is a good thought!

---

[269] Ephesians 1:17

[270] Genesis 15:1

There is abundant life waiting for you on the other side of this difficult process. There are plenty more good thoughts about you, your family and your future, in the inexhaustible, innovative, life-giving, wise and beautiful mind of Christ. The psalmist knew this and as he walked in God's presence, he considered every one of His thoughts precious.

How precious to me are your thoughts, God! How vast is the sum of them! Were I to count them, they would outnumber the grains of sand – when I awake, I am still with you. (Psalm 139:17-18)

## The Brilliant Mind of God

Have you ever stopped to think about the implications, in every area of your life, of having and enacting the mind of Christ?

*Our inner reality will eventually overflow into our external reality.*

In this book, there were many moments where you were challenged to confront and question some of your beliefs, but there are many more books out there which dissect the way the mind (thought processes which interpret self, others and the world), impacts and shapes reality within and around you. When we meditate on, and choose to believe in, the truth expressed in Jesus' words and actions, we position ourselves for transformation from the inside out. What happens within our hearts, our inner reality, is eventually going to overflow into our external reality.

Picture yourself walking hand-in-hand with Jesus, intimately connected with God, being fed, strengthened and wisely realigned by every word that proceeds from His mouth[271]. Whatever your circumstances, they pale into insignificance when His face shines upon you, and you experience His perfect, satisfying love. You can see clearly now. You know who you are in Jesus, you find your place and purpose in life and you grow and mature as

---

[271] Matthew 4:4

you become more like Him, every step of the way. From glory to glory, you are no longer in survival mode but you are thriving and touching the lives of those around you with the love and light of Heaven which flow from your words, your deeds, your hope, your joy, your Jesus-carrying presence.

This abundant life is not a fairy tale. Our heavenly Father went to great lengths to make this a reality we could access. He rescued us from death, futility and irrelevance when He purchased us back to Himself, pure, washed and cleansed by the precious blood of Jesus. His amazing Grace continues to be the central message of the Gospel of the Kingdom. The good news of eternal reconciliation orchestrated by a good and brilliant God, who made a way for us to rise up through the restorative, empowering and beautifying grace of re-creation

*This abundant life is not a fairy tale.*

## Re-created in Christ!

"In the beginning was the Word."[272]

By revisiting the first lines of Genesis, John intentionally highlights the beginning of a new time in the history of mankind: a new genesis, a new story of creation. When Jesus, the Son of God, entered this world, everything changed. A fallen, captive world, where the original glory had been dimmed and veiled, was in desperate need of truth revealing light. The living expression of the Father's perfect love came like a burst of irresistible light to dispel the darkness. A tidal wave of abundant *Life-Light*, redemption and restoration, ready to engulf a broken and fallen world and re-create it!

---

[272] John 1:1

*A whole new breed of sons and daughters restored to glory, shining His light.*

When light was first spoken into existence it took emptiness away. When the source of light walked among us, this world was impacted with His transformational and redemptive presence. When we choose to receive Jesus as our Savior, surrender our hearts to Him and make Him King of our lives, He doesn't just say "let there be light" but He Himself, the source of light, steps into our hearts to become one with us. The result: a whole new breed of sons and daughters restored to glory, shining His light in the world.

You are the light of the world. A town built on a hill cannot be hidden (Matthew 5:14)

Therefore, if anyone is in Christ, the new creation has come; The old has gone, the new is here! (2 Corinthians 5:17).

The original Greek word used in the second verse as "new" is the word *kainós*[273] which means *new* in *quality* (innovation), *fresh* in development or opportunity (because it is "not found exactly like this before"), "unprecedented", "unheard of", "of a new kind" in substance and nature. *Emmanuel*, God with us, accomplished His redemptive mission and became "Christ in us, the hope of glory"[274]. Through Him, we not only find our way back home, but we find out home is the Father's heart, unreservedly poured into our hearts as we live before His shining face and step fully into our glorious purpose and destiny.

---

[273] Strong's Concordance 2537

[274] Colossians 1:27

We have become his poetry, a re-created people that will fulfill the destiny he has given each of us, for we are joined to Jesus, the Anointed One. Even before we were born, God planned in advance *our destiny* and the good works we would do *to fulfill it*! (Ephesians 2:10 TPT)

## Defined by God

The apostle Paul, throughout all his letters, keeps addressing his brothers and sisters in the faith as "the saints". He did so because he had a revelation of God's sufficient grace released over us through Jesus' redemptive sacrifice. Although we can still be tempted to sin (which is a vital part of our freedom of choice), this is no longer our nature or heart's desire. In Him we are no longer

> *We are defined by our Father, not our past circumstances, and He says we are no longer sinners but saints.*

sinners but saints. Our old sinful nature was killed on the cross and we have been resurrected to life with Jesus[275], married to our Savior (as part of His glorious Bride)[276], one with Him! (It's a mystery how this works, but if you have a god you can fully understand with your mind, than I propose to you that your god is too small).

> *It's your Father's voice that should be feeding you, every step of the way.*

In this new beginning, which He has dearly paid for but freely given to us, we can really start with a clean slate. We are no longer defined by our past circumstances (divorce included), but we are defined by our Father. We are who He says we are.

---

[275] Romans 6:1-11 (I strongly recommend you meditate on this powerful passage, if you haven't yet)

[276] Ezekiel 16:18 / Ephesians 5:22-32

He says we are royalty, precious, valuable, delightful, hope-carriers, ministers of reconciliation, ambassadors of His Kingdom and powerful world changers! Stop listening to all the other voices who say something different. It's your Father's voice that should be feeding you every step of the way.

His voice doesn't come to accuse, condemn or torment us. That's the voice of the *accuser of the brethren*. Our good Father wishes to build us up, to restore us to the original glory He created us for. He longs to bring us closer and closer to His heart and He continues to pursue us relentlessly with a love that is fierce, passionate and incredibly joyful.

## Created for Bliss and Joy

"We have been grafted into Him and He is pure pleasure! This pleasure we find in Him is the reason we were created. God created Adam and Eve and placed them in the Garden of Eden. The word "Eden" in Hebrew means "the place of pleasure". What a revelation and insight this gives us into the intentions of God. He created you and me first for the pleasure and delight of knowing Him and being one with Him. Everything else flows out of this joy-filled relationship." (Stephen Bell in "Revolutionized by Grace")

*The colossal joy that sustained Jesus to willingly endure the wretched cross.*

Jesus carried the Father's brilliant redemption plan to completion "because of the joy set before Him" [277]. What colossal joy could sustain Jesus to willingly endure the wretched cross? The possibility of reconciliation and intimate, everlasting connection with His beloved

---

[277] Hebrews 12:2

312

ones, about to be re-created in Him. An extraordinary mystery, a new breed of sons and daughters who find their identity in Him as partakers of His divine nature[278] and therefore, commissioned to bring His life, freedom and glory into this world. Did you know that "Creation waits in eager expectation for the children of God to be revealed"?[279]

*For the creation was subjected to frustration, not by its own choice, but by the will of the one who subjected it, in hope that the creation itself will be liberated from its bondage to decay and brought into the freedom and glory of the children of God.* (Romans 8:20-21)

How did God bring life and glory into this world? He spoke the world into existence and expressed His divine attributes in His creation. Now it's you and me, the Children of God, the ones who are one with Christ, who are meant to bring that same creation into the freedom and glory we are walking in, so others can see God's beauty and majesty clearly expressed. What are we, the ones re-created in His image, speaking into existence? What are we expressing through the things we say, do and create?

## Creativity: our Nature and our Purpose

*In God's narrative, we were all given a relevant part to play.*

Aligned with the Gospel of the Kingdom, our sanctified imagination becomes a canvas for the Holy Spirit to paint expressions of the mind of Christ not only in us, but through us. He created us to be unique. DNA, fingerprints and other

---

[278] 2 Peter 1:3-4

[279] Romans 8:19

amazing peculiarities, are natural manifestations of a spiritual reality. Each one of us carries a unique, indispensable piece of the divine image. That's why loving, healthy families and communities, where there is unity in diversity, are a foundational requirement for the fullness of God to be manifested and reflected in this world[280]. We are all designed to participate in a narrative which is way bigger than our own selves. If we wish to embrace it, we all have a relevant part to play. When all the redeemed and fully restored pieces of this mirror are put together, we will see a clear, breathtaking reflection of His face.

Considering the expansive nature of our God (after all, He has no beginning and no end[281]), the possibilities are unlimited. It's no longer Ana, but Ana and Jesus creating together as one. It's no longer Mat, but Mat and Jesus creating together as one. It's no longer Mat or Ana and Jesus, but Mat and Ana, and Jesus in them, connected and creating together, as one. Can you see how incredibly powerful and promising this is?!

*God wants us to have fun creating with Him.*

I like to picture the moment when God invited His children [282], created in His image, to speak identity into other creatures[283]. It's like He saved the best for last because He knew they would have a lot of fun doing it together. Albert Einstein used to say, "creativity is intelligence having fun." I believe that one of the most significant ways God wants us to enjoy the freedom He has conquered for us is to also have fun creating with Him. When we do, dreams are awakened, hope arises, joy is released, connections are deepened and His glory is manifested.

---

[280] Ephesians 4:12-13

[281] Genesis 21:33 / Psalm 90:1-2 / Isaiah 57:15 / Hebrews 7:3 / 1 Timothy 1:17

[282] Genesis 5:2

[283] Genesis 2:20

If you have ever been involved in a creative project of some kind, one where you got to restore something derelict back to life, or one where you got to build or create something new from scratch, you have experienced and tasted the pleasure, joy and a sense of accomplishment or even fulfillment in that moment when you can finally say "It is finished!".

There is so much therapeutic value in creative activities. They present challenges, but also provide a space and a way in which we can tangibly express the unseen convergence of our triune, uniquely designed and diversely wired being. That expression, in whatever form, shape or medium, becomes something visible, audible, palpable and even palatable. Something which was hidden deep within and can now be seen, experienced and understood.

This is why I was very intentional in incorporating creative outlets and options for my readers to express their struggles, epiphanies, goals and dreams. Effective communication is a vital key in this journey to know and being known, and I am aware those activities can help make sense of disorganized or elusive feelings and thoughts, and lead to a more articulate communication of internal, emotional processes. There is great pleasure and joy in the moment two people really connect in this process and become aware that their creative or artistic expression is understood, received, celebrated and impactful.

There is a profound sense of purpose we get when someone is meaningfully impacted by something we have created or helped to create. The awareness that we have made a difference in someone else's life – even if for one single moment of personal discovery, liberation, inspiration, aspiration, joy or empowering hope – really satisfies our need for significance and for a purposeful existence. After all, we are created in God's image!

It always comes back to this: the more we know God, the more we will know ourselves and what good works He has prepared in advance for us. This discovery journey doesn't have to be weighty and boring. The world around us, even

*Creative activities can bring healing, clarity, joy and significance.*

creation itself, will always be impacted and liberated to see a higher reality, the Kingdom's reality, whenever God's glory and beauty is creatively manifested or displayed in and through our lives.

Make a careful exploration of who you are and the work you have been given, and then sink yourself into that. Don't be impressed with yourself. Don't compare yourself with others. Each of you must take responsibility for doing the creative best you can with your own life. (Galatians 6:4-5 MSG)

You can be creative in the way you host, in the way you treat your customers, in the way you teach, in the way you provide innovative services or offer innovative concepts in whatever area of society or field of the marketplace you move in. The mind of Christ has been made available to us and it is important we stay in the conversation He wants to have about solutions for the problems in this world. What if He is just waiting for us to ask Him the right questions about our family, our community, our city, our nation?

"But I have so much conflicting (and sometimes confusing) information that I have no idea what questions to ask!"

Then ask Him to give you the right questions. Ask Him what He wants you to prayerfully speak into existence, not just for your own sake but for the sake of the world: "If any of you lacks wisdom, you should ask God, who gives generously to all without finding fault, and it will be given to you" (James 1:5).

> *God has given us the power to speak like Him, to proclaim the truth of His Word into existence.*

We tend to forget that God has given us the power to speak like Him, to proclaim the truth of His Word into existence[284]. Created in God's image, our words, uttered with faith, can become spiritual truth, invisible but real, alive. A living, creative substance which pierces the spiritual realm to shift and change things, to make a way for the King and His Kingdom to come, bringing Heaven to Earth[285], impacting our reality in a tangible, visible and transformational way.

When we find our creative purpose in life we become more intentional and strategic, but also happier, more joyful and so much more fun to be around! It profoundly impacts our mental and emotional health and our relationships, especially our marriages.

## Your story is important!

The Bible has several stories of people who, while they were still unbelievers, were given prophetic dreams and visions by God. They were enlightened and guided by those around them who were close to God's heart and were available to become His mouthpiece. If you pay close attention to what the storytellers of our society are releasing, you will recognize in many of the movies, books, songs and even adverts out there,

---

[284] Proverbs 18:21 / 1 Peter 3:10 / Ephesians 4:29 / Matthew 12:36-37 / Proverbs 12:18 / Mark 11:23

[285] Matthew 6:10

characters and plot lines which are shadows of biblical narratives, including the messianic one.

Our Father continues to talk and pursue the hearts of His lost children in many different ways. His Spirit continues to whisper heaven's narratives to the storytellers who will make them visible, understandable, relatable, recognizable. Glimpses of heaven, glimpses of Him. Whispers which inspire us to aim higher, and speak to our deep desire to go up higher ourselves.

One day at church, during worship time, the Holy Spirit brought insight and revelation through one of those stories. He started by saying: "God has the last word. He has the better word and the last word. Just like it happened in the 'Sleeping Beauty' story. She was not dead, she was only sleeping. When He wakes her up everything changes, for ever and ever and ever."

*Our Father continues to whisper heaven's narratives to the storytellers who will make them visible.*

I immediately started watching, in my mind's eye, the classical Disney version of this story. I saw the moment when the wicked witch uttered a curse over the baby girl, and the glorious redemptive moment that followed when the good fairy counteracted those words with a different outcome, bringing back hope and a future for the princess and the kingdom. As I watched this, I was prompted to repent for all the times I had just listened to the voice of the 'wicked one' and had given up, left the throne room and didn't stick around to hear Jesus' last words: "It is finished, it is done, I have won the victory! I have given you a hope, a future and a purpose!"

In the background, the worship band was singing "Yeshua I love you, You are God, you are good, you are Jesus", and I prayed: "Jesus, you speak a better word and you speak the final word in my life and over your Church. I repent for every time I empowered the words of the enemy by believing his lies instead of proclaiming your words of destiny over my life and those around me. Yours are always going to be the final words, Jesus. I can walk on your words!"

*His life-breathing words prune us into holiness and fruitful growth.*

When His Word becomes our daily bread, a daily *source* of nurture, comfort and strength for our souls, our minds and our spirits, and when we invite Him to become the Author and the Finisher of our story, then our life script is no longer in our hands alone. The life-giving words He speaks and sings[286] over us, will forever change the course of our narratives. As they fall, one by one, on the white, cleansed by the blood of Jesus, pages of our destiny, His life-breathing words prune us into holiness and fruitful growth. When we listen and believe, we become who He says we are.

My honest desire is to empower, equip, inspire and motivate you to embrace and express your unique, creative expressions. I sincerely hope that the several creative activities you have engaged in throughout this book have brought healing, enabled you to take ownership and make sense of your own story, and gradually prepared you to express it in multiple ways, so when the time comes for you to tell your story, you feel ready to do it. Ready to witness to the world around you (which longs for a manifestation of the freedom and glory of God), the narratives of love, beauty and victory you, and your heavenly Father, have journeyed together. If we don't speak up, even the rocks will cry out![287] Our stories are a vehicle of worship, faith and prophetic potential. "The Testimony of Jesus is the Spirit of prophecy"[288]: an open door inviting others to be filled with the hope and belief He can do it again for them.

---

[286] Zephaniah 3:17

[287] Luke 19:40

[288] Revelation 19:10

Your story is not yours to keep or to hide *under a bowl*[289].Your story of deliverance, healing, restoration and redemption will become a place of encounter, a chest of treasures, a banquet of possibilities with the potential to not only impact your generation but to be passed on as a precious legacy to the generations to come, so they know, celebrate and worship God's multifaceted and extravagant goodness.

Write all this down for the coming generation, so re-created people will read it and praise the Lord! Tell them how Yahweh looked down from his high and holy place, gazing from his glory to survey the earth. He listened to all the groaning of his people longing to be free, and he set loose the sons of death to experience life. Multitudes will stream to Jerusalem to praise the Lord and declare his name in Zion! Peoples from every land, their kings and kingdoms, will gather together to worship the Lord. (Psalm 102:18-22 - TPT)

> *Stories of growth and victory are a precious legacy to the future generations.*

## You are qualified!

"Those are all encouraging thoughts but I don't really feel like I am the amazing new [creative] creation you have been talking about." Feelings are a very important part of us, but they don't always speak the truth. They can work against us by reinforcing or adding an extra weight to familiar lies or debilitating beliefs.

While I was writing this book, there were some moments when I felt stuck and unworthy, doubtful of my legitimacy to even write a book like this.

---

[289] Neither do people light a lamp and put it under a bowl. Instead they put it on its stand, and it gives light to everyone in the house. (Matthew 5:15)

Those were moments where I was painfully aware of the chasm between God's perfect, unconditional and sacrificial love and my still very limited ability to emulate Him in my relationships with others.

> *God NEVER disqualifies us!*

In those moments, my focus was again diverted to what I hadn't achieved yet, and the celebration of past victories was downrated and mocked by a tormenting inner noise. The enemy comes at you mercilessly and ruthlessly. His main purpose is to steal your hope and your joy, because then you are stripped of vision and strength. I kept hearing: "I'm a sham, a fake, I haven't arrived yet...who am I to be writing a book about anything?"

Thank God for the 'helmet of salvation'[290]: it protects the battlefield of the mind from succumbing to the lies of the enemy, by filtering everything through the reality of salvation and grace. His sheep know His voice[291] and I quickly snapped out of it because I knew that voice didn't sound like my good Shepherd. God never disqualifies us. The enemy disqualifies us, the grumpy, orphan-hearted "older brothers"[292] disqualify us, even we (in our unresolved insecurities) can disqualify ourselves, but He NEVER disqualifies us. "I don't have and never had one thought about you failing, Ana"[293], that's my God's voice!

He held nothing back but *of His own glory and goodness has given us everything we need for a godly life*[294], even His voice. I realized my writing had become both my weapon and my megaphone. The significant moments chronicled in my journals, and my life story with the Lord

---

[290] Ephesians 6:17

[291] John 10:27

[292] Allusion to the older brother's attitude in "The parable of the Prodigal Son" (Luke 15:11-32)

[293] Journal entry recorded in chapter 10

[294] 2 Peter 1:3

recorded in this book, spoke louder than the noise. Like living memorial stones, they looked me right in the eye and shouted in my face: "No, you are not a sham, this is all true, this really happened! There is a meaningful narrative which is a witness of things you have reason to be thankful for, and victories, conquests, breakthroughs and progress which will always be a cause for celebration."

> *Like you, I am an ordinary person with an extraordinary God...*

I am not teaching about a particular topic because I've mastered it, because I've become an expert. Like you, I am an ordinary person with an extraordinary God, in the process of discovering how extraordinary He has made me when He gave me the power to become His daughter[295]. I dare to write and to teach because I'm walking this road with God and His grace has been, and will continue to be, sufficient to walk this through, every step of the way.

## Embrace personal and relational development

You may argue this is easier for us because we did ministry school: "You have been trained and equipped and it impacted your life. We have no chance of that happening to us". Believe me when I tell you, you don't need to attend BSSM, or any other ministry school, to continue to grow. You will experience acceleration in your personal development if you can, and choose to, do a ministry school. However, you can continue to get equipped and grow right where you are.

You are not a victim, you are a powerful person and your Father says you are qualified for this. He has given you His Spirit to empower you[296] and guide you into all truth[297]. Mine, just like yours, is an open ended story: we

---

[295] John 1:12
[296] 2 Timothy 1:7
[297] John 14:17 / 2 Timothy 1:7

haven't arrived yet. Mat and I still are (and will continue to be) learning how to pursue deeper levels of connection. It's a lifelong goal.

In this pursuit for a deeper, healthier and more meaningful marriage, there are many tools and resources we have consumed with the motivation and wish to continue growing individually and as a couple. There is nothing more powerful than the truth revealed in the living Word of God but the following suggestions are effective because they are rooted in that very Word.

Here are some suggestions: Danny Silk's KYLO[298] curriculum and some of his courses at LOP[299] Academy, "The Story of Marriage" by John & Lisa Bevere, Barry and Lori Byrne's LAM[300] course, "Victorious Emotions" by Wendy Backlund, Graham Cooke's "Brilliant Perspectives" podcasts, and the blogs, declarations and podcasts of Steve Backlund on his "Igniting Hope Ministries" online platform. There are **many other** great resources available out there, but I can only recommend the above as we have tried and tested them and have been greatly blessed.

Before you dismiss this list, because "it's long and I don't have time to go through all this reading and extensive training", let me reassure you this is a list which has grown with the passing of the years. You don't have to feel overwhelmed. The secret is to ask the Holy Spirit where to start, pick that one and then just take as much time as you need, at your own pace, according to your specific circumstances and needs. Then, when you feel you're ready to move on, go for the next one. When you start seeing the benefits for yourself, your motivation for self-improvement and relational betterment will continue to increase, and so will your enthusiasm and proactivity.

---

[298] "Keep Your Love On"

[299] "Loving On Purpose"

[300] "Love After Marriage" (Nothing Hidden Ministries)

As you consider when and how to move forward with this, I would like to encourage you to cultivate a humble, open and teachable heart because when we empty our cups of the wisdom of this world, we make room for God's wisdom to fill us up to overflowing. And believe me, if you approach Him and embrace His wisdom, believing your life is going to change because "He is a rewarder of those who seek Him"[301], then you will taste and see His goodness.

> *Cultivate a humble, open and teachable heart to make room for God's wisdom to fill you up to overflowing.*

Journal entry:

*I woke up with a weighty presence of God in my bedroom. It was as if I could feel His breath upon my face. I breathed Him in deeply, with a joyful heart, and felt a warm wave of energy flow through my body, from head to toe. Then I could hear, in my spirit, my heavenly Teacher's voice:*

*"Abandonment, when you lay down everything, when you die to yourself. When there is genuine abandonment, an exchange will take place and you'll receive everything you need to fulfill my purpose in your life. Abandonment means you relinquish all control. It implies trust, because you can only willingly do it when you feel safe. It also indicates faith, because it can only be genuinely embraced from a place of true belief in what I've promised. When you position yourself in a place of readiness to receive, that*

> *Abandonment and readiness to receive tap into the Kingdom's readiness to give.*

---

[301] Hebrews 11:6

*readiness to receive will tap into the lavish gift-giving Kingdom reality[302], and draw from the Kingdom's readiness to give."*

May God's amazing grace become the highest and most significant reality in our lives and, with a surrendered, hungry and childlike heart, may our prayer be: "Father, I'm ready to receive what you are so ready to give!"

Every gift[303] God freely gives us is good and perfect[304], streaming down from the Father of lights, who shines from the heavens with no hidden shadow or darkness and is never subject to change. (James 1:17 - TPT)

---

[302] Ephesians 1:4-6 MSG (v6 "He wanted us to enter into the celebration of His lavish gift-giving by the hand of his beloved Son").

[303] Or "legacy" (TPT footnotes).

[304] The Aramaic word used here, *mshamlaita,* means "complete, wholesome, abundant, sufficient, enough, and perfect" (TPT footnotes).

# Q & A

## M y s e l f  &  G o d

❏ Well done for persevering to the end. You have come so far! I am excited as I consider what God has been speaking to your heart and doing in your life, and for what is yet to come!

- Turn your attention and affection to the Lord and ask Him how He feels, and what He thinks about your perseverance.

- Make your own 'tracking map' with the help of the Holy Spirit: tick covered ground, and ask the Holy Spirit to bring His perspective on your personal transformational goals (we are different people on different journeys, so you don't want to limit or box Him in). Ask Him where He's taking you next on your inner transformation journey.

- Ask the Holy Spirit which book of the Bible He wants you to explore with Him.

- Make a reading plan tailored to your circumstances so you can sustain and strengthen this reading habit.

- Will you continue journaling your story with God? Have you considered sharing your story with others? How are you going to do it? (words, drawings, paintings, photos, songs, sculptures, dance choreographies, a clothing line, bumper stickers, special recipes, knitting, quilt making, film directing…); Ask the Holy Spirit and embrace this adventure with Him.

- Picture yourself in your favorite place in nature. Can you see God in creation? How? Tell Him.

- Create a token or memento made with something you find in nature (pebbles, wood, sticks, pine needles or cones, dried flowers, leaves, etc.) which will remind you to celebrate the godly attributes revealed in nature; If you are in a relationship, you can make a "split peace" (so you hold or carry one half and give the other half to the other person).

# T o g e t h e r
*(For those who want to work towards the restoration or improvement of their marriage)*

❑ Your perseverance has been, and will continue to be, rewarded. My sincere hope is you have grown closer to God and to each other. If you have, you are on the right track and you will keep moving forward and growing stronger.

- Share with your spouse what the Holy Spirit told you about your perseverance.

- Exchange your personal 'tracking maps'; give honest and loving feedback.

- Adapt and adjust your individual 'maps' so the two can become one. Take a moment to thank God for His hand upon you, because He has sustained you and brought you here; Also thank Him for everything He is still going to do.

- As a follow up, speak words of blessing over your spouse and over your future as a couple filled with God's presence and favor.

- Share with each other how you are going to journal your story with God and what is your purpose in doing it.

- Try to guess each other's favorite place in nature; share how you see God in creation.

- ✱ Plan a fun creative project together to celebrate God's grace. Ask the Holy Spirit to inspire you so your project has elements of deep joy, awe and wonder. His grace is FLABBERGASTING!* (You can ask Him for another word).

*Final journal entry:

When I asked the Holy Spirit to give me one word to describe God's grace He enthusiastically replied: "FLABBERGASTING!". When I looked it up[305], this is what I found:

- Amazing
- Astonishing
- Astounding
- Blindsiding
- Dumbfounding
- Eye-opening
- Jarring
- Jaw-dropping
- Jolting
- Shocking
- Surprising

---

[305] Merriam-Webster Online Dictionary and Thesaurus

- *Startling*
- *Stunning*
- *Stupefying*

*WOW! I couldn't believe my eyes when this banquet of adjectives was laid there before me, waiting to be creatively projected into the atmosphere, and I burst into song: "Your grace is flabbergasting! I am flabbergasted[306] by your grace!*

*I sang and danced in circles like an exuberant child making these words loud and alive. I knew this was a God moment, because the childlike joy, awe and wonder which flooded my heart were not from this world. In that moment I could sense God's face shining, smiling upon me, as if He was saying with His eyes, "That's my girl".*

---

[306] Overwhelmed with shock, surprise and wonder!

# LifeLine

Revelation & Transformation log          ____/____/____

# Beauty for Ashes!

If you would like to share your story, I would be very happy to read your testimony and celebrate your progress. I would also like to give you a platform on my website to exhibit the works of art you have produced during your healing and restorative journey. Whenever we share our breakthroughs with the world around us in a creative way, we are setting the stage for glory and beauty to be released, and this will always inspire and catalyze more healing and restoration.

Email: definedbygod.always@gmail.com

Website: www.definedbygod.com

# ABOUT THE AUTHOR

Ana Redding is happily married to Mat. She has lived in Portugal, the UK and the USA, and she is a Christian author and speaker with a background in teaching. She is a radical lover of Jesus who understands the power of a redemptive testimony filled with encounters with the kindness and transforming presence of God. The changes that are visible in her person and in her life have happened as an outcome of a relational process with the Lord through His Word and the person of the Holy Spirit. Ana continues to pursue mind renewal and deeper levels of connection with God, her husband and those who run the good race with her.

Made in the USA
Monee, IL
28 July 2020